Cultural China

Chinese Landscapes: Themes and Motifs in Literature

中國山水

LONG RIVER PRESS
San Francisco

This book is edited and designed by the Editorial Committee of *Cultural China* series.

Managing Editors: Naiqing Xu, Youbu Wang, Ying Wu, Zongpei Jia
Compiler (Chinese): Lihong Zhao
Editor (Chinese): Ruqi Xu

Translation: Xiaozhen Wu
Executive Editors: Ying Wu, Chris Robyn
Interior and Cover Design: Yinchang Yuan, Jing Li

ISBN 1-59265-050-3
Library of Congress Control Number: 2005934435

Published by

Long River Press
360 Swift Ave., Suite 48
South San Francisco, CA 94080
USA
and
Shanghai Press and Publishing Development Company
1110 Huaihai Middle Road, Donghu Villa F, Shanghai, China (200031)

Computer typeset by Yuan Yinchang Design Studio, Shanghai.
Printed in China by Shanghai Donnelley Printing Co. Ltd.

1 2 3 4 5 6 7 8 9 10

CONTENTS

CONTENTS

Preface

Zhao Lihong

In order to compile this book, I have been engrossed in research and consequently read a large number of landscape essays. The experience was both enriching and pleasant. The essays took me on imaginary trips to fantastic sights all around China. Famous or little known, great or insignificant, China's mountains and rivers were vividly presented.

It has long been a tradition in Chinese literature for writers to excel in landscape essays. Over thousands of years ancient writers have produced innumerable oft-quoted travel logs. And almost all Chinese writers since the May 4th Movement, who write in vernacular Chinese, have turned out articles on Chinese landscape. Some are about their respective hometowns, others on what they saw and heard on a trip. Mountains and rivers crisscross the vast Chinese territory, so much so that each place claims its own distinctive scenic spot. China boasts the steepest mountains and the most tortuous rivers in the world. Nature has created all sorts of sights, while our ancestors have left their own wondrous imprints. A place becomes famous if there is a natural wonder or some enchanting historic relics. If both criteria are met, then the place becomes known throughout the country. However, the scenery in writings may not necessarily be ones of national renown. Writers are more concerned with fate and life, but in discussing these, must describe the surroundings. So the environment, be it a mountain, a river, a village, a town, or even grass or a tree, is then immortalized. On the other hand, some previously obscure places have

gained a high reputation thanks to essays with a fusion of feelings with the natural setting. At the time when Ba Jin wrote A Paradise for Birds, few people knew the small island in Xinhui, Guangdong Province, where thousands of birds dwell. Whereas by now it is the most important local scenic spot whose name has henceforth been changed into Xiaoniao Tiantang (Paradise for Little Birds).

It is impossible for an anthology of this size to assume the role of an encyclopedia on China's landscapes, or a comprehensive dictionary of travel notes. It is out of the question to include all the best landscape essays and introduce all scenic spots in China in just a hundred thousand words. Compared with China's overall landscape, it is just a corner of the garden. Compared with all landscape literature by Chinese writers, it is but a drop in the ocean. The selected works in this book span 80 years of the 20th century and several generations of writers. Chinese social life changed greatly during these eight decades, and we can witness these changes through the descriptions of scenery. Despite the passing of time and the vicissitudes of humans, China's landscape is as charming as ever. I believe that a careful reading of this book will bring readers some knowledge of China's landscape, probably a desire to see it in one's own eyes, and an interest in landscape writings by Chinese authors. This interest is comparable to one felt by a person who longs for a tour of the entire garden after an inspection of a single flower, or a view of the vast sea after a look at one drop of water.

At the Four-Step Study, September 20, 2001

At the Foot of Mount Emei

Guo Moluo

My hometown is located at the foot of Mount Emei, 75 li (or 37.5 kilometers) from the city of Jiading. The Dadu River flows here from the southwest, changes its course between the second and third peak of Mount Emei, and then turns northeast. My village was therefore named Riverbend. Cradled between the mountain and the river, it sees the sun rise over the Dadu River, and sink behind Mount Emei.

The high, green mountains change very little. They are sometimes enveloped in fog or capped with snow when winter sets in.

The river has broken free from the restraining mountains upstream and flows with abandon. The vast river is dotted with islands, where young weed trees grow. These trees are lush and green in spring and summer, but sparse and bleak in winter. The water is a velvety dark green, but turns red during the summer floods. Waves lash at the both banks, echoing each other.

People from the outside always admire the beauty here, with its mountains and river on a much grander scale than those in the south of the Yangtze River. Maybe they are right, but somehow I do not see where the beauty is. Is it probably because I have grown used to it? I spent 13 years here before going down to school in the city of Leshan, and might very well have come to look at it with unseeing eyes. Indeed, even now I don't feel nostalgia for it. These kind of olden-time feelings have already dried up in me. Maybe they shouldn't, but I am not going to pretend. By contrast, there are some places in Leshan that I do miss - areas around Mount Wuyou and the dam across the river. I miss them not because of something old, but because of something new.

I attended boarding primary and middle schools in Leshan for four years. Strangely, not once did I cross the river to visit Mount Wuyou.

There is nothing worth mentioning about Leshan. Although Wang Yuyang once remarked: "Landscape at Sichuan tops the world, landscape at Jiazhou tops Sichuan", I take it that he was not referring to the city itself.

The Dadu River meets with the southward-flowing Min River to the northeast of the city, and goes on travelling east. Across from the city on the northern bank, facing the three peaks of Mount Emei, stand Mount Lingyun, Mount Wuyou, and Mount Horsesaddle. During the Tang Dynasty when Wei Gao garrisoned Sichuan, Monk Haitong chiseled a statue of the Buddha out of the side of Mount Lingyun, which squats facing the river and towers as high as the mountain. On top of the mountain there is an ancient building where the great writer Su Dongpo (1037-1101) once studied. For these reasons Mount Lingyun has always been frequented by men of letters.

Mount Wuyou was originally named Mount Wuniu (Ravencow), because its foliage is a luxuriant raven black, and its shape like that of a cow. Some people claim that it is exactly the Mount Li chiseled out by Li Bing when he was Governor of Sichuan in the Qin Dynasty (256 BC-206BC). It is a towering island standing aloof from the bank. Wang Yuyang polished its name up into Wuyou. The Wuyou Temple houses the Er Ya Pavilion where Guo Sheren of the Han Dynasty annotated Er Ya (or Near to Correctness, the earliest Chinese dictionary compiled between 221BC- 220 AD). Mount Wuyou is superior to Mount Lingyun in its secluded charm.

It is strange that during my four-year stay in Leshan, when I was an adolescent aged from 13 to 17 consumed by wanderlust, I visited Mount Lingyun many times, but never once set feet on Mount Wuyou. It was in 1930, during the Anti-Japanese War and 26 years after I had left my hometown, that I visited Mount Wuyou. Mount Lingyun was at that time completely vulgarized and a scene of dilapidation. With a plastered face, the stone Buddha had lost its dignity. Stragglers and disbanded soldiers quartered at the Dongpo Hall. The Inkstone Washing Pool was overgrown with weeds. However, Mount Wuyou was refreshing, undoubtedly because it was my first visit.

The Wuyou Temple was also a vulgar place with nothing commendable. Yet the mountain itself, together with the woods and the trails, were delightful. The Er Ya Pavilion was built on the edge of a cliff that overhung the river, where, thanks to the dense foliage, one could not see the river but only hear the lashing water, which was just right. These were the things I liked. I also enjoyed boating at the foot of the mountain at dawn or in the nightfall, quiet, uncluttered, and joyful.

These must have been the things that Wang Yuyang appreciated, mustn't they? I myself missed only these parts. Besides, the Hu's Dam across from the mountain was so vast that it cheered and opened one up. However, I experienced those feelings on my return to Leshan in 1940, but never during my school days there.

The city of Leshan may be loosely defined as my hometown, but the pity is that I do not feel nostalgia for it. Is it because of my drained sentiments, or because of the times? Mount Emei remains a mystery to me. Although I lived more than a dozen years at its foot, I never paid a visit. Therefore I do not know how nice it could be. For curiosity's sake, I would not object to climbing up to the Golden Dome if such an opportunity arises. To me, Mount Emei is not different from Mount Tai.

(December 22nd, 1946)

About Scenery

Mao Dun

A trailer of the movie *The Stormy Frontier*, which I saw the other night, reminded me again of the desert beyond the Gorilla Gorge. Not having attained "Gobi" status yet, it is only a nameless dot on an ordinary map, although it is boundless to the naked eye. At noon when the sun is directly above, its pure strong reflection will irritate your eyes. There are no undulating dunes, nor a single mud shed in sight, just a vast expanse of nowhere. It is so level that not a single kariz [underground channel-connected well system] could be located, so monotonous in color that the occasional tiny white glow from the skeletons of camels or horses never manage to stand out, so quiet that the only sound audible seems to come from the hissing hot air. Nevertheless, you can't deny the existence of "scenery" here. When a first black dot emerges on the horizon, when more dots form a line or a team, when the light breeze sends the gentle jingling of bells into your ears, and when finally those stately camels, in neat phalanxes, approach in composed and firm strides, when the scarlet oblong leading flag dazzles your eyes, when your ears are filled with the harmonious clattering, — you may not utter a word there and then, but surely you will marvel how imposing yet how charming it is! Where Nature displays its most monotonous side, human activities render it a new look. Isn't it a kind of "scenery"? Nature is great, but man is even greater.

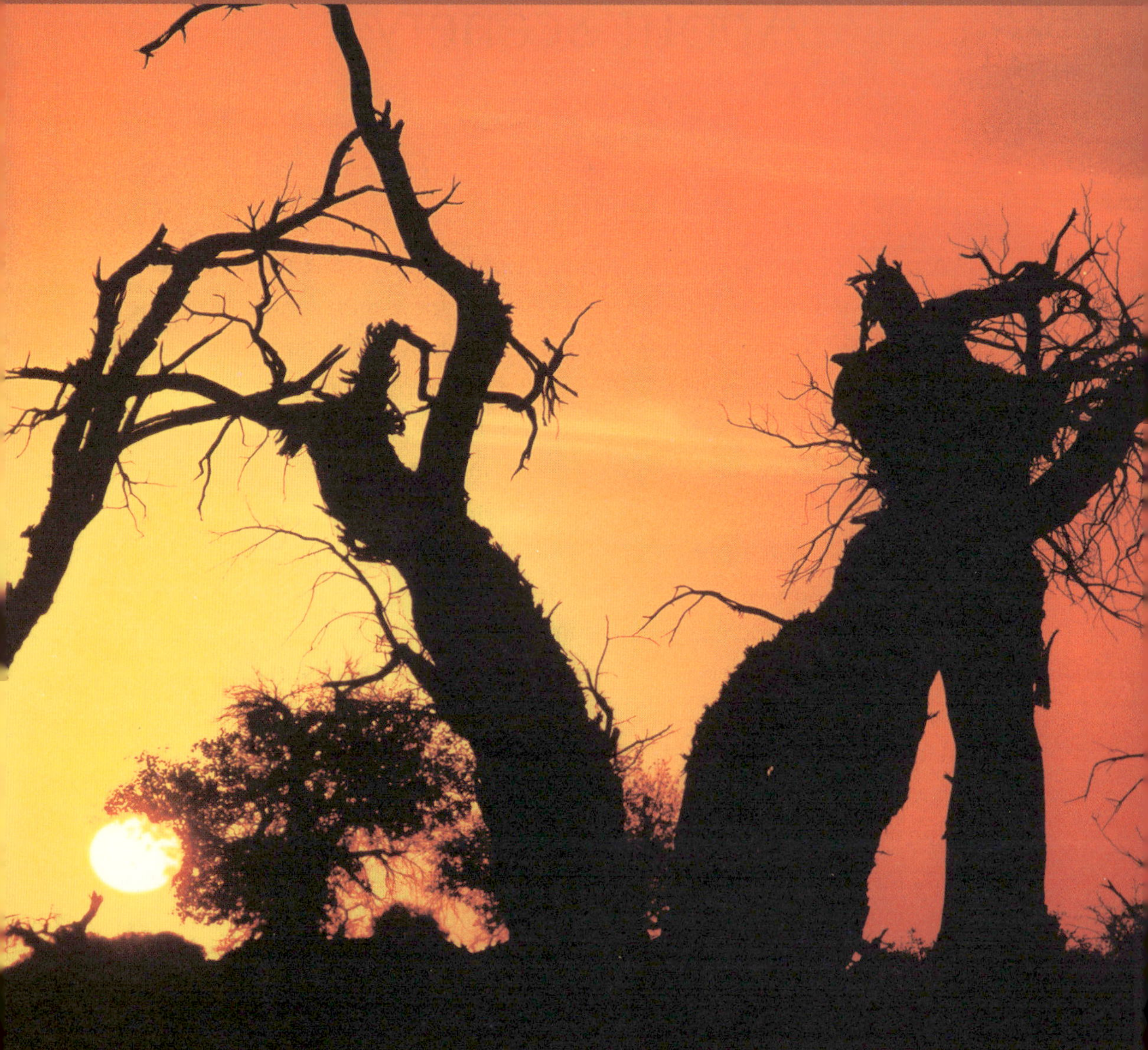

Then I recalled another scene on the so-called "Loess Plateau"! Most hills there were barren, but terraced fields had transformed those bald heads into favus-affected heads with some scattering hair. Particularly attractive were those long-stalked crops, which stood tall and in order like a parade expecting inspection, and which swayed in the night breeze. Moonlit nights were even better. The sky was so blue that it was almost transparent. The moon seemed to be no more than a few feet away from the hilltop. Viewed from a distance the dense, erect millet on the hilltop resembled bristling hair on a human head. Suddenly two ox horns appeared on the ridge, then the entire ox, then two or three plough-shouldering persons, and maybe a kid. They walked down in a leisurely fashion, cutting a silhouette against a background of blue sky, black mountains, and silvery moonlight. A pastoral poet who sees this will definitely regard it as the best subject matter. But there was even more. These late-returning farmers were singing short simple songs, whose pleasant melody wafted down from the hilltop. Even after they had disappeared into the col, their songs lingered under the blue sky, bright moon and among the dark mountains.

Another time, another scene. The sun was setting. The parched yellow earth was emitting the heat it had accumulated during the day. The swift stream looked as if it could wash away all the pebbles on the shallow riverbed. In a col along the stream there was a team returning from their "production", in whose excited conversation at least seven or eight accents were distinguishable. Suddenly they started singing masculine songs in unison. Their hearty laughter was echoed by the similarly hearty river. Take a look at their hands. This hand had used to hold palettes, that pair had played a violin accompaniment to the "Song of Production" the day before. This hand had often been seen woodcarving with a knife, while that had written voluminously with inspiration. But right at the moment they had all grown callous, thanks to laboring with hoes. At the foot of the slope the team was greeted by another group. Here, beside the flaming campfire, hands that had once applied rouge and powder were done with preparing golden cooked millet and green rape. By then the sun had set, leaving behind it a sky covered with rosy clouds. The stream ran even more loudly, splashing against rocks to produce snowy foams. People stretched their mud-stained feet in the stream and let it do the washing, or they scooped up some water to clean their faces. With hills behind and the stream in front, with the solemnly quiet nature and vigorous human beings, the place had become a fantastic picture.

Here, the blue sky, the bright moon, the barren hills, the monotonous yellow earth, and the shallow rapids seemed to be the most appropriate background, and also irreplaceable. Nature is great, man is greater, but human activities inspired by lofty ideals are the greatest among the great!

We have all seen a man in suit whisper to his lover in perm, cheongsam and high heels on a bench under the shade in a park corner. But imagine, on a rainy day, you were riding along an embankment between a tawny turbid river and rugged cliffs. Despite the horse's cautious probe into the mud with its hooves, sometimes it still staggered. Judged by the usual criteria, all was quiet and grayish yellow, nothing lively or vivid. However, as you looked up you suddenly caught sight of some natural caves on the high cliff, where, in a structure similar to a third-floor back room, a couple were sitting knee to knee. Only the difference in hairstyle allowed you to conclude that one of them was a woman. Driven there by the rain, they must have chatted long enough, so much so that by then their heads drew close together over an open notebook. Just think how different it is from seeing a couple snuggle up to each other whispering on a park bench! At the first sight of lovers in a park, it will occur to you that "there is a couple here". Whereas there and then, upon seeing such a pair in such a dull rainy day, among desolate hills and in a primitive cave, you would feel it a "miracle" which gave instant luster to Nature! It did not matter whether they were lovers or not. What you saw were two vital human beings who had a clear understanding of the meaning of life. Under no circumstance would they feel tired or bored, let alone seeking excitement from mischief. Instead they would stick to their way, feeling happy and contented. But what was the enabling force lying behind?

Nevertheless, let's go back to "scenery". Here man still dominates the "scenery", without whom there is little else worthy of mentioning. Furthermore, is there anything else worth cherishing in the absence of man with a rich inner life?

Take another example. If you agree that a score or so of peach trees make a wood, then here is one. Blooms had given way to green leaves long before, but there was not a single peach in sight. A half of an old millstone was the prettiest round table. A broken stone tablet or an old stone step became rare long tables. Stones of various sizes acted as ready-made stools, and they were perceived as luxury items. The odd-looking furniture was necessary because there was a teahouse here. In front of the peach wood there was buckwheat planted by villagers, as well as long-stalked crops such as hemp and corn. The blossoming buckwheat looked like a pink carpet from a distance, while the hemp and corn were screens arranged on its edge. The sun shone through openings in the foliage onto the earth and stone furniture, leaving golden streaks here and there. From time to time some insect chirped. A horse tethered to a tree on the edge of the wood stretched to rub its neck against the trunk, and, feeling contented, neighed. "This is not bad." You might say. Right, the place did claim some components of a "scenic spot"! But that might not be the case. In the strong plateau sunlight people enjoyed the shade here as an outdoors resting place, so they added a teahouse and turned it into a "scenic spot". However, it would make a laughingstock if such commonplace objects as the score or so of peach trees, half a millstone, some broken stone tablets, plus buckwheat, hemp and corn are considered major components of the so-called scenic spot. In a vast country like Chin, this place pales into insignificance by comparison with numerous other so-called scenic spots. What's the big deal about it? So there must be another perspective. Now please sit down, order a cup of green tea and twenty cents' worth of dates, and become a patron of the peach orchard teahouse. You'd like to observe female customers first? O.K. There are several right over there. One of them might have received some remittance from home, so she has invited friends here. Still another group sits around a stone table, but in place of dates and tea they have brought their books. Apart from them, two robust young men who had "walked the hardest walk on earth" are sitting quietly like gentle girls. A group of men and women, some seated, some squatting, are debating a philosophical issue and constantly breaking out into laughter. Nearby, a person lie on an oblong slab of stone with a book covering his face. These would be enough to look at. In a word there was something special in the air, but nothing odd. People came here to relax after work. If they had money they helped themselves to some tea; if they had no money they would simply chat. In the eyes of the leisured who want to find some way to kill the time, the seats here are uncomfortable, the food and drink too coarse, delights too few. At most they would come once, and a second visit would certainly bore them to death. However, those people who did not see any reason for killing the time valued the simple and crude place highly, so the peach orchard became well-known.

Hence the "scenery" here is worth recalling with nostalgia. Lofty human spirit makes up for the lack of Nature and adds beauty, both in form and in content, to the latter. Man has created a second Nature!

The last recollection is about northern China in May. At dawn, when a touch of light had come in through the window paper, a loud and clear trumpet broke the silence. I suddenly recalled the first photo I had seen on an album the day before, wherein the pale black silhouette of a trumpeter stood against a background of silvery white. His thrust-out chest and outstanding brows conveyed gravity, resolution, bravery and high alert. As I ruminated over the skill of the photographer, I detected gravity, resolution, bravery and high alert in the blowing trumpet. So I got dressed and went outside to have a look. The air was extremely chilly, and the hill to my left was shrouded in the rosy clouds of dawn. I saw the young trumpeter on the peak. His forehead shone in the morning glow. Yet what made me exclaim with admiration was a gun-carrying soldier who stood solemnly facing east like a statue in a place nearby. The only moving object was the piece of red silk hanging from the trumpet that swayed in the morning breeze. The soldier's bayonet that gleamed coldly in the pink dawn conveyed strength. I stared in a daze, as if the two of them were the embodiment of our national spirit.

If you too take it as "scenery", then it is the true scenery, the greatest among the great!

(The Misty Date Hill Pass, December 1940)

The Quietness of Fangyan

Yu Dafu

Fangyan is located 25 kilometers northeast of Yongkang County. There are buses covering the over 50 kilometers of distance between Jinhua and Yongkang, but from there on one has to either hire a sedan or walk to reach Fangyan. The day when we went there, it was cloudy and the rain was around the corner, so we all hired sedans to travel east after getting off the bus at Yongkang. The Jinshan Village was seven and a half kilometers away, and in another seven and a half kilometers we reached Zhiying, a big town of around 1,000 households, the majority of which carried the surname "Ying". We stopped for a short break there and purchased some oilpaper as our protection against the increasingly heavy rain. About five kilometers later, mountains appeared on both sides of the road. Ancient trees stretched their limbs over the grotesque-looking peaks and rocks. They assumed different shapes in the drizzle. The sedan carriers pointed out each and every one of them:

This is the Husband and Wife Rock. Those are the Tiger Rock... the Rat Ladder, etc. In another kilometer or so we arrived at Yanxia Street at the foot of Fangyan.

Those who have been to Jinhua must have had the following experience: once you had checked into a hotel, some quiet and scholarly country gentleman in a long gown made from black cloth would come to cross-examine you:

Do you plan to worship at Fangyan? How many times have you been to worship there? Where did you stay?

If you replied that this would be your first visit, he would produce a business card and recommend you to stay at the Fangyan address printed on it. They are agents sent by Yanxia Street house owners whose job resembles that of a hotel receptionist but in a slightly modified way. Judging by those agents working hundreds of miles away from Yanxia Street, you could well imagine how attractive Fangyan is to worshippers, and how fierce the competition is among the five hundred establishments on Yanxia Street.

There are about three to five thousand people in the hotel business in Yanxia Street whose livelihood depends on the Revered Mr. Hu's Temple. Most of them belong to either the Cheng or the Ying family. They value learning and have accumulated considerable wealth. There are three stories in their houses, most of whose ground floor is built in the valley, the middle floor opens onto the street, and the top floor overlooks the street. The number of rooms for each hotel ranges from 30 to 50. Each of them is said to be overcrowded during the peak season. Pilgrims swarm in from Shaoxing, Chuzhou, Hangzhou and nearby counties. Some have traveled from as far as Fujian Province.

A zigzagging path of a couple of miles leads you from Yanxia Street to the foot of the mountain. There is no way to count all the closely-packed steep stone steps spiraling up the mountain. It takes an hour to reach the front gate of the Revered Mr. Hu's Temple.

The given name and substitute name of the Revered Mr. Hu are Ze and Zizheng respectively. A Yongkang native during the Song Dynasty, he was later promoted to Vice Minister of War. The temple was built in his honor because he had once presented a memorial to the emperor persuading him to exempt inhabitants of Quzhou and Wuzhou from poll tax. The Revered Mr. Hu studied at Fangyan when he was young, so the temple there must be authentic. What's more, the spirit of the Revered Mr. Hu has made its presence felt from time to time. Some of his most outstanding supernatural deeds are as follows:

In the reign of Emperor Hui of the Song Dynasty, Yongkang locals took refuge from bandits at Fangyan, where there was a pit capable of accommodating a thousand people with an overhanging vine. As the bandits were climbing up the vine, a red snake appeared, to gnaw at the vine. It broke, and all the bandits fell to their death.

Some bandits from Qingqi made their lair at Fangyan. One night their chief dreamed of a god watering his horse at Fangyan's pool. At dawn the pool was found to have dried up. The scared bandits fled helter-skelter.

During the Taiping Uprising (1851-1864) many neighboring villages and towns were robbed, yet Fangyan was spared.

In the third year of the Republic of China (1913), the admirers of the Revered Mr. Hu at Sheng County who built a temple in his honor sent people to steal the head of Mr. Hu's statue at Fangyan and planned to relocate it to their own temple. The Revered Mr. Hu appeared in the dreams of the local magistrate and peasants. As a result all thieves were caught. That winter a fire broke out in a village in Sheng County to take the lives of all those who had conspired to steal the statue's head. In the following August two people from the same village died on their pilgrimage to Fangyan.

There are countless other tales like those mentioned above. Consequently Fangyan attracts worshippers all year round, especially in the spring and autumn. Pilgrims come and go in an endless stream for hundreds of miles around. Those Jinhua natives who have migrated to other places built their own temples in honor of the Revered Mr. Hu. Superstitious as it is, it reveals the unexpectedly profound influence of the Revered Mr. Hu and the reason why Fangyan is so widely known. However, it was for the purpose of enjoying the unusual quiet and beauty here that we had taken the trouble to travel to Fangyan from afar.

Ranging from 600 meters to 1,000 meters in height and covering an area of two to four square kilometers, all mountains around Fangyan rise steeply into the sky. There is not much difference in size between the top and the foot of the mountains. Either square or round in shape, they look like huge pillars holding up the sky. The flat tops are overgrown with bushes. The gravel cliffs are hardly climbable. Rushing waterfalls and fantastic trees are scattered among the mountains. From dawn to dusk, rain or shine, the scenery is ever changing and unpredictable. They must be the grandest of the grand mountains, mustn't they?

I had used to find the bold, vigorous strokes in depicting odd-shaped rocks and sheer cliffs in traditional Chinese painting incredible, but now as I stood at Fangyan scanning the surrounding mountains, I found them inadequate. When I first started learning English at school, *The Great Stone Face*, a short story by American Puritan writer Hawthorne, enthralled me. Here at Fangyan I realized what an ignorant youngster I had been. The number of great stone faces similar to that in the novel was beyond counting in this area. Not having been to Egypt, there was no way for me to judge whether the Sphinx in the desert could rival the rocks here. The Five Peaks Academy at the Shou Mountain, a couple of miles north of Fangyan, was particularly quiet, so much so that one's hair would stand on end in such a natural environment.

A few peaks to the north, which stretched to the west where they slanted to the south, encircled the place. The towering precipice formed a top-heavy stone wall. Half-way down the wall, or about six to ten meters from the ground, a huge cave like the gaping mouth of a monster came unexpectedly into view. Rocks formed the walls of the cavity, while the Five Peaks Academy, the Beautiful Pool Memorial and The Book of Changes Lecture Hall had been constructed between the upper and lower jaws. Not a single rafter or tile was necessary in such a setting far away from the madding crowd, where there was shelter from the wind and rain, and where neither the summer heat or the winter cold could penetrate. The precipice was even more sheer as it abruptly turned southeast, where the five fantastic peaks of Sturdy, Waterfall, Peach Blossom, Inverted Cauldron and Cockcrow rose to the sky one after another. As giant as the mountains at Fangyan, they varied in shape and color. As I stood on the upper floor of the Five Peaks Academy, the only sound that reached my ears came from nearby waterfalls. I raised my eyes to find the sky narrower and yet the birds fail to fly across it. I gazed at the five green and purple peaks, but they kept reticence. Looking out to the east, I caught a glimpse of the snowy clouds and distant trees floating in the wedge-shaped opening in the sky. A sense of tranquility, freshness and greatness welled up. The reason why Confucian moralists such as Zhu Huiweng, Lu Donglai and Chen Longchuan lectured only here, while other Song Dynasty Confucian scholars preferred to teach at caves and secluded places was probably that they took advantage of the mighty nature to suppress human desires. It was impossible to see through the trouble they had taken without personally experiencing Jinhua's scenery.

In the drizzle, we toured around the Five Peaks Academy and the Revered Mr. Hu's Temple on our first day at Fangyan. The sizeable temple was on the top of Fangyan, along the front and back streets on which many hotels had prospered thanks to the Revered Mr. Hu, as the tradition had been in China that when a man attained immortality, even his pets ascended to heaven. The statue of the Revered Mr Hu turned out to be a red-faced, long-haired gentle old man. Besides the statue in the front hall, there was another identical one in the back hall. Probably one of them was used at temple fairs. We happened to arrive on the first day of the tenth month of the lunar calendar. Therefore village theatricals were being offered in the temple's front hall. People of all ages and both genders crowded in front of the stage, breaking into tears when moved. Not comprehending a bit of the plot or the lines, we inquired of a nearby middle-aged mandarin-speaking gentleman who appeared to be a local inhabitant. According to him, it was a local troupe performing some dramas like *Kill the Dog to Persuade the Wife* that advocated filial piety and righteousness.

We went downhill from the Revered Mr. Hu's Temple to return to the Cheng's Hotel where we would stay for the night. Supper was ready in the lounge where two giant red candles had already been lit. The meal was sumptuous, with many courses of pork and chicken, yet without fish or seafood: they were not that palatable.

We got up at dawn the next day and took the sedans that had carried us here back to Yongkang via the Fushan Temple at Lingyan. The scenery on the way was again quiet and unusual.

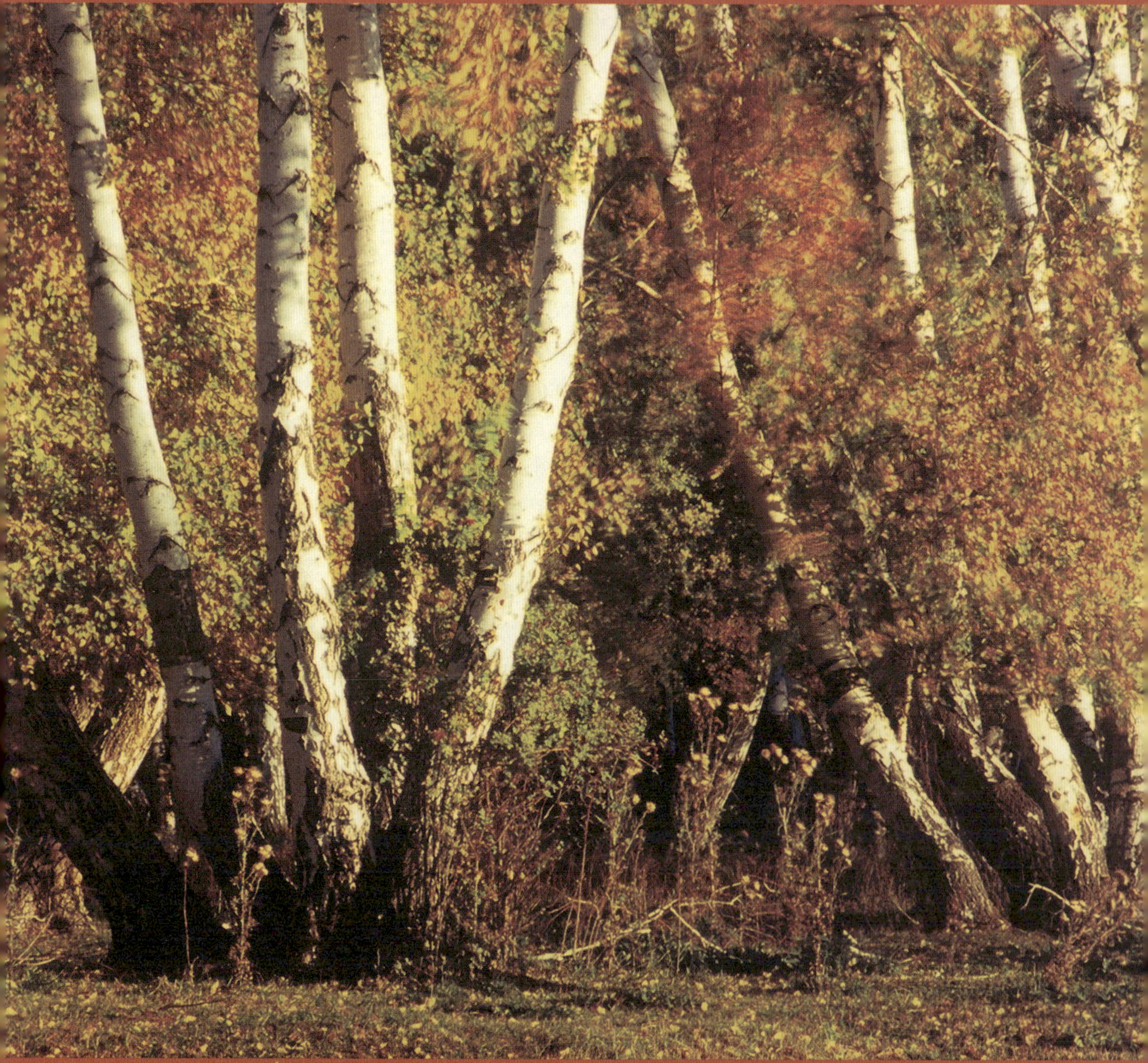

Sketches from the Tianmu Mountains

Xu Zhimo

"Buddha told the world
I would be with him
At His words
Doubts and regrets were all gone
Yet at first
Surprised and bewildered I was
Might it be Devil
Who disturbed the peace of my mind"
(Metaphors, Lotus Sutra)

All may not be quiet in the mountains. Temples hide among towering trees. Morning and night, the wind blows, pines whisper, bamboos murmur, birds sing, insects chirp. The huge bell in the tower, fish-shaped wooden blocks in the hall, and thick hollowed bamboo poles on both sides of the temple (used to draw spring water) are all like natural pipes and flutes that echo sounds issued from the sky or earth, sometimes slow, sometimes rapid. It is not quiet at all, but the mountain sounds, be they produced by earthworms in the mud or by sedan carriers at night as they sing a rhythmic tune, have some distinctive features, i.e., they are pure, clear, penetrating, refreshing as a glass of iced water. Similar to a bath in the spring water that cleanses you, those mountain sounds, though seemingly ordinary, are evidently purifying.

At night, crisp sounds lull you to sleep. In the early morning they wake you up.

It is bliss to live in the mountains but even better to live in a multi-storied house in the mountains. My window on the upper floor opens out into an immensely dense forest, backed by a sea of clouds! The sun shines, the moon caresses, stars sparkle, and they are all mine. Through this one-meter-square window I take in changes in nature; through this one-meter-square window I consider my changing feelings with contentment.

When I woke up this morning, rosy clouds lit up my mosquito net. Birds were singing a song of praise; I joined them. They offered their clear and melodious voice, while I contributed with profound silence.

The bell tolled once at the bell tower, the majestic sound echoing through deserted mountains. The toll stirred a tide of thoughts in me. No, the word "tide" is too much. Let me say a stream of thoughts, instead. The way Christians say "Amen" and Hindus say "o — m" is similar to the way a bell hums, an infinite undulation starting from inclusive round lips to an exclusive shut mouth. It apparently expands, but at the same time delves deep. Things are both in its periphery and at its center: at once the peel and the seed, the axle and the wheel. This great and profound "om" gives one a sense of action and another sense, of inaction, at the same time. Inaction implies action, while action entails inaction. From perching to flying, and from flying back to perching; from this world to the other world, and from the other world back to this world: —

"Buddha's gentle voice was heard, profound and subtle."

What an amazing force! What a wonderful enlightenment! It tolerates all conflicting phenomena, and for an instant widens one's outlook. This single and pure sound purified my soul. Flowers bloom and fall, meteors shoot across the sky and fireflies fly over the fields, pines soar straight up into the sky, precipitous crags lord over a dangerous sea, love between man and woman, jewelry's sparkle, volcanic lava; an infant soundly asleep in its cradle.

Day and night, the bell on the hill goes on nonstop, averaging one toll every five minutes. The monk who is in charge lives alone in the bell tower. He is said to have tolled the bell for eleven consecutive years and made a pledge to go on until strength fails him. The bell tower also houses some Buddhist idols. The bell monk seats himself beside the bell. Every night he sleeps in a sitting posture, one hand holding the bell club, so accustomed to the arrangement that sleep never interferes with his duty. "This monk," I said to myself, "must have attained the Way! Most other monks haven't. A moment ago the monk in charge of receptions mistook the seven apertures in the human head for the six sense organs, and then got confused by the one surplus nostril or ear. The abbot frequently cited some military and provincial governors in the conversation. The monk in charge of the pavilion halfway up the hill was the very embodiment of greediness and displeasure, breaking two innocent teacups for no reason. But this bell monk is in no way mediocre. He must be paid a visit!" He is about 50 and has been a monk for over 20 years. Yes he is in charge of the bell tower and sounding the bell (he went over to give it a toll as he spoke), and yes, he sits sleeping every night. However, besides that, he doesn't appear much different in my layman's eyes. What a pity! He dusted the shrine, pedestals and kneeling cushions, renewed candles and incenses, drew a jar of water, washed a bunch of green vegetables, took out a handful of rice, dried his hand before accepting alms from worshippers, and then turned around to gave the bell another toll. Buddhist practices had not made him lean in the face, yet he did not have insomniacs' tired look, instead he smiled big smiles from time to time. What kinds of scriptures does he chant? No. Just "Amitabha". He might be illiterate. "What are the mountains over there, Master?" "We are at the Tianmu Mountains," he said. "I know. I mean the mountains over there," I pointed with my hand. "I don't' know," he answered.

There is another monk who lives farther up the hill in a place where Crown Prince Zhaoming used to study. There are a few houses, called thatched sheds, with Buddhist statues inside, which are also controlled by the temple. But they are not as frightening as the thatched sheds on Mount Pudu, where the monks who practice Buddhism either sitting or leaning are all thin and gaunt, like ghosts. Most of them do not speak. Whatever alms you put in the basket or plate in front of them, be it gold bullion or iron bar, they will never open their mouth or utter a word. Popular legends are even weirder. Some are said to have not eaten or stirred for half a year, but still alive and lost in the unseen world. They may soon attain Buddhahood. Just look at their black and lifeless complexion, which differs little from stones or earth. "Some of them," according to worshippers, " have become Living Buddha. Our grandmothers saw them sit like that 30 years ago!"

However, the thatched sheds and the monk inside on the Tianmu Mountains are not that legendary. The sheds are shelters from wind and rain, and the Buddhism practitioner a lively human being, yet no less interesting to us. He is a tall, dark-faced, slow-moving middle-aged man, who has been a monk for about ten years, sat in meditation three years before, and is currently perfecting himself in the shed. Originally he was a businessman, with parents, brothers and sisters at home, probably a wife too. Instead of explaining why he chose to become a monk in his middle age, he simply said, "I've committed too many sins as a layman. It was better for me to follow the Buddha." However, judged by his calm voice and discreet manner, he must be a person who had not only experienced vicissitudes in life, but also acquired the ability to tell right from wrong. His mouth and eyes revealed self-restraint and traces of Devil's fight with Buddha. You might believe that he had once committed murder and arson, or that he was a returned prodigal. The bell monk was untainted and unsophisticated, whereas he was evidently an escaped prisoner from the mundane world. Three years in meditation and another three years in the shed had not put out the fire inside him. "I've committed too many sins as a layman. It was better for me to follow the Buddha." Wasn't that from a trembling penitent soul? I was curious — how possibly could I learn his thoughts as he sits cross-legged deep in the night?

"Buddha told the world
I would be with him
At His words
Doubts and regrets were all gone
Yet at first

Surprised and bewildered I was
Might it be Devil
Who disturbed the peace of my mind"

Or maybe I was seeing too much out of it. Those of us who are influenced by a Western outlook on life tend to take life too seriously, want too strongly a place in this world, and would not willingly step back. We would rather put our entire body and soul under life's rolling machine, not grudging a single drop of bodily juice; we would not admit defeat, or withdraw, or lower our flag unless at the end of our rope. What's more, even after admitting despair, we would rather take our lives than retracing our steps dispiritedly. We would kill ourselves, a resolute end to life, instead of becoming a monk, a denial of life. Yes, Westerners do go to monasteries or nunneries, such as Abelard and Heloise, but they do it out of some emotional upheavals and convert human love into love for God. The perceiving self is unequivocally existent and active. For Orientals, to become a monk or a nun is to dispose of all emotions. Buddhists and Taoists alike, they aim at removing the self. Besides, the concept of renouncing the mortal world by becoming a monk or nun did not originate in China, but was imported from India together with Buddhism. As to why India gave birth to such thoughts, scholars offered an interesting array of philosophical or even physical theories. It is worth researching why China tolerates such thoughts and why in fact the number of newly initiated monks and nuns do not decrease nowadays (Recently a friend of mine almost became a young monk!), since this is far more than simply an issue of the extent of knowledge or even consciousness. There might be a lot of fascinating explanations. Ignorant as I am, I would like to hear form our scholars.

Morning Moon Over the Lugou Bridge

Wang Tongzhao

"Melancholy is the sun over Changan, Sobbing is not the river from Longtou."

A Qing Dynasty poet wrote the beautiful line above in memory of the Lugou Bridge. Does it make difficult reading because of the classical allusions to "the sun over Changan" and "the river from Longtou"? However, if you know their sources well, if you possess the power of association and imagination, and if you are reminded of the surroundings, scenery and historical changes of the place, naturally you will feel that such "classical" allusions do add to the greatness and beauty of the Lugou Bridge.

Open a detailed map and you will locate the historically well-known Sangqian River in current Hubei Province, or the Capital District of the Qing Dynasty. The Sangqian River has been no stranger to wars since ancient times, or poets reminiscing about the past and grieving over the present. Yet few people seem to have heard of the three proper names of the Zhi River, the Xi River and the Lei River. Besides, those who have been to Beiping (the old name for Beijing) always remember the Yongding River outside it. Even if they do not remember the Yongding River, surely the name of Yongding Gate, the south gate of the Outer City, rings a familiar bell to each and every one. Although I am not here to discuss textual research or to comment on waterways, in my essay on the Lugou Bridge I have to mention the river underneath it.

The Zhi River, the Xi River, the Lei River, and the commonly known Yongding River refer in fact to the same river - the Sangqian River.

There is another large river whose name is less strange but hardly remarkable in ordinary geography books - the Hun River. It originates from Hunyuan, a place close to the famous Hengshan Mountain. Because of its turbid water, it is also known as the Yellow River, Jr. It feeds into the Sangqian River in Shanxi Province. The latter winds through Huairen, Datong and arrives at Huailai County of Hubei Province, where it bends southeast inside the Great Wall, heads like a yellow dragon through the mountains of Changping County for over 100 kilometers until it finally reaches this majestic ancient bridge at Wanping County.

Right, the river is not from Longtou. The torrential river under the bridge is actually a convergence of the Sangqian River and the Hun River; or rather, a convergence of the so-called Zhi River, the Xi River, the Lei River, the Yongding river, and the Hun River, the Yellow River, Jr., and the Black Water River (a popular name for the Hun River).

The bridge was built neither in the Northern Song Dynasty nor at Beiping under the Mongolian rule. The wooden bridge spanning the river was not replaced by a stone one until June of the 29th year of Emperor Dading's Reign in the Jin Dynasty, when the Jin people in Northern China were fighting the Southern Song Dynasty in the south. Evidence is found in a Jin Dynasty imperial edict, which reads, "Upon the completion of the bridge in March of the second year of Emperor Mingchang, We confer the name Guangli on it. An eastern corridor and a western corridor are built for the convenience of travelers."

When Marco Polo came to China and served in the imperial court of early Yuan Dynasty, he saw this mighty construction and sang high praises of it in his *Travels*.

The bridge was renovated in both Yuan Dynasty and Ming Dynasty, but renovation was carried out on a much grander scale in the ninth year of Emperor Zhengtong's reign, to which the existing stone balusters and lions may possibly be attributed. Several major rebuilding projects were undertaken during the Qing Dynasty, especially the two in the 17th and 50th year respectively of Emperor Qianlong's reign, which did add luster to the bridge.

"The bridge is 220 meters long, 8 meters wide. The balustrade is 0.8 meter in width. There are 140 stone balusters and 11 arches. The sixth arch is right above the river center."

From the above explanatory note of the bridge based on statistics after the renovation in the 50th year of Emperor Qianlong's reign, people (those who have not been there) may have an idea of its magnificence.

In former times, counties in the neighborhood of Beiping were under the jurisdiction of Shuntian Prefecture, or the so-called Capital District. As a result of literary commemoration by celebrities, eight scenic spots in the District have become well known, such as the Western Hills Shimmering in Snow, the Great Wall Surrounded by Lush Greenery at the Juyong Pass, and the Rainbow Floating over the Jade Spring. They all have scenes of quietude and beauty except for the poetic sounding Morning Moon over the Lugou Bridge, where there is just a bridge. It goes without saying that "the setting moon over willow-lined banks in the morning breeze" struck the deepest chord in travelers of the past as they set out at daybreak. Moreover, there was such a majestic stone bridge over a current rolling from afar acting as a vital passage to the

Capital. No one knows for sure how many officials, scholars, businessmen and farm laborers there were who were driven to the Capital, center of fame and wealth, in pursuit of career and life or for the purpose of sightseeing, and consequently passed by this ancient bridge at dusk or dawn. Think about this: in a time when means of transportation were far less advanced than they are today, people riding horses, in carriages, wearing bamboo hats and carrying loads on shoulder poles came and went, each of them keeping their own worries, happiness, joy and sorrow to themselves, yet all burdened with the heaviness of life. Here the spectacular scene was transposed into their worries, happiness, joy and sorrow. Whatever outlook they held on life, owing to intricate shifts in time and space, overwhelmed by this lofty construction, anyone who was not an idiot could not help but feel touched. How they were touched depended on individual qualities as well as the context. Hence the Lugou Bridge was generously rewarded by becoming a part of people's memory and artistic heritage.

However, it is said that there is another reason for citing the "morning moon" to describe the beauty of the Lugou Bridge. When the day breaks on the last day of the lunar month, the third-quarter moon unveils itself fully nowhere else but over the Lugou Bridge. The folklore sounds dubious. The Lugou Bridge rises just so above the ground; why is it that in the same time slot the last-quarter moon over the Western Hills or the White Pagoda (at the Beihai Park) in Beiping is less clear than it is over here? Yet let us not be that rigid. The creativity that led an imaginative artist who had been on the spot to pair the "morning moon" with the Lugou Bridge is not meant for scientific verification. As the saying goes, "The day's work is best begun in the morning". And here we are talking about travelers setting out at dawn. The misty morning air set off the thought-provoking moon - one afloat in the azure sky while the other set among the white stones of the giant bridge. The battlement of the Capital was dimly discernible. Clouds over the Western Hills appeared now clear, now vague. The wilderness was vast and the yellow current torrential. Although the scenery might change with time, whether it be a chilly spring morning or a desolate autumn dawn, if neither rain nor snow fell, such light, such colors, such a place and construction, the moon at daybreak on the last day of the lunar month, the white stones, the vast wilderness and the yellow current would inevitably turn into a beautiful painting that lingered in the minds of travelers and inspired aesthetic feelings.

Don't you agree that "the morning moon" and the "green Lugou grass" (Liu Lufen of the Qing Dynasty started a stanza entitled *Lament at the Wayside Pavilion Out of Town* in his *The Gull Dream Ci Poem* with: "I lament over the cold spring moon. The green Lugou grass rolls out into the distance.") are a perfect match?

Whether you have been to this place of historical significance or not, by now you must have gone beyond "musing over things of the remote past". In fact, there is much food for thought even if you simply muse over the remote past! What's more, the blood-stained stone lions, the bleached bones on the bridge, the boundless stretch of wind-blown sand, and the sobbing river form a solemn epic of their own. It is for sure that even the everlasting "morning moon" will greet you with a wan smile and an icy stare, instead of the gentle, quiet and beautiful look that used to stir your "refreshing perception".

The yellow current under the bridge is sobbing day and night. The soaring noble spirit is keeping company with the silent countryside....

They are all waiting for the day when brightness descends and torrents surge - the early morning of that day.

Spring at Big Bright Lake

Lao She

Spring does not last long in the North. Moreover it is often blown off by the fierce wind. Jinan's blossoms of peach, plum, crab-apple and so on are ravaged by sandstorms almost every year. When the sandstorm sweeps by, it turns dark all around, fallen flowers twirling in the wind. When it is light enough for the eyes to see again, spring has already gone! I remember once, at two or three o'clock in the afternoon, when lilacs had just bloomed, it was so dark that lights had to be turned on indoors. The wind grew gustier and gustier, and the sky turned from gray to yellow, to dark yellow, to yellowish black, finally to pitch black. The next morning I went out to check the two lilacs in the courtyard, only to find that the petals were so damaged that they seemed to have been cooked, and barely any tender leaves were left intact! Winds are rare in Jinan in autumn and winter. Maybe they are all saved up for spring.

With winds like that, there is hardly any spring in Jinan, neither is there much of a spring at Big Bright Lake.

The top three scenic spots in Jinan all have pleasant, ringing names: Thousand Buddha Mountain, Bouncing Spring, and Big Bright Lake. Upon hearing "Big Bright Lake", one has a mental picture of bright spring and a beautiful landscape. However, the truth is, it is neither big, nor bright, nor even a lake.

At present there is no clear expanse of water in the lake, but "fields" divided by earth ridges. Outside the "fields" are several ditches, along which pleasure boats sail in the name of sightseeing. Deep water is unnecessary for paddy fields, so the water here is dark instead of clear. Neither is rapid water required, thus the water here runs still. Lotuses and cattails scatter here and there. Earth dikes block water flow, while cattails blocks lotuses from view. There is no scenery whatsoever, just "crops" of various heights. Boats sail on the water as if they were zigzagging through Chinese sorghum fields, steaming hot and perhaps horribly stinking. Summer is better. If the water isn't that smelly, one may take in some fragrance of lotus blossom and certainly some green leaves. However, in spring, there is black muddy water underneath the boat and shabby dams on both sides. The wind is so wild that those fresh greens have to struggle for life. Therefore, it is neither big, nor bright, nor even a lake.

On the other hand, the lake has long been considered as a scenic spot. The reason why it is neither big nor bright is because the lake is no longer a lake. If we reclaim all the "fields", remove all the earth dikes, dredge the lake, it will immediately become big and bright - the lake covers a wide area, and Jinan abounds in cool spring water. This may only be wishful thinking right now. However, even now, even when nothing is changed, it is still a scenic spot, for it is no easy job finding such a wide expanse of water in the cities of Northern China. People would not care whether Thousand Buddha Mountain, which is no match for the lake, is counted as a scenic spot or not, for mountains are found everywhere in the North. By contrast, water is a rare blessing. Jinan is said to have 72 springs within its city walls and there is a river outside the city, but a lake is still an absolute necessity. With springs, ponds, the river and the lake all gathered together, Jinan is unique. Being the one and only "water town" in the North, it cannot go without a lake. On a boat trip we may see the ditches instead of the lake. But if we climb to a higher altitude, for example, to the top of Thousand Buddha Mountain, and look northward, we will see a stretch of grayish green-Big Bright Lake, and a curve of shiny gray running between Mount Hua and Mount Que outside the city - Yellow River. Then we will see why Jinan is unique, for there is not just some water, but plenty.

Besides, even if there is not much to recommend about the lake itself, its produce is worth mentioning. Gourmets probably outnumber aesthetes. Those who have been to Suzhou often remember the dim sum there, those who have visited the West Lake always miss the Dragon Well Tea, lotus root starch, water shield and so on. Perhaps food in the stomach lasts longer in one's memory than a glimpse of beautiful scenery. That granted, the cattails, wild rice stems and lotus roots from Big Bright Lake might be important contributors to its fame. Anyway, those aquatic products have the distinctive flavor of Southern China. Of all the northern cities, only Jinan could "afford" to sell bunches of huge white lotus flowers together with green vegetables in summer.

I once wrote a novel entitled *Big Bright Lake*, which was destroyed by fire at the Commercial Press during the January 28th Incident (in

Shanghai in 1932). I had a vague memory of a passage in the novel about autumn at Big Bright Lake, but the exact wording fails me. Mr. Sang Zizhong painted for me an oil painting of autumn at Big Bright Lake, which is still hung on the wall in my house. Both he and I focused on autumn at Big Bright Lake. There might be something there. Yes, it is because only in autumn that Big Bright Lake is somewhat striking. Jinan is at its best in autumn: sunny, warm, windless, clear and bright everywhere. Take a walk on top of the city wall in this season, and you will look down at a mirror of a lake decorated with faded lotus flowers and withered willows. Even those shabby earth ridges are now merged perfectly into the autumn landscape: a broken lotus or two on an occasional earthwork, some withered vine, a few scattered reed catkins. With all the "crops" harvested, the lake appears bigger, therefore brighter. And there are more. The yellowish Thousand Buddha Mountain stands to the south, on top of which sits a placid "peg"-probably a tower — of the Kaiyuan Temple. The open and vast river lies to the north. By now the mountain and the lake, the city and the river are "bright" indeed. Mr. Sang painted his picture on the northern city wall. In it he painted a few willows around the lake and one single pleasure boat on the lake. The lake water is grayish blue, and the willow leaves a touch of brown. In the background he added Thousand Buddha Mountain. The lake and the mountain form a bright and quiet autumn scene, with an imperceptible breeze caressing the tip of the willows.

Forgive me! I should have been writing about spring at Big Bright Lake, but somehow I digressed to autumn at Big Bright Lake. But maybe it is because Mr. Kangde assigned me the wrong topic!

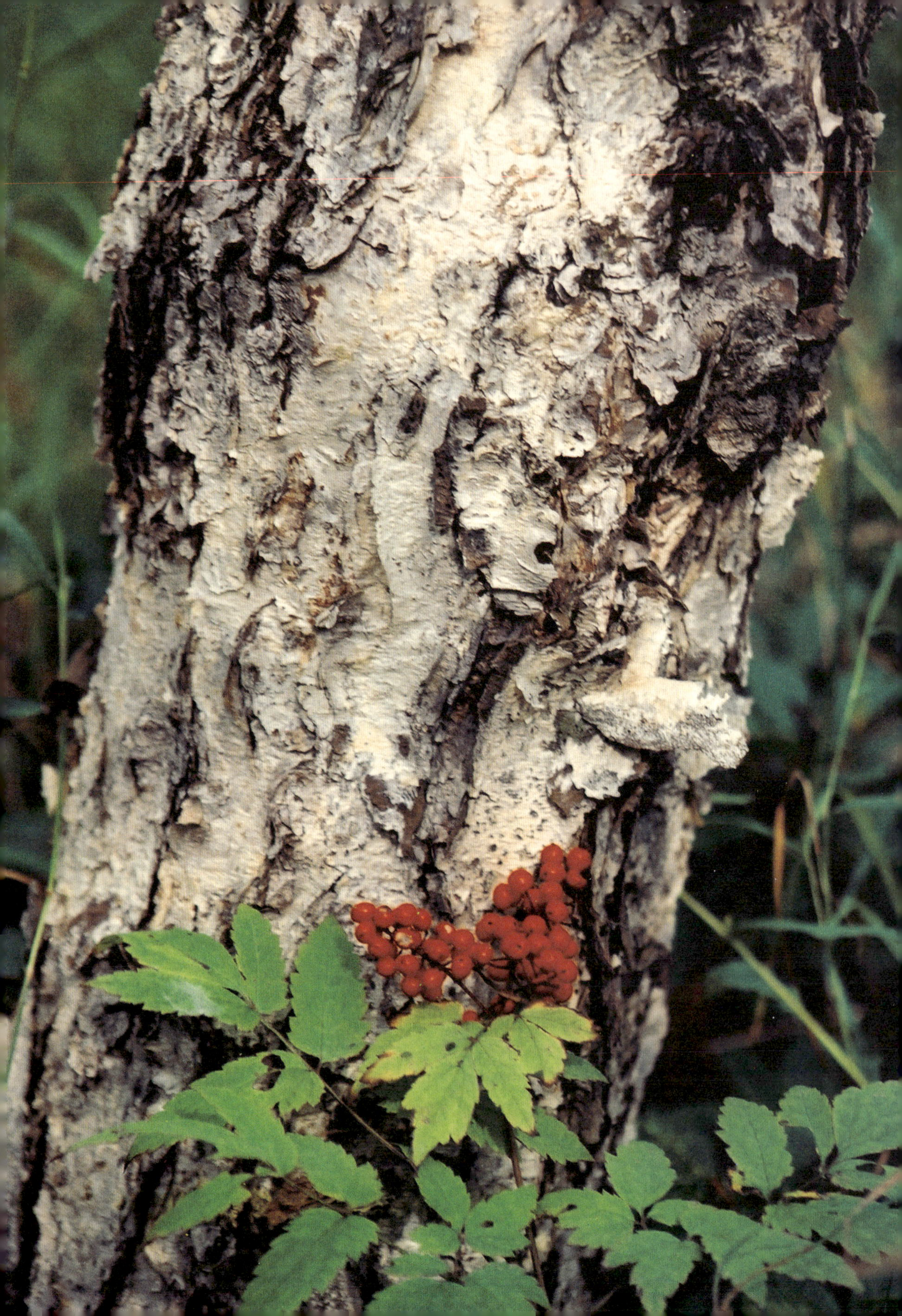

Paradise for Birds

Ba Jin

We had supper at the primary school where N worked. The heat had abated. The sun had set behind the hills, leaving a streak of rosy dusk over the horizon, on hilltops and tree tips.

"Let's go boating!" suggested N as we stood admiring the mountain view beside a pool in front of the school.

"O.K," other friends happily agreed, so did I.

We followed a pebble path and reached the riverbank in no time. Going through a grass-thatched pavilion there, we discovered several small boats moored under some huge trees along the bank.

One after another we jumped into a boat. A friend untied the rope, dipped the pole into the water, and the boat slid slowly towards the middle of the river.

Three friends rowed as I sat looking around.

Far in the distance there was a tower on top of a hill, surrounded by green trees. Towers like that are rare in this area. My friend Y's hometown is right over there. The next day I would set out for it, to climb that hill and that tower.

The river stretched out white, wide and not a stir. The boat glided over the surface. The rhythmic paddling of the three oars sounded like music to the ear.

The river narrowed down at one place where clusters of green leaves projected over the water. The tint was so pretty. They were the leaves of many banyans, but I couldn't locate the tree trunks.

The moment I said "many banyans" my friends corrected me. One friend said there was only one banyan, while another claimed two. I had seen quite a number of big banyans, but never one as big as this.

Our boat gradually approached the banyan. Thus I had a chance to have a good look at it. Indeed there was only one tree, with numerous branches. Many roots that had grown out of the branches hung down and found their way underground. A number of branches bent and touched the river, so much so that from a distance the whole tree looked as if it were lying on the river surface.

The banyan was flourishing (it was bearing small fruits, many of which had since come off) and seemed to be presenting us with its full vitality. All those clusters of leaves piled one upon another, leaving not a single chink in between. The bright green lit up our eyes, as if there were a new life rejoicing on every leave. What a beautiful southern tree!

Our boat stayed for a while under the tree. It was wet on the bank, so we did not land. My friend called it "Paradise for Birds", since lots of birds nested on the tree and the farmers forbade bird hunting. I seemed to hear wings flapping, but when I searched with my eyes, I could not see a single bird. There were just countless roots standing like wooden stakes. The ground was wet, maybe it was frequently flooded when the river tides rose. No bird in "Paradise for Birds", I could not help wondering. Then a friend poled the boat slowly back towards the middle of the river.

Some litchi trees lined the path along the river. It was tempting to see the red fruits hanging heavily among the foliage. Our boat headed for them. A friend guided the boat into a small ditch with his oar. When the boat stopped beside the path, we all jumped onshore.

Two friends climbed quickly up the trees, picked some litchi with leaves still on to throw down to us. N, Y and I stood eating the litchi right under the tree. After they had climbed down, we ate on the way back to the boat. The litchi was not ripe yet, so afterwards we all gave up.

The next day we went to Y's hometown, the place with the tower on the hill. We started from N's primary school and passed the "Paradise for Birds" for a second time.

It was in the morning when the sun brightened up the water and the tree. Again we lingered a bit under the tree.

At first it was all quiet. Then a bird sang a note. N clapped his hands. Immediately we saw a big bird flush, then a second, then a third. We kept clapping. Soon the wood was bustling with birds. Some were big, some small, some spotted, some black, some singing on the branches, some flying, some flapping their wings.

I was engrossed. My eyes could hardly take it all in. If I looked at one bird I would miss another. When I caught sight of one bird another flew out of view. A thrush fluttered out, got scared at our clapping, flitted back to the wood, landed on a twig and started chirping excitedly. What a sweet song!

"Time to go," urged Y.

On our way towards the village at the foot of the tower, I turned round to look at the exuberant banyan. I was a little bit reluctant to leave. My eyes had deceived me the day before. That place is indeed a paradise for birds!

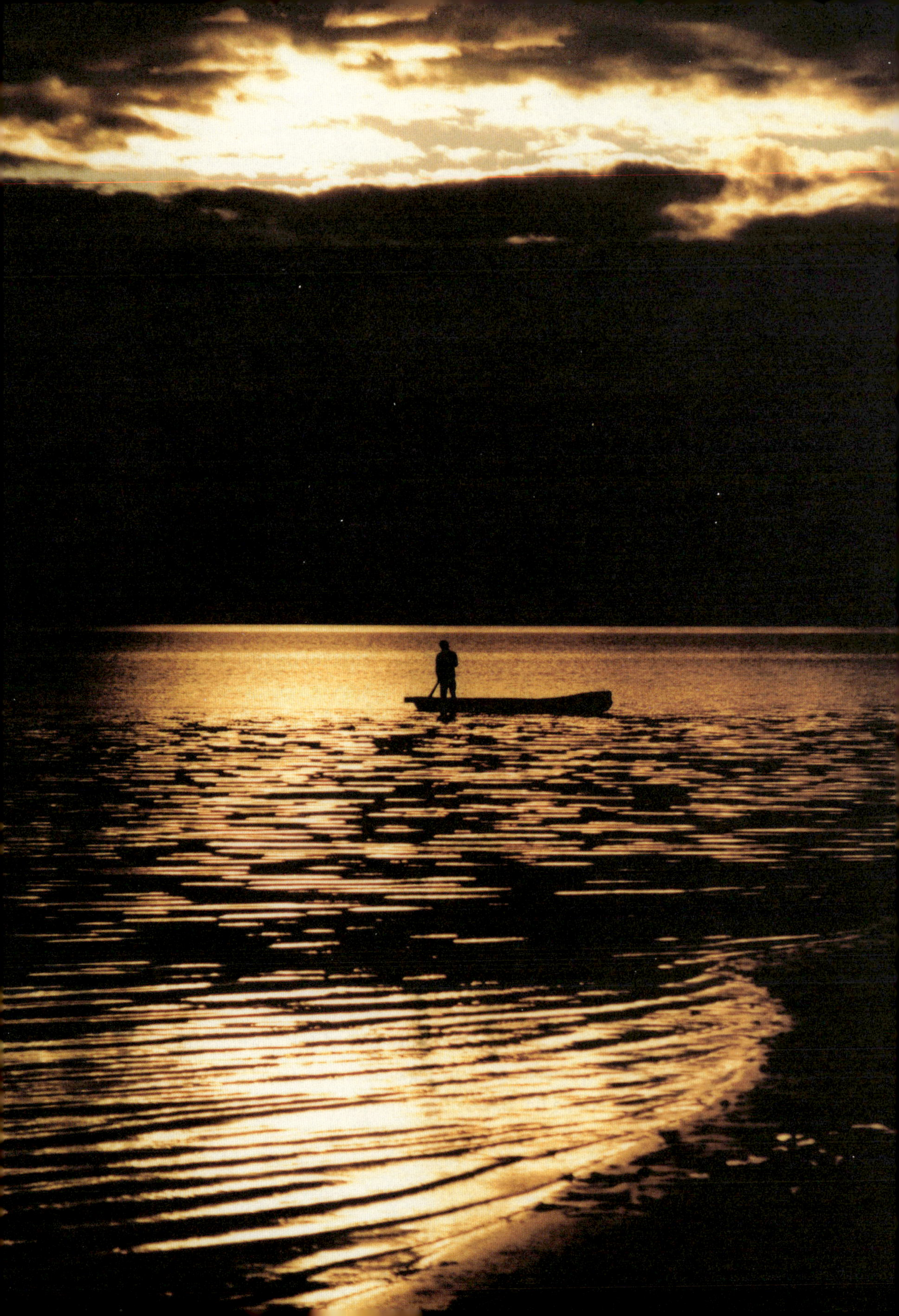

Travel Notes on the Taihu Lake

Zhong Jingwen

During my two-day sojourn in Suzhou I not only set foot on the fragrant grass of Zhenniang's tomb at Tiger Hill, but also had a drink from the No. 1 Spring of Southern Jiangsu Province and Northern Zhejiang whose water was as blue as king crab juice. Afterwards my companion Mr. Li and I exerted our remaining strength on a tour of the vast Taihu Lake at Wuxi. The itinerary had been set in advance, not decided on impulse or because of an unsatisfied desire for sightseeing.

A night train on the Shanghai-Nanjing Railway dropped us at Wuxi at nine o'clock in the evening. I will never forget how we arrived on a dark night lit up with myriad lights and how in a daze we were absorbed into it, accompanied by a drizzly spring rain.

Tired and comforted by the passable bedding at the hotel, I was able to sleep soundly through a spring night despite the uneasiness any journey entails. It was well past seven o'clock in the morning when I woke up. The sky was still gloomy but the drizzle was gone. We were delighted.

Each having pocketed a copy of *The Complete Tourist Guide to Wuxi* from the hotel front desk, we settled into a rickshaw that would take us to Taihu Lake.

I guess it is an experience common to average tourists that on your way to a well-known scenic spot, either you (as a first-timer, of course) can't help fishing for information from the rickshaw man or the sedan carrier with enthusiasm, or the latter starts an exhaustive briefing without being invited. (He has his intentions, not so good as to be a selfless volunteer teacher.) That was exactly what happened to us. My fellow traveler Mr. Li asked for all sorts of details; whereas I limited myself to the few absolutely necessary inquiries. As the Q-&-A session went on between them, I browsed The Complete Tourist Guide in silence. Published for promotion, it certainly was fascinating to some extent. What especially enthralled me, a fan of verse, were poems by celebrities in the appendix.

At last we reached the Huishan Hill, known for its "unrivaled scenery". The numerous food stalls and toy stores lining the path beyond the gate seemed to prove how attractive this hill was to visitors. The rickshaw man took us to the Huishan Temple, where we bought a dozen or so of pictures of the scenery. The Rising Cloud Building was not very tall, but tastefully decorated. One could not only climb up and look out, but take a short break inside to enjoy the tranquility as well. An ancient poet left the following poem on the building, "A sorrowful traveler in a desolate hill of late autumn, sat meditating in a house with loosened clothes. The red trees in the valley were going to endure the frost, and bronze percussion instruments produced clear melodies at the temple deep in the hill." Right now it was "the blooming season" of spring (The second line of a couplet on the upper-floor pillars reads, "Commanding the best scenery of the hill and the blooming season." What a beautiful line!) instead of the late autumn when "trees were dyed red by the frost". Therefore I was free to sit in the building "meditating with loosened clothes," yet without the sighs of "a sorrowful traveler in a desolate hill".

The No. 2 Spring under Heaven, what a sensational title! Although we were not there "alone with the small round moon in the sky," we did "come to try the No. 2 spring under heaven"! The spring was encircled by rocks and on top of it there was a pavilion. On the stone face near the pavilion were inscribed the characters "No.2 Spring under Heaven". In addition, there was a stone tablet with Emperor Qianlong's poem on it by the side of the spring. I could not refrain from remarking how interesting it was for this Manchu emperor, who was well-versed in both polite letters and martial arts, to have left poems or inscriptions here and there on his inspection tours of areas south of the Yangtz River, adding to the number of places of historic interest and scenic beauty, providing later tourists with things to enjoy and meditate on. Then it occurred to me that the age when Pi Rixiu wrote "From time to time I gathered fallen leaves at the monk's hut, and boiled stream water under the pine tree" was far gone. A sense of melancholy surged up.

Pressed for time, we, like Wen Zhiming (1470-1559, painter, calligrapher and poet), had to apologize to the Huishan Hill for "failing to climb the green and purple mountain in front of me." Neither did we find time to visit the many gardens, terraces, temples and courtyards scattered around the hill. The thing I regret the most is that I did not set foot on the Five- Li Street! Friends, listen to this:

The Huishan Street is five-li long.

The shoes are scented after a journey through flowers.

And this:

A willow branch coils around peach blossoms,

The red and green colors form a harmonious picture five-li long.

How attractive the Five-Li Street is in those popular poems! We arrived on a bright spring day when the willows had just turned green and the beautiful peach trees were in full blossom, yet I "missed" the scene. It suffices to say that there are always things contrary to one's wish in this world! Certainly I also realized that I might have felt disappointed or bored if I had had this "journey through flowers". However, regretful as I was, could I really find relief in such reasoning? If yes, then human emotions are just too vulgar.

We went to the Xishan Hill, which was on our way. There was the Longguang Temple on the hilltop and a tower behind it, but we turned back halfway for fear of not being able to return to Suzhou in time. I wondered if such haste had made us a laughingstock to the mountain deity. It might be unnecessary or even impossible to make excuses, but would it forgive the helplessness of such transient guests as us?

Having inferred from friends' remarks and *The Complete Tourist Guide* that the Plum Garden was a major scenic spot in Wuxi, we were naturally filled with expectations and joy upon arrival at its entrance. Judged by the name, the garden must claim a sizeable number of plum trees. The pity was we visited at the wrong time when the scene of "thousands of trees blossoming together to keep each other company" had been replaced by that of "green leaves making shade and branches weighted down by fruits"! Yet why such a fuss over missing the season? In the garden, peach trees, pear trees and other unknown flowers had succeeded the plum trees in their efforts to decorate the spring landscape by blooming in a riot of red, white, blue and purple. The moment we stepped into the Crane-Attracting Pavilion, we were reminded of the Crane-Releasing Pavilion on the Gushan Hill. I was amused when Mr. Li said that the crane released at the West Lake were attracted here. Looking out from the pavilion, I saw the glittering Taihu Lake and the towering mountains around it. My stress and worries gave way to a sense of enlightenment. Without thinking I started reciting a poem that I had read in the past, "Have a drink at the Crane-Attracting Pavilion, the Chu mountains are smiling and the lake glimmering". It was not so much enlightenment as intoxication.

After the Plum Garden, we strolled around an orchard where peach trees were in full blossom, then a couple of miles of fields and mountain trails over green grasses, through secluded woods. We stayed for a while at the Hall of Vast Expanse at the southern foot of the Guanshe Hill. The hall was built on a vantage point by the lake, where one had a nice view of the vast expanse of lake water, the imposing mountains, and the boats on the lake. There was a King Xiang's Shrine (Xiang Yu, 232-203BC, leader of the uprising that overthrew the Qin Dynasty) next door to the hall. Probably it had been because of the enhanced image of the tragic hero in Sima Qian's accounts that I loved and sympathized with him since childhood, and wrote articles against the traditional evaluation of him, as well as poems extolling his deeds. Of the articles, I could not recall a word, but the poems were still intact in some old manuscript. As I grew older I was no longer that much into things extraordinary and radical, but my perception of him was no worse than that of his enemy (the lucky station head [Here the author is referring to Liu Bang, 256 or 247-195BC, who beat Xiang Yu and founded the Western Han Dynasty]). I didn't walk into his shabby shrine without anticipation. In my mind his statue should at least resemble those of commonplace ancient warriors, with superhuman bravery and awe-inspiring strength. Yet what I saw was "a pale-faced, black-bearded, scholarly-looking man in emperor's ceremonial dress and hat" instead of a peerless hero capable of lifting a mountain! People in Southern Jiangsu Province and Northern Zhejiang Province had deprived him of his heroic spirit and turned him into a pedantic scholar.

Shortly after that we boarded a small steamboat at the foot of the Guanshe Hill to go to the Turtle Head Islet. This islet at the foot of the Chongshan Hill was named after its turtle head-like shape. There were a few other buildings and pavilions apart from the stately Temple of the Floral Goddess. The peach trees, which blossomed like a piece of red brocade stretching for hundreds of steps, formed an intoxicating picture of spring. When wind rose, the lush pine wood near the temple soughed like raging billows. A great number of odd-shaped rocks assumed myriad shapes on the islet. We paced up and down taking in the view: in the bright sun the surrounding lake, which expanded to meet the horizon, glittered like a vast pane of glass or a snow-covered suburb. Several pilgrims' boats traveled full sail in the lake. The few hills that rose proudly into the sky away from the mortal world made the lake all the more magnificent.

Lost in thought, I recalled my hometown, Shantou (or Swatow), whose coast shared similar features with what was in my view. Back when I had taught there, I would walk by myself along the beach at breezy dawns and moonlit nights. With the roaring of waves in my ears, I gazed into the distance. I would first feel lost, and then stand in awe. It was not until the scenery had changed appearance a few times or the moon had crossed to the other side of the sky that I returned to the noisy schoolhouse. The experience had taken place a few years before, yet the memory had not faded away. If life can be compared to pictures, would these count as some meaningful snapshots?

According to friends, the Taihu Lake was at its best at sunset. Yes, it would be sublime and fantastic to watch from the distance the scarlet sun sink slowly into the vast expanse of gentle water, but I couldn't afford the time to wait.

I imagined that the lake would be at its best not only at sunset, but more so in the moon light. I remembered a poem by Shu Liren entitled *A Trip to West Taihu Lake on a Moonlit Night* which went to the effect that, "The moon goddess polishes her mirror shiny, the dragon princess irons her piece of silk smooth. When the silvery water pours into the sea to the east, the Moon Palace joins the Crystal Palace." No wonder that in such an exquisite environment the poet exclaimed "How lucky I am to be in a boat on such misty waters on such a night", and posed the question "Was there a moon like tonight's when Fan Li eloped with Xi Shi on a boat?"

Afterwards we had a cup of tea at the temple. We wanted to linger, but time was running out. As we got on a bus at the foot of the Guanshe Hill and bid farewell to the lake, the parting sorrows stirring my heart were even more forceful than the waves stirring the lake.

On the Gan River

Feng Zhi

It is a perilous trip on the Gan River from Ganzhou to Wan'an. Boats frequently run up on rocks. However smart a boatman is, when his boat is on this stretch he would not trust himself, but pay a local navigator to guide him through. The navigator is familiar with every rock in this part of the river, as if it were a farm or a house inherited from his ancestors. He stands at the stern, holds the rudder, steers the boat away from rocks, smoothly and gracefully, like a snake gliding in the grass. When the dangers are left behind, he gets off at a proper place, and wishes you prosperity.

We boarded a boat on the Gan River on a balmy late October day. Since the boat was sailing downstream with the southerly wind, we covered quite a distance in two half-day trips. However, by around three o'clock in the afternoon, the wind started to blow harder and harder from a different direction. The navigator laid down his rudder, saying, "Ahead of us are the Shoal of Heavenly Pillar and the Road to Death; let's anchor here for the night" In such a gust the shoal ahead sounded too perilous even for an old hand like him. What's more, names like Shoal of Heavenly Pillar and the Road to Death gave one the shivers.

It was only four o'clock in the afternoon with the sun still high in the sky that our boat drew alongside and the boatman cast the anchor. There was no village in sight. Confined for too long in the boat, we jumped onshore, did our usual deep breathing, and felt relaxed. However, this time around us there were neither villages nor other boats, just sand and barren hills. Although kids from our boat frolicked on the sands, one felt an indescribable fear upon hearing the gustier wind and seeing the cloudier sky. Even the rocks seemed to break through the river surface in a ruthless manner.

My wife, who had been sick these past two months in Ganzhou, was lying in the boat, unable to sit up. During the few days when she was so sick that she lost consciousness, I sat beside her bed holding her icy hands, as if guided by her on a trip to the kingdom of shadows. By now she was recovering, but I understood from the way she spoke and acted that I could not expect too much too soon. After pacing the sand a few times in all the silence, I went back to the boat listlessly.

"Where are we?" she asked.

"I don't know. There is no village around."

...

The wind blew against the river. The river swayed the boat. Floating clouds blocked the nearly full moon from view. The kids on our boat were the first to fall asleep. I too was lost in fantasies and became oblivious of the surrounding world.

Soon I dreamed about making futile attempts at finding my way out of a forest, although I could hear people talking in the distance. When I woke up to the reality in the boat, the forest had gone, but the talking was still audible. Who else would be talking in such a deserted place? Then K, a fellow passenger, made a slight coughing sound.

"Is there any other boat nearby?" I whispered.

"I think I saw one not too far away," answered K. "Listen! There are people speaking, probably on the bank."

"It's half past twelve —" K struck a match to look at his watch. His words made me all the more worried.

Other people onboard were still sleeping soundly.

I went back to half-sleep in the hope that nothing would happen. An indefinite number of minutes went by, then the dog in our boat barked sharply, waking us all up. The talking voices in the distance didn't cease; instead they sounded closer and closer. I thought there might be something wrong.

Neither the dog barking onboard nor the talking voices outside stopped. Moments later, K bravely put on his clothes and sneaked out of the cabin. By that time everyone was awoke but held their breath. Only some furtive rustling could be heard as people tried their best to hide important belongings in obscure corners: in faggots, in stove ashes, inside cabin chinks... We all got ready for something unusual.

There were shoals upstream and downstream. Our boat was stranded in the wind, as if it were at the mercy of some magician. I stayed with my convalescent wife, not knowing what else to do. Suddenly a shaft of light entered through cracks in the cabin roofing. It shifted gradually from the front of the cabin to the back. Evidently its source on the river outside had moved by our stern to the bow. Not long after the first shaft of light had died down, another shaft followed suit an moved along the same way.

It was quiet but uneasy in the boat. My wife's heart was pounding. The kids were the only ones undisturbed in their sleep.

K came in and whispered that there had been two small rowboats passing by, one after another, both lit up by a fire on the bow. There were two guys on each rowboat. Were they spying on us?

Upon hearing that, I too went out. The landscape was bathed in dim silvery moonlight. The two spots of firelight traveled rapidly away on the river. Had they gone to inform fellow gangsters, or had they changed their mind because there were too many of us onboard?

I stared blankly at the two bright spots. Dogs had stopped barking, voices from the rowboats were no longer audible. Apart from the suspicion and fear permeating the boat, there was only the inhuman, vast and primitive world.

Eventually the boatman approached me; the unease of the passengers might have stirred him out of bed. He told me not to be afraid because it had always been a safe place around here.

"Then what are these two rowboats doing deep in the night?"

"Fishing. During the day there is too much traffic on the river for fishing. At night, it is the best time for fishing. Fishes gather around lights. Look, God knows how many fishes there are under these two rowboats..."

His words opened my eyes instantly, and the expression "lights on fishing boats" came to my mind.

...

The wind died away the next morning. As our boat was getting ready to set sail, two fishermen rowed their boat towards us from the other side of the river. They sold us two fleshy and delicious mandarin fishes, as if they had come to make up for the false alarm the night before.

Having been born and raised near the sea, my wife was used to fish and shrimps. Upon seeing those two fish skipping and jumping about, she smiled her first healthy smile since recovery.

(Kunming, 1939)

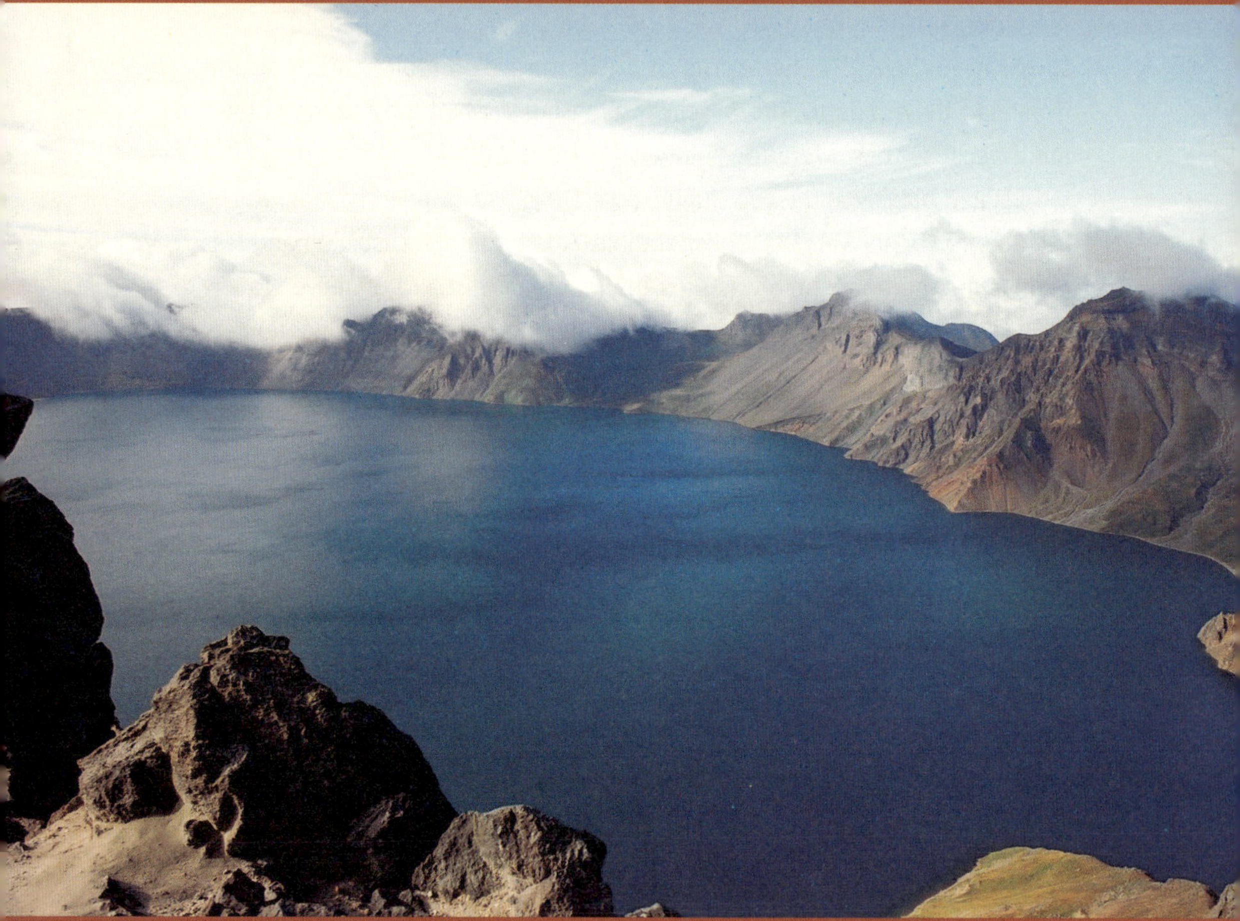

Mirror Lake

Zang Kejia

There are many famous lakes in our country. Upon hearing the names of the Dongting Lake, whose "vapor shrouds the Yunmeng lakes and waves pound the city of Yunyang", and the vast and majestic Taihu Lake, I can't hold back my yearning. Take West Lake: I have walked on the Su Causeway to take a good look at its beautiful scenery, and sailed on a solitary boat late at night to admire the reflected moon at Three Pools Mirroring the Moon. As to Big Bright Lake, which is located in my hometown, I have been a frequent visitor: in midsummer I rowed a small boat charging around in arrays of lotus, and, back in those dark days, I went there more than once with friends at cold night and sang wild songs to give vent to our feelings at the Li Xia Pavilion.

Yet I am a stranger to Mirror Lake. Starting from July, I had spent a month and a half covering 1,500 kilometers between Shenyang, Changchun, and Harbin, touring scenic spots and historical sites, visiting landmarks in industrial development. I managed all these despite my poor health, which amazed friends, who called it a "miracle". However, comrades in the Northeast told me, "A trip to the Northeast will not be worthwhile without a visit to Mirror Lake." They mentioned the delicious red crucian carps there and sang its praises. Descriptions of a scenic spot sound better than the real thing. My interest was aroused. But at the thought of the long journey, I hesitated and felt the kind of melancholy one had when a beauty was within sight but beyond reach. Guests staying at the same hotel left for it one group after another, among whom was an 82-year-old well-known doctor who said humorously, " I won't rest in my grave if I haven't seen Mirror Lake.

"Let's go!" His words helped me make up my mind.

A ten-hour's train trip took us from Harbin to Mu Dan Jiang, a city as beautiful as a flower blooming on the edge of the Great Northern Wilderness. The story of eight female soldiers drowning themselves in the river there in the face of Japanese invaders has won it national renown. In another two hours we were in Ningan County of Heilongjiang Province, where Mirror Lake lies.

We disembarked from the train and got into a "Gaz 69" truck. It had been a fine day the day before at Mu Dan Jiang, but rain had fallen on the Mirror Lake area. Once we had settled down, the light truck started running smoothly at a rapid speed on an open and flat road for a dozen kilometers. Light breezes spread ripples over the green Chinese sorghum and millet fields until where the green hills met the blue sky. Absorbing the scene before my eyes, I marveled at the vastness of our country. It was near early autumn, but the wheat here had just come out. What a drastic difference in climate inside and outside of the Great Wall! Our wagon was like a grasshopper boat braving waves in a sea of green. A huge tiger-like object approached us from the other direction with billows of smoke and dust, as well as howling gusts. It turned out to be a heavy diesel truck hauling five or six trailers on which lay bulky timber leaving the forest to contribute its willing share to the socialist construction! From time to time we passed graceful women from the Korean ethnic group in threes and fours, a jar on each head, dresses swaying. At the end of the smooth road came a rough dirt trail where holes had become water puddles. Our truck bumped along as if going through dancing motions.

The green mountains that had been discernible in the distance were out of sight. Our truck was halfway up the spiraling mountain path. On both sides of the path were all kinds of exotic flowers and rare herbs, some like strings of pearls, some like red lanterns, some like blue dangling bells, some like bright yellow trumpets. They lined up along the road to give visitors a cordial greeting with their beauty and fragrance. A hunter emerged from the deep forest, birds hanging from his long-barreled gun, a dog following at his heels. The sights refreshed visitors, in whose minds one after another brightly vivid images formed a colorful chain. But where was the lake?

"We're going around it," answered the comrade who had come to receive us.

As the truck made a last turn to the hilltop, the driver exclaimed, "Look!"

Ah, Mirror Lake — through chinks of the green trees I glimpsed your long silvery waist! You have guided the wagon to speed towards its destination and at the same time you have been chasing it enthusiastically as if you had caught sight of some beloved ones inside. My eyes, my nose, and my soul were all immersed in the wonderful atmosphere of Mirror Lake.

Novel-looking log cabins of various styles and colors stood close together or across a small path from each other. In the cabins lived different types of personnel and their families, as well as scientists, writers and well-known doctors from Beijing, Shenyang, Harbin... They would spend the last portion of summer here beside the quiet and secluded lake.

Lying in bed at night with lights turned off, I saw from the windowpanes the reflection of the lake, tender as the glances of a demure maiden. There was not a single insect chirping or waves breaking; it was tranquil, mysterious, and hazy, like in wonderland. The next morning I woke up totally refreshed, and then I realized that I had been sleeping in her gentle and cool arms.

I walked along the sunlit morning path towards her. There were people angling from the footbridge and three or four small boats were awaiting patrons. The lake expanded to the distant south and north, mirroring on its tranquil surface continuous green mountains. Neither cicadas nor birds sang. An occasional cormorant shot arrow-like from the rosy morning sky to the water. I stood on the bank to take in the surrounding precipitous peaks and the deep clear lake, forming a mental picture of a violent ground-shaking volcanic eruption a million years ago which drove torrents of water out of the earth's core to "form a lake flanked by towering gorges". Located 350 meters above sea level, she was a beauty who had lain down to stretch her slender body. Peaceful and natural, she was all by herself in seclusion. Was it out of fear of disturbing her that even in summer, birds, cicadas and insects kept quiet?

There were a few people on the path, some adults, some children. Upon meeting each other naturally they would nod, stop and talk for a few moments, as if they were old friends meeting again after a long separation. A group of kids walked out of the deep forest, mushrooms in hands, some of which were like yellow bread, others like small red umbrellas. Even old people in their 80s behaved like kids in nature, with a walking stick in one hand, and evergreen in another, showing the latter off to others as if they had found a treasure. The lake was a treasure lake. The turtles, crucian carps and red-tailed fish in it tasted so delicious that you would never forget it all your life. It was able to generate a huge amount of electricity, transport thousands of timbers to the outside world. The mountains were treasure mountains, too. Countless rare animals like otters, foxes and leopards made their home here and were by now enclosed in the depth of mountains by live wire netting. Those who had a stroke of luck in the forest could bring home infant-like ginseng, roots of large-flowered skullcap, etc. The area is abundant in medicinal herbs. The beautiful lake and mountains were not only rare scenic spots in the country, but also places of origin of precious produce.

In the pale setting sun, a small steamboat carried us towards the upper reaches of the lake. The lake surface was so smooth that our boat seemed to be gliding on a pane of glass. The clear ripples looked like fine wrinkles on silk, sleek and light green. The color gradually deepened into dark green in the distance. Looking up, one saw clouds floating leisurely in the sky; looking down at the lake there was another sky with hovering clouds. Hills on both sides stood inverted in the lake, all of them green and accompanying visitors with deep attachment. It seemed that the end was drawing near, but after a turn there were similar mountains and similar water. How one wished for some change! However, it remained the same across 60 kilometers from the north to the south. Indeed there was a green mountain beyond the mountain, and a lake beyond the lake. Compared with the rolling Dongting Lake, Mirror Lake was quiet and peaceful. In contrast to the vast and perfectly round Taihu Lake, Mirror Lake was more like a slowly-flowing river. By her side, Big Bright Lake was only a pool of clear water. Compared to her — an unaffected and chaste girl — West Lake in Hangzhou was a beautiful and glamorous young woman who had applied makeup to her brows and eyes. Mirror Lake was not artificial but naturally beautiful. There wasn't a single temple or other manmade spot on her banks, as if she were "afraid that any makeup would ruin her natural looks". In the morning she could be a mirror for goddesses to do their daily toilet. In the evening she could offer the Moon Goddess a chance to look at her own beautiful image. During hot summer days, if fairy maidens descended to bathe in the secluded lake, absolutely no one would steal their silk dresses to keep them from going back to heaven.

On the mountains surrounding the lake were luxuriant green woods. They were all "young growth" planted after liberation. Japanese invaders had burned down all the tall ancient trees in primeval forests during the enemy and puppet regime! The boat moved slowly in a light breeze as if traveling in a scroll of painting. Patches of chlorella bobbed slightly on the lake surface in reaction to the motion of the small steamboat. Large fish suddenly showed above water, bringing forth cries of surprise. The aquatic products company had cast nets with long strings of buoys. It was reported that the day before one net had hauled in over 12,000 kg of fish. Imagine, how beautiful it would be to haul in glittering fish in the golden lights of sunset.

Several glaringly red tile-roof houses abruptly came into view in the remote mountain area to the left of the lake, which enlivened the simple and plain scene of nature. We asked our captain, "What is over there?"

"It's is a hydropower station. The Anti-Japanese Amalgamated Army once wiped out a Japanese garrison force there." Those words set me thinking about the images and life stories of the martyrs in Harbin's "Museum of

Northern China Martyrs" which I had visited twice. They also reminded me of the anti-Japanese leaders I had met at Mu Dan Jiang's sanatoriums, some of whom were still carrying on their faces unhealed wounds from the Anti-Japanese War. The lake and the mountains were beautiful, but they were once bathed in blood, for more than one battle had taken place in this area. Therefore, the scenery was particularly beautiful and fetching!

There were eight major scenic spots on Mirror Lake. Mount Gu Major and Mount Gu Minor looked like their namesakes in the Yangtze River. The Pearl Gate was formed by two pearl-shaped hills, through which boats traveled. The "Hanging Tower", actually a natural waterfall at the north mouth of the lake, was the most famous. I had already admired its magnificence from color photos and paintings by masters. Water from Mirror Lake thundered down like a crystal curtain 20 meters from the dustpan-shaped mouth into the deep pool below, sending up a mist of millions of pearls. She was in no way inferior to waterfalls at the Lushan Mountain in either vigor or beauty, although she had not won great renown yet. The pity was that we arrived after rain and were consequently blocked access to it by flood on the other side of the mountain, so much so that we could only stand at a distance and catch a glimpse of the foamy water through green trees. Was it because it was too proud of its own beauty to be seen? We stayed nearby for five days and checked out the flood every day. Yet it did not subside. Time was running out, so we had to bid farewell to Mirror Lake in a wistful mood, feeling the trip a little bit short of perfection. Perhaps the "Hanging Tower" had done it on purpose to "hook" us back sometime later.

(Beijing, September 3rd, 1962)

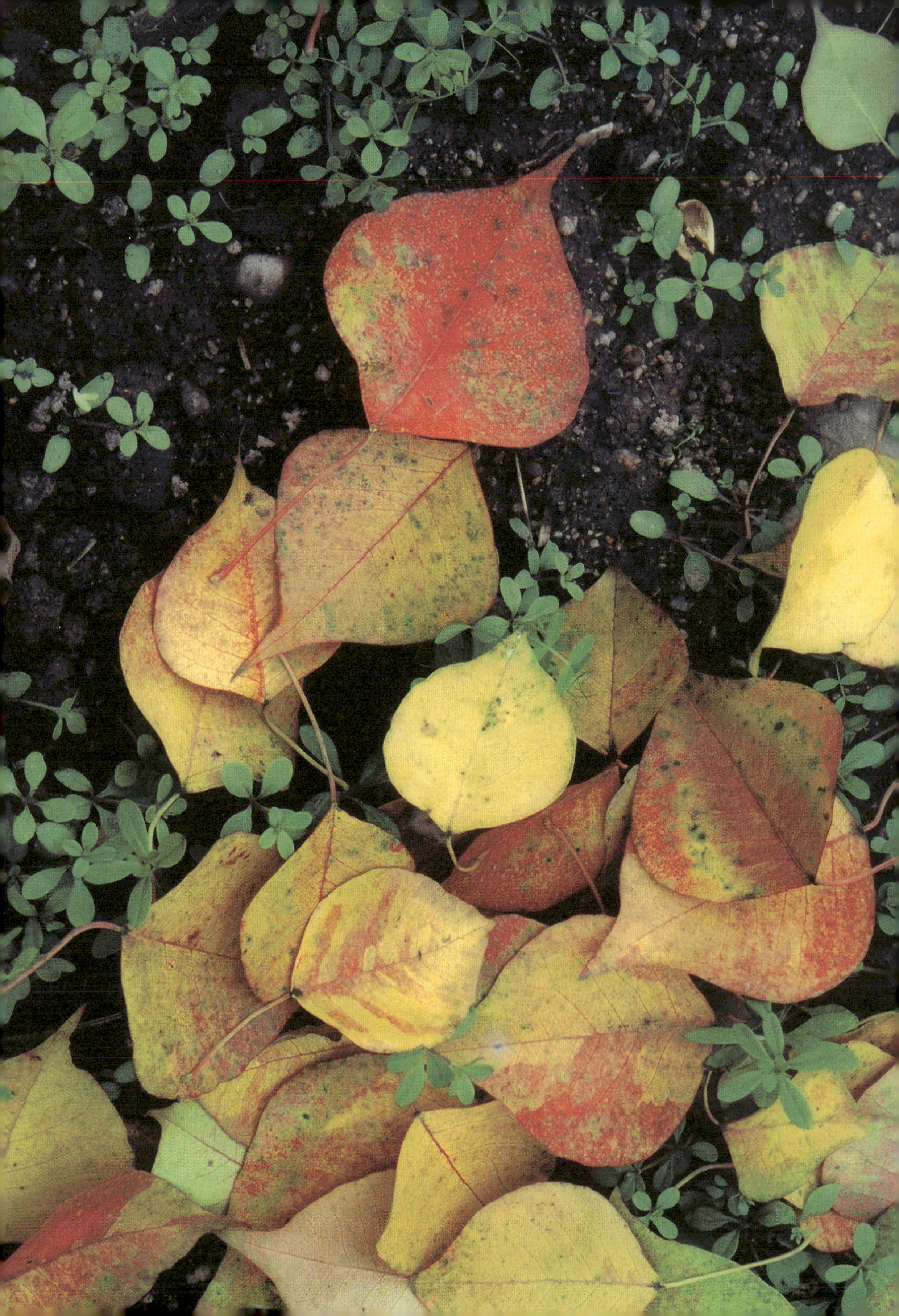

The Looks of Lushan Mountain

Feng Zikai

"Within reach but blocked by rainstorm, Lushan is not fit for climbing. Deep in the mist and fog, I suspect there are monks of the Six Dynasties remaining" (by Qian Qi). Despite this Tang Dynasty poet's advice against climbing the Lushan Mountain, we made it by car to the top within two hours. During these two hours the climate changed rapidly from midsummer to late autumn. It was 95 degrees Fahrenheit when we got into the car, and during the journey we first gave up fans then put on more clothes, later as we got off it was just over 70 degrees Fahrenheit. On the way to the No. 3 Guesthouse our car passed the Main Street, which gave me the initial impression of the Lushan Mountain as an arcadia: level and broad land, majestic buildings; facilities such as tea houses, restaurants and department stores; people, old and young, who were happy and pleased with themselves. However, they were not "shocked" at the sight of us, since there were such a great number of people coming up to spend their summer holidays. We barely managed to get two rooms at the heavily-booked guesthouse. The Lushan Mountain indeed lived up to its name as a celebrated summer resort. It was clear and sunny that day. I stood at a window gazing into the distance, and found nothing nearby but tall ancient trees whose shade screened off the sun, along with undulating hills in the distance where snowy clouds appeared and disappeared. Sometimes a stretch of wood submerged into a sea of clouds; on other occasions numerous towers and pavilions emerged from behind vanishing flakes of white clouds. As I stood gazing, a whitish cloud floated through our window. Hermits and persons of refined tastes would certainly open the window wide to welcome its company. However, lowbrow as I was, I immediately shut the window to our visitor. For my part, those white clouds are to blame for my failure to get the real looks of the mountain.

There are many scenic spots and historic sites in the Lushan Mountain area, of a reported total of above 200. Nevertheless in our ten-day visit we only covered places such as the Small Heavenly Pond, Flower Path, the Heavenly Bridge, Fairy's Cave, the Mouth Holding the Poyang Lake, Yellow Dragon's Pool and Black Dragon's Pool. Yu of the Xia Dynasty (c.2100BC - c.1600BC) once climbed the Dahanyang Peak while conquering floods. Kuang Su of the Zhou Dynasty (c.1100BC - c.771BC) used to lead a recluse's life here. Dharmacarya Huiyuan of the Jin Dynasty (265-420) planted pine trees in front of the East Woods Temple. Wang Xizhi (303-361,calligrapher) washed his writing brush at the Returning Sect Temple. Tao Yuanming (c.376-427, poet) inhabited the Lili Village near the hot springs. Li Bai (701-762, poet) read books at the foot of Wu Lao Peaks. Bai Juyi (772-846, poet) chanted poems in praise of peaches at the Flower Path. Zhu Xi (1130-1200, philosopher and scholar) lectured at the Academy of White Deer Cave. Wang Yangming (1472-1528. philosopher) took a walk at the Self Sacrificing Cliff. Zhu

Yuanzhang (1328-1398, founder of the Ming Dynasty) fought against Chen Youliang at the Heavenly Bridge: There are too many renowned historic sites to be counted. Yet it was quite troublesome to pay them a visit. What was more, a visit would come to nothing because they could not possibly inspire me, as I was no poet. Therefore I only paid my respects when convenient. Sometimes with my wife and children away at some places of seclusion or adventure, I would rest my head on a high pillow in the house on the hill 1,500 meters above sea level, browsing photos of Lushan's landscape or guidebooks and so on. With the mountain view right at the door, clouds and trees close to the window, away from the hubbub, cooled by the bamboo pillow and bamboo mat, I felt totally away from the summer heat. When I saw photos of the Heavenly Bridge, my interest was aroused, so much so that I went to search for it with my children. On our way up to the cliff top, a professor wearing a Nanjing University badge told me, "It is hard climbing up there, why don't you stop here as you are quite advanced in years? The bridge-like rock may have already fallen down. There is nothing except for this cliff." I looked up, and sure enough, the scene was different from the one in the photos. In the photos there are two cliffs facing each other, with a huge slab stretching out from the right cliff but falling a meter or two short of reaching the left one, as if one could stride over the gap. Yet in reality there was no slab but two cliffs a dozen meters apart, and we were climbing the one on the left. I said to myself, as this place was named the Heavenly Bridge, there should have been a slab serving as a bridge, but now the slab had fallen down. We sat on the cliff top to watch clouds rising and listen to enjoy the chirping of birds.

We took a few pictures and then walked back to the guesthouse in a carefree mood. At supper I inquired of someone from the Administrative Bureau as to when the bridge had fallen down. He replied that there had been no bridge in the first place, and that photos shot from a certain angle created the impression of a bridge. Ah, suddenly I saw it all: I did see a not-so-huge slab reaching into the air from where I had my conversation with the professor from Nanjing University, i.e., a dozen or so meters away from the left cliff. If a photo was taken from a place near the slab, in perspective the distance between the slab and the cliff would be wiped out, hence the pictures I had enjoyed so much. I was slightly displeased, as if I had been trapped by commercial advertising. Nevertheless, as far as photography is concerned, I could not criticize it as a sham, just that it was a bit "too" clever. The name of the Heavenly Bridge is weird too: Why is it called the Heavenly Bridge when there is no bridge at all?

The Mouth Holding the Poyang Lake faces the Yangtze River to the left and borders the Poyang Lake on the right, which is so spectacular that one should not miss it. One day we did climb up to the pavilion on top of the highest peak, only to find thick whitish clouds blocking both the river and the lake from view. We spent a long time in the pavilion, drinking tea and waiting for the clouds to disperse. Yet they hovered on and there was nothing to see but the vast expanse of whiteness. At that time a man walked into the pavilion holding a palm-leaf fan. He greeted us as a fellow townsman upon hearing the five of us speak the dialect of our hometown. It turned out that his hometown was Huzhou, a city close to our Stone Gate Bay, and our dialects were similar. So we started chatting in dialect. It was delightful talking in one's dialect, because every word of it went to the heart of the matter and gave full expression to the finest sentiments. This Huzhou guy was quite cultured and spoke elegantly. He said he lived in Shanghai, and on his way back from visiting his son in Jiujiang he had got off the boat to tour the Lushan Mountain. I asked why he had brought a palm-leaf fan along, and as a reply he listed its many uses: cooling the owner when it is hot, sheltering him from the scorching sun, acting as an umbrella when it rains and a cushion when one sits. He compared it to the palm-leaf fan held by the Divine Monk Ji Gong, which was why later we would refer to him as "the Divine Monk Ji Gong". While telling each other about our trip, he said he had arrived only the morning before. Upon learning that there were fixed time slots for restaurants on the main street to sell meal tickets, he bought one at 11 a.m., purchased a bottle of wine to bring to the Small Heavenly Pond where he offered it to the martyrs buried there, toured around, and then took the bottle of wine back to the restaurant to have a hearty meal. I too was heartened by his account. Whitish clouds were unyielding in their efforts to hide the Yangtze River and the Poyang Lake from us. As we were running out of time and there was a car waiting at the foot of the peak, we had to part with "the Divine Monk Ji Gong" and return to the guesthouse. Since then "the Divine Monk Ji Gong" became a subject of our conversation. Not having his name or address, or any real hope of another meeting, we had started treating him like some character in a novel. However, as luck would have it, when we were having dinner at Jiujiang's Xunlu Restaurant after leaving Lu Shan Mountain a few days later, "the Divine Monk Ji Gong" appeared again, palm-leaf fan in hand. It turned out that he also had gone there to wait for a boat to Shanghai. Again, we described to each other our travel experiences since parting company. This gentleman, traveling all alone and sometimes deep into deserted areas, had covered far more places than we had. I only remember the episode during which he climbed up to the top floor of an ancient pagoda only to find a flushed yellow weasel. In Huzhou dialect he remarked, "I gave it a fright, and it gave me a fright!" I felt the line almost poetic, lacking just the rhyme. Wasn't the line of poetry by Yang Wanli of the Song Dynasty, which went to the effect that "I wandered into a no man's land, starting up mountain birds which in turn gave me a start" describing a similar experience? Nowadays some free verses in vernacular Chinese discard rhymes, allot a vernacular sentence, or even a single "but" or "no" to each line, and make it really hard for me to see what they convey. On such occasions it would occur to me that if they could write as poetically as our "Divine Monk Ji Gong" spoke, I would not mind the absence of rhymes.

Eating at Jiujiang's Xunlu Restaurant seemed to be quite similar to dining out in Shanghai. But it was different in the mountain. The No. 3 Guesthouse, where we had stayed, was a kilometer or two away from the main street and there was no other restaurant around. We could only have meals in the guesthouse. The food was cheap and aplenty. But it was the table d'hote rather than a la carte, and there were fixed hours for serving meals. So it was not a restaurant, but a canteen, like the ones at school. Not having eaten at a canteen for 40 years, I felt rejuvenated in my old age. There was a restaurant a kilometer or two away on the main street, but it too had fixed hours. Besides, the food supply was so limited that, without purchasing a meal ticket in advance, one may quite probably go sightseeing with an empty stomach. In the boat to Jiujiang, passengers were divided into five or six eating shifts, with each shift an allowed time slot of 20 minutes. Meal tickets had to be purchased in advance. There was a notice put up in the canteen which read "No drinking please". A fellow passenger observed, "To eat is to fulfill a task." I said to myself, it was understandable when such a small canteen onboard a ship had to cater to so many people, but surely things would be better in the tourist area in the mountain. Yet restaurants in the mountain were no better. I do hope that there will be improvements in the coming years. Why? After all this is a tourist area! Not a school or a training center! People seldom find time to go sightseeing. When seized with the desire to tour around, they would inevitably delay meals. If hungry they would certainly long for some snack. Wouldn't it be even better if areas of tourist interest allow sightseers to make the most of their trip by offering them food and drink whenever such need arises? However, the Lushan Mountain has always impressed me favorably, and the catering there has been no exception. As we opened a bottle of Tsingdao Beer the foam sprayed yards beyond. I thought that Tsingdao Beer seemed to be much more foamy than my favorite brand of Bright Beer in Shanghai. After returning home I hurried to buy some Tsingdao beer, but as I opened the bottle there was no splashing foam, exactly the same as Bright Beer. Well, the atmospheric pressure at 1,500 meters above sea level had a hand in it! How delicious beer in the Lushan Mountain was!

(Shanghai, September 1956)

Revisiting Bei Dai He

Chen Hengzhe

We must always associate two things with Bei Dai He, one being westernization and the other, fashion. Unfortunately, I could not rid myself of my native characteristics despite my overseas experience, neither am I good at following fashion. Therefore, there must be something else prompting me to visit Bei Dai He, and what's more, to be eager to go there and reluctant to leave.

There might be a thousand kinds of sports and martial arts, but none agrees with me, which is one thing I regret in my whole life. Come to think of it, I learned to ride a horse in my childhood, and later as an adolescent I learned to skate, play tennis, and ride a bicycle. But none of them seemed to have agreed with me. One after another they came knocking at my door, then one after another they departed unobtrusively, without leaving any trace in my mind, or any feelings of attachment and melancholy. However, the god of swimming has found an unexpected disciple in me, a good-for-nothing.

As soon as I leap into the water, I feel an indescribable pleasure comparable to that of a thirsty person getting a hearty drink of water. After some swimming, I lie face up on the water, and all my muscles will relax, my mind getting a better rest than in sleep. Waves are lashing by my ears. My body is swaying up and down with waves like a feather. My mind is in peace and the world means nothing.

Apart from swimming, there is one more thing at Bei Dai He that attracts me profoundly — the boundless sea. If you take a rickshaw at the train station, soon you will see a curving expanse of light. Your heart will leap, and your depression will be dispelled instantly by a sense of pleasant coolness. This time I spent six days there with Shuyong. In the first four days, it was sunny and clear during the day but cloudy and moonless at night. Yet every night we went down to the beach to watch snowy waves pound the shore and to hear billows roar. Although thick clouds blocked out the moon, in the dim light one could sense another aspect of the greatness of Nature.

One day, when the sun had just set but there was still some light left, both the sea and the beach were deserted. The vast sky met the boundless sea in the far distance. Suddenly three lone birds flew from the distant east, gracefully and in step with each other. They flew over where we sat towards the west, gradually turning into three small black dots. The dots grew paler and paler until they merged into the smoky sky over the horizon. Somehow I was suddenly seized with a profound sense of loneliness and sorrow. Three lone birds, coming from some place unknown and going to some other place unknown, met with the two of us solitary travelers in the vast expanse of sky and water at a desolate dusk, never to run into each other again. The mountains, rocks, the sea and tides are there forever, but such a chance encounter will never repeat itself.

Since the sun rose from behind the East Hill, we could only see the rosy clouds of dawn, but not the morning sun itself. When the sun was finally visible, golden rays had already lit up the sky, and human shadows were long on the ground. Similarly, sunsets took place behind the West Hill. Only the crimson clouds gave us a hint as to what went on over there. The one thing that was visible was the moonrise. We went to wait for it on the beach every day, only to find an overcast sky. On the fifth night, we kept waiting until half past seven, but to no avail. There was no one else on the beach and it was darkening. All was quiet and mysterious. Suddenly Shuyong cried out in surprise, arousing me out of my reverie. Do you know what had happened? It turned out that a stripe of red light had leapt out in the east where the sea merged with the sky. The light expanded gradually into a huge red fireball hovering over the horizon. In no more than a quarter of an hour, a wheel of a cool moon had presided over the sky and silvered the vast sea below. Our five-day-long pious attendance was finally rewarded that day. We hurried back to the hotel, grabbed some supper, hired a rickshaw to get to the Mountain of Continuous Peaks, lay down on the Lotus Stone in the pinewood at the Lotus Stone Park, and started enjoying the moonlight both in the sky and over the sea. The clouds that night were especially lovely, some dispersed and light, others thick and layered in good order. They changed the shape and glow of the full moon from time to time, making it all the more adorable. However, out on the sea you might hope that the sky would be clear so that you could appreciate the greatness and fresh charm of the boundless silvery waves.

On the last day, we spent quite some time at a friend's on the East Hill. There I learned a new style of swimming. In the evening we went picnicking with our host, hostess and their children at Dove's Nest. It was only after the red moon had emerged from below the sea and human shadows had fallen on the ground that we returned reluctantly in the moonlight. After a reluctant farewell to our host and hostess, we took a rickshaw to head for the train station. On the way the shimmering waves and flitting clouds accompanied us on the other side of the wood.

The beach at Bei Dai He stretched from the east to the west, lying to the north of the sea. So the seaside area could be roughly divided into an east section, a middle section and a west section.

The east section centered upon the East Hill. Inhabitants there were mostly related to churches. The education they had received was neither too modern nor too traditional, neither too much nor too little. Families were the axis of their life. Usually the wives and kids would spend the whole summer there, while the husbands only came to stay occasionally. Nine tenths of them were foreigners, especially Americans. The other one tenth were Chinese, mostly working for the Union Hospital or related to churches. They probably came here every year, so they knew each other, but they were also friendly to outsiders. When I swam there, I would frequently come across some acquaintances in the sea. They would introduce me to someone else, make us shake hands standing in the water and say "nice to have come to know you" to each other. Yet how possibly could we get to know each other? A person's appearance and facial expressions are greatly different in the water than on land.

The middle section centered upon the Stone Hill. Most inhabitants there were businessmen, with a large number in recent years of Germans and Russians who had suddenly become rich by doing business in China. The axis of their life is not family, but society. There were a few exceptional wives with kids, but those were far from typical. The typical middle section symbols were scarlet lips, provocative glances, and magnates' paunches. They "made love" boldly and resolutely, intimate as flies with honey, as if to make up for the insufficiency and dullness of sexual life since Adam's time. However, with closer observation you will sense a kind of insouciance in the dissolute and sensual life. It seemed that they only wanted to enjoy while they could.

There were few Chinese among them, let alone Chinese women. When I swam there, they all paid me surprised attention. Their attitude towards the Chinese was typically "Shanghai-minded". Let me tell you a story to illustrate how prevalent this attitude was among this type of foreigners. A friend of mine once went on a trip with her husband to the top of the West Hill. The trek down the hill was quite rough. While walking they saw two French kids, a boy about ten and a girl seven or eight years old. The girl, frightened by the steep hill and shivering, begged the boy for help. But the boy refused and rapidly went down by himself. Disgusted, my friend made her husband leave her to help that girl. Afterwards at the foot of the hill, the grateful girl tried to strike a conversation with them by inquiring about their nationality. My friend asked her to guess. She ventured, "Are you British?" "No. Don't you see my yellow skin and black hair?" A bit surprised, the girl tried again, "Are you Japanese?" Wrong again. "We are Chinese." Believe it or not, the girl was so shocked that her lips turned pale, her eyes went blank, and her facial muscles started quavering. She shouted her brother's name like crazy. The boy who had not gone far was in turn shocked. He immediately came to hold her hand, showing dependence on each other in times of difficulty and danger. At once angry and sympathetic, my friend deliberately stared and bawled at them, "Don't you dare to leave!" Even more frightened, the two kids did stand still. She told them, "If I don't teach you a lesson today, you'll grow up into two international vermin. Listen, go home and tell your parents about the two frightful and contemptible Chinese you met today. Tell them that the Chinese lady had her husband help you, young girl, to go down the hill although she herself was having a hard time, while your own brother wouldn't lend you a hand. Ask your parents, how do these two Chinese gangsters compare with French gangsters? And with your French gentlemen? Go now. I hope today's event is an eye-opener for you!" The boy was after all an elder brother, so he shamefacedly held out his hand, thanked them, apologized, then took his sister back home, turning his head now and then in astonishment.

The west section centered upon the Mountain of Continuous Peaks. Besides diplomats, inhabitants there included wealthy Chinese and retired nobility. It was they who organized the Society of Public Welfare. Although we don't think we belong there, when we think of those arrogant foreigners, whether scarlet-lipped and plump-armed, or bald-headed and glib-tongued, we can't help being grateful to those venerable, eminent, influential and wealthy public welfare activists for saving a bit of our national dignity.

We felt less inhibited swimming in the bathing place belonging to the Society of Public Welfare, and much happier than swimming in the one in the middle section. Moreover, there were life guards who followed you and relieved you of the fear of drowning.

Quite a number of Chinese lived in the west section and many of them were female. But the majority of those whom I saw swimming or horse riding were teenage girls. Most women in their twenties would just sit there gracefully holding an umbrella and simply watch. At most they would slowly peel off their stockings, hold their pretty fashionable cheongsam and walk cautiously on the sands. As to women in their thirties, I hadn't seen a single one during my six-day stay there. Yet there were young couples romancing, although in a manner entirely different from the Westerners. The Westerners living in the middle section made love boldly and resolutely, while the "fashionable" class in the west section, as I saw it, would only walk along the beach and talk to each other under the cover of moonlight and rising tides, rather secretively and bashfully. Besides, seldom did a couple venture out alone. Instead, five or six couples would come out together and then break up near the beach. What I learned form the few days' stay there may be limited, but this phenomenon might well represent the freedom of and restraints on the social life of some Chinese youth living there.

September 1932

Climbing the Taishan Mountain in the Rain

Li Jianwu

In the past decades there had been more than a few times when I looked out of a train window at the Taishan Mountain and felt indebted to our age-old cultural tradition, as the saying "When Confucius stood at the top of the East Hill, the Lu Kingdom looked smaller, while the world was much smaller once he had climbed the Taishan Mountain" popped up in my mind. Du Fu dreamed of "ascending to the summit (of the Taishan Mountain) to find all the surrounding mountains dwarfed". So did I. Yet I had always been in such a hurry that I let opportunities slip.

On the day I scheduled to climb the Taishan Mountain, the weather was not helpful. It was raining. The drizzle seemed to be gnawing at our hearts instead of falling on the ground. The sky was gloomy, and so was our mood. We had agreed to set out in early morning, but the rain was falling more and more heavily as all of us gathered together. Should we wait until it cleared up? It was downright depressing "waiting" for the uncertain. When the sky finally lightened up at half past eleven, I could not wait any longer. "Let's go!" I urged the young guys to gather their things and together we headed for the Daizong Archway in high spirits.

We could not tell whether it was smoke or mist that met our eyes. Anyway the entire mountain was enveloped in an indistinguishable gray, making the ancient Taishan Mountain all the more imposing. Shortly after the Daizong Archway a deafening roar attracted us to the dam of the Tiger Hill Reservoir. Seven columns of torrential water cascaded out of the arches like seven bolts of glimmering yellow brocade down onto jagged rocks , sending up splashes of white foam which in turn descended upon the whirlpool below. The place was named the Bend of Small Horned Dragon. The dragon was said to have been brought up to heaven by Lü Dongbin, but at the sight of the churning water one might wonder if it had returned home. We made a detour around the Tiger Hill to stand on the dam; to one side of which there was a placid lake that hardly stirred in the gentle breeze and drizzling rain, while to the other side thousands upon thousands of ferocious troops seemed to be hiding under the exquisite yellow brocades. The comparison to yellow brocades was made for convenience's sake, in fact they were more like strands of spun yarn carrying delicate patterns in the absence of any warp and weft, or pieces of transparent white cotton with similarly transparent yellow designs. Maybe only the Spinning Damsel could weave such a spectacular scene.

As the rain gained strength we turned into the Shrine of Seven Deities behind the Temple of the Queen Mother of the Western Heavens. There were seven statues. Lü Dongbin stood in the middle flanked by his friends Li Tieguai and He Xiangu, while his four disciples waited on either side, hence the name the Shrine of Seven Deities. There was nothing outstanding about the statues of Lü Dongbin and his two friends, but the two pageboys in niches and the old man opposite the Willow Tree Sprite had been bestowed with unusual vividness. Average temple statues are often either insipid or uncanny. The few original ones did not look Chinese, neither could they rival this lifelike and easily accessible old man. The obscure sculptor must have had a profound knowledge of how human appearance changes with age. I would have gone on admiring the artistry if the young guys had not called my attention to the time.

We started on the route uphill in the rain. There were three stone archways in a row: the First Heaven Gate, The Place Where Confucius Rested, and the Celestial Steps. The sound of water faded away, while grand red doors blocked the mountain from view. Once through the doorways we found ourselves in a bright open space, face to face with the mountain. As we climbed upwards, water flowed downwards. The Mid Creek that eventually fed into the Tiger Hill Reservoir accompanied us until the Mid Heaven Gate. A mixture of rainwater and spring water oozing from cracks on sheer precipices ran along the slope into the mountain creek. Gradually the trickling developed into a thunderous roar. Sometimes the wind would tear an opening in the clouds, through which we caught a glimpse of the South Heaven Gate which seemed to be standing erect on the hilltop not that far away, along with the Steeper Eighteen Bends that lay prostrate like a grayish white python across the gorge. But more often black clouds blotted out the sky, so much so that the mountain ranges were transformed into landscape paintings in Chinese ink and wash. We waded across the shallow part of the Mid Creek and reached the famous Jing Shi Valley in no time. The flood had run over a plot of level stone ground one-*mu* in area on the smooth surface of which had been inscribed the entire text of *Vajracchedika-sutra*. Each character was as large as a *dou*, a traditional Chinese measure for grain, but as the years went by floods had scoured most of them illegible. Afterwards we went back to the main route. The rain had stopped without our noticing it. Sweaty as we were, we were only too glad to peel off our raincoats and cool off. As luck would have it, we found ourselves in a cypress wood where it was so dark that we felt as if dusk had fallen ahead of time. Sweat was gone and chill crept up. That explained why people called it the Cypress Cave. Gathering ourselves up, we climbed at one go up the Huangxian Ridge via the Hutian Pavilion. The reddish yellow gravel there made it self-evident why the Mid Creek was so turbid in color.

I leaned against the stone archway at the Mid Heaven Gate and looked around, feeling both proud and worried. I was proud because I had covered half of the trail, worried if I could manage the other half. The clouds dispersed while the mist had risen again. It was past four in the afternoon after all that climbing and break-taking. Hardship did not seem to be looming ahead, for what stretched in front of us was a smooth downhill dirt path. The young guys scampered down, and I, suddenly feeling rejuvenated, followed them, talking and laughing.

Before we knew it the downhill path had given way to an uphill one. The climb became harder and harder as it gained gradient. All the time the path remained wide. Only when you leaned forward would you stare into an unfathomable gorge. You could see but not hear water flowing down there. Looking up to the west, I saw a white ribbon less than a meter in width hanging across the sky and swinging ever so with the wind. A closer look would be ideal, but the vast gorge separated us from it. We were still showering praises on it when we ran right into a drizzle in front of a stone bridge. It turned out that there was another waterfall right next to the bridge ready to give us a big surprise. Six to ten meters in breadth, it rushed down a short length, and with a roar crashed into the odd-shaped rocks under the bridge, sending spurts far and wide. From then on, the mountain creek turned from the left side of the path to the right. The babbling accompanied us all the way up to the South Heaven Gate.

After the Cloud Walking Bridge we were on the winding path up the highest peak of the Taishan Mountain. The South Heaven Gate should be closer, but we lost its sight thanks to all the bends along the path. Weeds and wild flowers of all shape and color crowded over precipitous crags. Old as I was, I gathered some of them like a kid, held onto them until the leaves and flowers all shriveled up, and then apologetically threw them into the mountain creek to let the water wash them away. However, what cleansed the soul were those "twisted and robust pine trees that feed on rosy clouds". High altitude posed no problem to them. They struck root in the cracks of sheer cliffs, twisted their trunks like coiling dragons carved on pillars, spreading out their branches in mid-air, as if fighting against gusts and dark clouds for the light of day, or teasing the gentle breezes and whitish clouds. Some pines grew so impatient expecting you that they went up to a vantage height to keep vigil. Other pines were waiting for you with green umbrella-like crowns. Still others appeared content with their lot. Anyway they made you feel that they were the natural masters of the Taishan Mountain, and that both were integral part of the scenery. The mist coiled up the gorge down the Pine-Facing Hill. Darkness was falling. Putting one foot forward, then another, I lost count of the steps I had climbed, as if the climbing had been going on all my life. What fun, and yet how rough it was! Finally, the end of the Gentler Eighteen Bends came into view. I raised my head at the Ascending to Heaven Archway, only to find the Steeper Eighteen Bends leading up to the South Heaven Gate like a long, long ladder. My courage was receding. The newly paved stone steps were so narrow that they could not hold the entire sole. No wonder Ying Shao of Eastern Han Dynasty wrote in *An Account of the Ceremony on the Taishan Mountain Offering Sacrifices to Heaven and Earth* that, "Viewed from below the Heaven Gate is comparable to a hole through which one has a glimpse of the sky. Along the 3.5-kilometer-long narrow winding footpath there are thick ropes to help climbers up. Aided by two attendants on both sides and another in front, the climber sees both the soles of the person ahead and the crown of the head of the person behind. Together they form a human ladder. What a rough climb it is to scale the rocky cliff and touch the sky." An old man leaning sideways in his ascension overtook us. An old lady carrying a pilgrim's sachet passed by us with seeming ease despite her bound feet. Just as Ying Shao had mentioned, my eyes followed them but my feet did not. I clutched at the iron railings and gripped the young guys, stopping to catch the breath every dozen steps. Eventually, I got to the South Heaven Gate at seven o'clock.

The heart was still pounding wildly and my eyelids quivering, but I had actually made it to the top. How could it be possible for me to manage the neat but endless winding footpath down below? I strolled along the Heaven Street as if I had had nothing to do with all that hardship. The small hotels lining the street were otherwise indistinguishable except for a mark: a bamboo strainer hanging from the door, a pair of parrots at the window, a wooden club, a golden ox, etc. The more spacious ones had tea tables, while the small ones could only afford small low tables on heatable brick beds. They were caught between towering rocks on the back and a vast chasm in the front. There was something unique about the rocks too. Ancient poets described the Taishan Mountain as "rocky". If you read the annotation you would see that by "rocky" they referred to the way rocks had amassed. In fact once you were on the summit you were confronted with them. There were rocks resembling a lotus petal, an elephant head, an old man, and a crouching tiger. Some were scattered about to form a bridge. Some stood aloof like a pillar. Some bent to touch the sea. Some stared angrily at you. Others were just a blackish mass resembling nothing but a blockade in your way. Numerous legends had emerged with the passage of time. The Imperial Sacrifice Platform reminded you how spectacular it had been when emperors offered sacrifices to heaven and earth. A stone tablet at an unremarkable spot told you that it was right there that "Confucius had found the world smaller". A mountain pool was named the Hair Washing Basin because the Jade Maiden had used to wash her hair there. The White Cloud Cave was known for emitting white clouds in the past. Although clouds had stopped emerging from the cave, they were still floating among the hills. On a sunny day as you were enjoying the "boundless greenery of the Qi and Lu Kingkoms", a sudden gust "conjured up layer upon layer of clouds", and in a moment there was "a sea of clouds around you" as Song Zhiwen described in *Personal Reflections on the Three Days at Guiyang*. Were they really clouds? Evidently there were clouds over your head. So they might be piles of snow or cotton fiber that stretched continuously towards the horizon where the sea met the sky. A streak of sunray gilded the clouds, then lit them up and burned them away, revealing the true look of the earth below. There were two zigzagging white lines, one being the Nai River and the other the Wen River. A black dot crawled ant-like among the greenery with a wisp of smoke. As you stood gesticulating and making comments, the mist rose to wipe off illusions together with what was real.

We missed the spectacular sunrise. For that purpose you had to visit on a clear autumn day. However, we had some exclusive pleasure: the waterfalls we had seen in the rain were less impressive two days later as we went downhill. Smaller ones had dried up, while larger ones had shrunk. We followed the West Creek uphill and down dale, passed through the fragrant Apple Orchard, and lingered for quite some time near the Black Dragon Pool. We would have lingered longer had we not had a train to catch. There the mountains and water were of another style, different but still harmonious.

A mountain without water is as inanimate as a person without eyes. Our boldness to climb the Taishan Mountain in the rain was rewarded by the awe-inspiring waterfalls we saw on the way. Besides, the Doumu Palace offered us shelter as the rain turned into a downpour. We enjoyed the scenery in the rain without getting wet, so naturally the trip was all the more fascinating.

The Fuchun River, Where the Green Mountains and Blue Water Form a Pleasant Contrast

Zhou Shoujuan

A few years ago I had an impressive trip to the Fuchun River with several old friends. We had planned to go up the river until Yanzhou, but as soon as the sightseeing had been over at the Fishing Terrace, a fellow traveler who preferred the bustling West Lake to the tranquil Fuchun River bribed the boatman into telling us that what lay ahead was a dangerous zone frequented by bandits. We headed back for Hangzhou in haste. Later when the conspiracy became known I felt upset. Although the idea of a revisit came back to me from time to time, there was always something more pressing to attend to. Who would have thought that my wish would eventually be fulfilled when, at the end of my three months' secluded life at the town of Nanxun, Zhejiang Province after the August 13 Incident of 1937, I boarded a Jiangshan boat that was to take me to Nanping Village

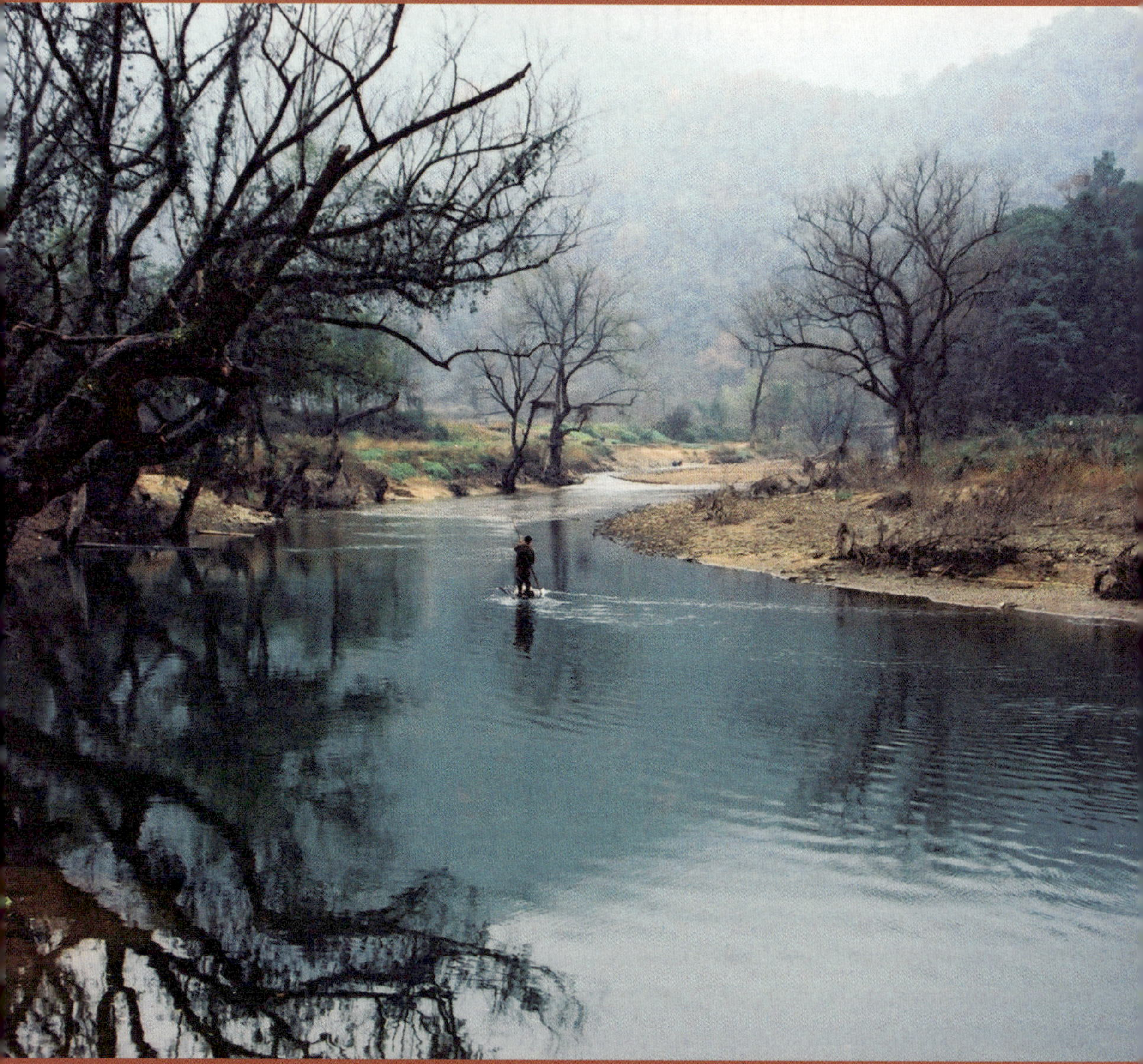

of the Yi county, Anhui Province via Hangzhou over the entire length of the Fuchun River, enjoying the blue water and green mountains to the fullest extent. The picturesque scenery made me imagine myself part of the long scroll painted by Huang Zijiu for the Fuchun River. I felt as if I were in paradise. Yet on the previous occasion a number of us came looking for signs of spring, while I took this trip alone to seek asylum from war. How time had changed!

The most beautiful scenery of the Fuchun River was to be found at a section called the Seven-Li Rapids, or the Seven-Li Shoals, a 3.5-kilometer stretch west of the Fishing Terrace. There, screens of green mountains lined the banks. The water was so shallow and limpid that the fish and pebbles on the riverbed were clearly visible. The rapids were rare wonders with torrents and whirlpools. Well, since my poor writing could hardly communicate the beauty, let's find proof in the fine works of ancient poets. For instance, Liang Jinzhu from Qiantang wrote in his *Long Poem Composed As the Wind Stopped Us at the Seven-Li Rapids*, "Range upon range of mountains disdain to duplicate one another. I sit by the boat window having an eyeful, for there is nothing like those in my hometown. Now a hare flushes out and a falcon swoops down, now a phoenix hovers in the sky accompanied by a crane, now crouching like a ferocious tiger, now coiling like a legendary dragon. Now enclosed, now open, now a long wall. The green is like that of the emerald, the reddish brown that of the coral. The rock held up by a deity is less craggy, and the mountain painted by Mi Dian is less delicate. White silk cascades down jade peaks. All the time there are fantastic rocks and misty clouds. The rapids lock up the torrents, and around the bend hills rise to the sky. The passage ahead seems to be blocked by reeds, while the way back leads to Shagri-La. Woodcutters sing in the distance, and boats sail in the setting sun. The Eastern and Western Terraces stand halfway up the steep mountain, forever in the memory of hermits. I come to admire their integrity and stop under the Azure Clouds Rock. I start scaling the mountain finding foothold among vines and cracks. After hundreds of bends I finally make it to the summit that towers aloft. What a pity that I take the journey alone, and find the only companion in an old man in sheepskin. A strong wind forebodes a coming storm. A haze rises among green mountains. The river becomes so wild that the boatman dare not go any further along the dangerous shoal; instead he lowers the sail to anchor by the ferry. The fish angled at at Yan Ziling Fishing Terrace becomes my supper onboard, together with juicy bamboo shoots. After the storm the moon comes out at daybreak, when thrushes chirp all over the peaks." And then there is a *ci* poem entitled *A 100-Character Poem* by Chen Lanfu from Panyu. A short preface comes first: "On a summer day when I passed the Seven-Li Rapids I was caught in a cool shower. I pushed open the boat window to look at the newly washed mountains cast exquisite shadows in the water. As the boat sailed through all the green, I washed my brush in the river and composed the following poem. If a fairy sings this poem to a flute, all mountains will echo." And the *ci* poem reads, " The thousand-li river has been dyed dark green by mountains. Thrushes chirp incessantly on the banks, and the wind sends the boat travelling full sail. The piled rocks, the wisps of smoke, and the clear river lined with trees seem to have come out of General Li Jr.'s painting. A sudden mountain shower conveys coolness to the boat. I'd like to row among the reeds and have the fisherman lend me a spare straw hat. Not that I want to taste the juicy perch or drink the delicious wine, but that I enjoy the hazy scenery. Fishing in the wilderness and whistling to the moon on a high terrace, isn't there unconventional life in every dynasty? The rain stops at night, but the stars and clouds still seem wet." From the above poem and the *ci* poem you will conclude that the Seven-Li Rapids does measure up to its fame.

Boats navigating the Fuchun River are called Jiangshan boats. Some are six to ten meters in length, while others are as long as twelve to sixteen meters long. The hull is made from China fir and polished as bright as new with yellow tung oil. The sturdy awning over the deck in the shape of a half moon is weaved from reed leaves and bamboo; there are doors in the front and the back, windows on the left and right, and berths for passengers underneath. Smaller boats accommodate four berths, while larger boats find space for six or eight. The crew consists of the family members of the owner plus three or four hired hands. The latter will jump onshore to tow the boat at shoals or shallows. How exciting it is to see them work in full cooperation!

It took our boat a good thirteen to fourteen days from the Qiantang River to Tunxi. And among them, six to seven days were spent on the way from the Fuchun River to the Yanjiang River. What a luxury it was to watch the seemingly endless beautiful scenery unroll in front of us! We greeted the morning glow at sunrise, bid farewell to the sun sinking among rosy clouds, counted the array of stars, basked in the clear moon, bathed by mountain rain and combed by river wind. Our ears took in torrents, waterfalls, songs by fishermen and woodmen, the chirping of thrushes, and the soughing of pines. The feast for my eyes and ears was so sumptuous that I felt as if in fairyland and wouldn't change my place with a king. I sat either by the window or at the bow, rain or shine, for fear that some splendid scenery would slip under my nose. However, to my regret, every day the captain ordered to unmoor before daybreak, so I must have missed something. But then luck had it that we would inevitably cast anchor close to a mountain village or small town, together with other boats. There was another kind of distinctive joy to sit by a candle under the awning and listen to the river babbling, people murmuring. I wrote a *ci* poem to the tune of *Pouring out My Heart,* " The boat moored under a bridge at night. The Fuchun River. Small boats were our neighbors. The river reflected the moon whose light streamed in through the boat window. I sat quietly listening to swift current rushing over stones." The bright moon over the river lingered in my memory. The crimson Chinese tallow trees in daylight also left me a deep impression. By the time we sailed in the Fuchun River in the late-autumn season of mid-November, the Chinese tallow trees along the river had all turned dazzlingly red, forming a pleasant contrast with the blue water and green mountains. We could not have enough of them, so much so that we had the boat pulled in to shore, walked for a couple of miles, took a close look under the trees, or brought back to the boat a few twigs with blood-red leaves and snow-white fruits as souvenirs. There is no need for me to sing praises of the Chinese tallow trees along the Fuchun River, for the renowned ci poet, Guo Pinjia of the Qing Dynasty, had already done an excellent piece to the tune of *Maipitang*. In the short preface he wrote, "On my way to Fuyang I saw a recent frost had turned the Chinese tallow trees into alternating red and green; mountains cast their shadow in the river, sails and masts flit over the water surface, a stretch of bank here, and a solitary house there, all worthy of a painter's brush. I could not have enough of the scenery, hence the following *ci* poem in its memory: However high the surrounding mountains are, the river never fails to capture their image. The green displays a little of its talent in decorating the sparse woods. The red seems unable to settle down yet. Together they greet the glorious glow in the morning, and set off the lingering rosy clouds at dusk. Sails and boats are dimly visible. Depression vanishes as soon as the window is open. With my cloth hat on askew I stare at the frosty scene in a drunken stupor. The path along the river is familiar for I have twice traveled over it. This time I happen to arrive when the first frost falls. The birds that hover leisurely in the sky laugh at my graying temples. As the wind rises I fear that the fallen leaves would bury the trail leading to secluded places. On this returning trip thousands of trees sigh in the wind, hundreds of mountains are covered with snow. How desolate it is!"

The few hundreds of miles from Fuyang to Yanzhou on the river were comparable to a long scroll of landscape painting. The green mountains would brighten your eyes, and the green water would cleanse your internal organs. No wonder Yan Ziling would rather live as a hermit on the Fuchun Mountain and amuse himself by angling than taking a prominent position in the imperial court. I had twice passed by Fuyang, a large county known for its straw paper production, but there had not been a chance for me to go sightseeing because our boat did not stop over there. Yet its prosperity was perceivable from the row upon row of houses in the distance, as well as the innumerable boats moored along its bank.

Tonglu was located west of Fuyang. The ancient county was established in the Wu Kingdom during the time of the Three Kingdoms. It was under the jurisdiction of the Yanzhou Prefecture in the Ming and Qing Dynasties, but since the founding of the Republic of China it received orders from Jinhua. Both tourists to the Fishing Terrace and traveling traders to Anhui Province must pass through here, which explained the boom along the river.

The Fuchun Mountain was about 20 to 25 kilometers west of Tonglu. On it there were two terraces, the Eastern Terrace being the place where Yan Ziling of the Eastern Han Dynasty had fished, the Western Terrace being where Xie Gao of Southern Song Dynasty had shed tears for Wen Tianxiang. Both places were well-known historical sights. Although we, pressed for time, did not pay our respects to them, the thought of a hermit and a loyal court official sharing the scenery on two terraces facing each other added quite some luster to the Fuchun landscape.

There were too many good things for the eyes to feast on, from the Fishing Terrace to Yanzhou. Yanzhou used to be a prefecture seat established in the Ming Dynasty, and was renamed Jiande County at the beginning of the Republic of China. I spent a half-day at Yanzhou, chatting over tea with the venerable Wu Xianshu at a riverside teahouse while taking in the splendid view. That night I slept in the boat and came up with four poems of four lines each. "The boat is like a floating house on the river, the frequent croaking of oars sound like folk songs from the former State of Yue. The dripping rain lulls me into an afternoon nap, and while I'm dreaming the boat has reached Yanzhou." "An exquisite tower stands lofty, a carefree conversation over a cup of tea. The tower's reflection is as graceful as a beautiful lady, and the river greener than tea." "The blue water ripples like crepe silk; fishing boats return with nets hung up high. Means of livelihood are plenty on the river; with cormorants perched, they come to peddle fish." "Lights and stars twinkle as the water ripples; travelers' boats crowd outside

Yanzhou. At night a drizzle on the boat roofing falls, and tomorrow the green river rises."

There were many rapids as the Fuchun River fed into the Xin'an River and finally reached Tunxi. According to the captain, there were 72 major rapids and over 100 minor ones. There was no way to know whether he was exaggerating. But tension ran high as we passed through rapids. It was with all their strength that the crew held the rudder, punted the pole, towed the boat, and cried out. What follows is an excerpt from the writing of my son, Zheng, describing such a process: "The raging current crashed loudly into the boat. The captain stood valiantly on the bow, thrust a thick long iron-tipped pole in between the numerous stones on the riverbed with great force, nestling the thicker end of the pole in the hollow of his shoulder. At the same tine he stepped onto a horizontal bar of the bowhead and twisted his body. The veins on his neck were showing, and his face blushed scarlet. As he stretched his legs as long as he could and protruded his belly, a sound of heave-ho escaped his throat. It was only then that the boat advanced slightly. Despite repeated punting, the boat was still trapped, so he pulled down from the mast with all his might a rattan hoop on which were tethered seven or eight tow ropes. Now it was all up to the boat trackers to tow the boat. The captain went on poling and shouting. The gray-haired man at the stern held the rudder with both hands and shouted in chorus with him. Sometimes the torrential water pounded the stern and in an instant the boat was turned at a right angle against the flow. The old man leaned out of the boat in his efforts to control the rudder, his shouts louder than the roaring torrents. On the bank the boat trackers were immobile. Their bodies were bent close to the ground at a 30-degree angle. Only

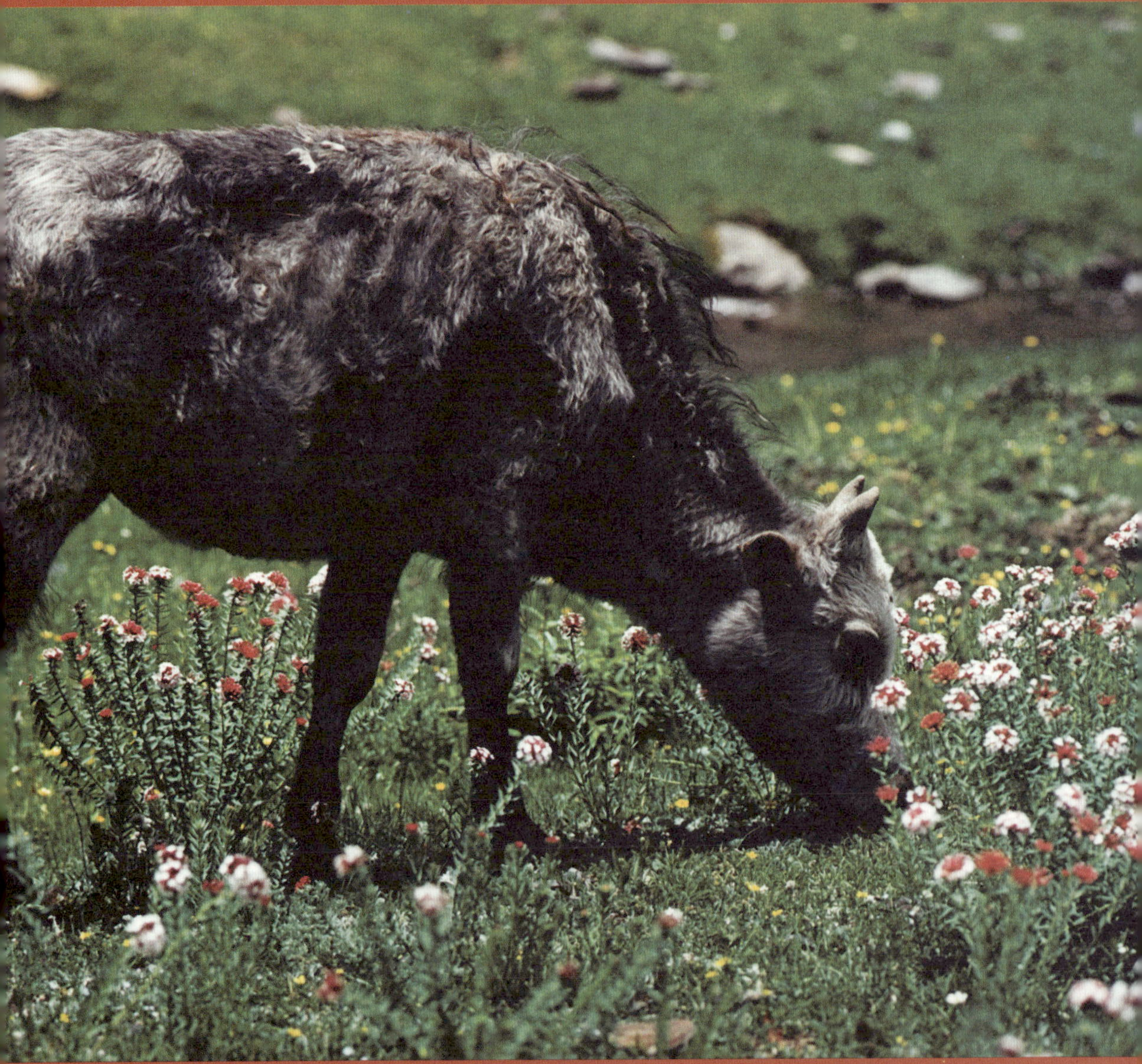

long after the foot in front had taken a firm stand did they drag another foot slowly ahead. There could not possibly be any slower slow motion. Each and every one of them gritted their teeth, clenched their fists, drooped their head, and flexed their leg muscles. The tow ropes were like arrows on the bowstring and the situation was extremely precarious. Finally great human strength got the upper hand of the ferocious water and the boat rushed down. The uproar of the river gradually lowered its volume. Man is the final winner!" Childish as the writing was, it was quite vivid in describing the perilous scene. The Cormorant Rapids and the Angry River Rapids were the two most well-known ones along the Fuchun River. I wrote a poem on my way through the Angry River Rapids: "The river flows swiftly at the Angry River Rapids, its sorrow and indignation easy to perceive. I sit on the bow watching the raging waves, at a time when the country is seething." Zhang Xianghe of the Qing Dynasty wrote in his *Going Against the Rapids*: "The boat trudges against the rapids, one *li* is as hard as ten *li* on a smoother section of the river. The river turns and twists since the Tongjiang Station. The constrained current shoots forward like an arrow. The water is so clear that you can count the fish and see the pebbles scattering over the river bed. All of a sudden the river is much deeper and huge stones crouch in its midst. The boat swerves around rocks and the heave-hoes fill one's ears. Can the Yanyu of the Qutang Gorge possibly match the peril here?"

Thrushes are song birds with yellow or black feathers. White thrushes are rare. They have distinctive eyebrows. [Translator's note: Their name in Chinese literally means "painted brows".] Although their native habitat is said to be in Sichuan Province, there were a great number of them in the Fuchun River area. As your boat sails among the green mountains over the blue water, you hear birds sing melodious songs on the banks. They are the thrushes. That explains why thrushes were frequently mentioned in ancient poems extolling the Fuchun River. I loved the thrushes as well as the Fuchun River. Although they were nowhere to be seen, their sweet songs were comparable to water rolling over the tip of the tongue, or continuous chains of links. This kind of natural sound was much superior to man-made music. I referred to thrushes in my four-line poem *Song of Triumph at the Fuchun River,* " The general splashes river water to the sky, and washes off the bloodstains there. The million-strong army take off their armor all together, accompanied by the triumphant songs of thrushes as they return home." There is another specialty in the Fuchun River, i.e., hilsa herrings. Legend has it that red, lipstick-like specks would appear on the lips of hilsa herrings as soon as they pass under Yan Ziling's Fishing Terrace. Just imagine how beautiful the fish is with silvery scales and scarlet lips. On my two trips over the Fuchun River, one around the Pure Brightness Festival and another after the Mid Autumn Festival, I did not taste the hilsa herrings. I did try the mandarin fish at the peach blossom season, but still I was not satisfied. According to the annotation by Zhang Xianghe to poems in memory of the Fishing Terrace, "The smaller hilsa herrings, also known as herring maids, are only to be found under the Fishing Terrace." What an unusual name the herring maid is! I wonder if it was recorded in the dictionary *Near to Correctness*. Neither do I know how small they actually are. Once I ate a kind of small fish, considerably larger in size but no longer than one inch, which was sold in bottles by Tonglu locals. They were delicious and reportedly captured under the Fishing Terrace, too, hence the name Ziling Fish.

Travel Notes on Mount Stone Bells

Ji Xianlin

When I read *Notes on Mount Stone Bells* by Su Dongpo as a child, I admired its eerie and vivid description so much that I could barely take my eyes off it. Having read it aloud time and again, even today I can still repeat it from memory without a single slip. However, I never dared to imagine that one day I could visit it in person. It was indeed like a dream to chance upon the scene today, and, quoting Jin Shengtan [1608-1661, a renowned literary critic], "what a pleasure!"

A mere 50-plus meters above sea level, Mount Stone Bells is dwarfed by its lofty neighbor, Lushan Mountain. However, the buildings on it have a style of their own. In an extremely limited space, there are "houses every five paces, pavilions every ten paces, with winding corridors and projecting tiles on roof edges, in harmony with the terrain, angular and masculine." At present they have been restored to resplendent magnificence. It seemed complicated climbing uphill. Starting from the Pavilion in Memory of Su Dongpo, one ascends through buildings, exquisite courtyards and winding corridors, Buddhist temples and brightly lit halls, luxuriant trees and exotic flowers, green and tall bamboos, tortuous paths leading to secluded spots, Buddhist adobes hidden among flowers and trees. There is unforgettable charm at every turn.

Engraved tablets abound around here. There are inscriptions of various sizes and different styles on almost all the rocks. Su Dongpo, Huang Tingjian, Zheng Banqiao, Peng Yulin, as well as numerous other calligraphers or obscure figures left their original calligraphic work here. The number of poems by celebrities is even more shocking. From the Northern and Southern Dynasties to the Qing Dynasty, there were over 700 poems in honor of Mount Stone Bells by well-known personages such as Tao Yuanming, Xie Lingyun, Meng Haoran, Li Bai, Qian Qi, Bai Juyi, Wang Anshi, Su Shi, Huang Tingjian, Wen Tianxiang, Zhu Yuanzhang, Liu Ji, Wang Shouren, Wang Yuyang, Yuan Zicai, Jiang Shiquan, and Peng Yulin. Present at the scene and recalling those men of letters in the past 2,000 years who once lingered around here, one can hardly refrain from nostalgic musings over the past.

Situated at the convergence point of the Poyang Lake and the Yangtze River, it has long been a place of strategic importance where a number of fierce battles in the Chinese history took place. In a flash, one could almost picture arrays of gunboats that blotted out the sun, beacon-fire and dust that shrouded the battlefield. However, nowadays peace prevails and the landscape is all that remains to glorify our country.

I stood on a sheer precipice overlooking the immensely deep and vast water. Looking up, I could see the misty mountains and beautiful land of Jiangxi, Anhui and Hubei provinces. Looking down, I could see the yellow Yangtz river converge with the green Poyang Lake, with a clear line of demarcation in between. The two streams of water would flow for tens of miles without mixing. Wasn't it a miracle of the universe to have "a vast expanse of Chu River at one's foot and the peaks of the Lushan Mountain within easy reach"? Looking into the far distance of the Chu skies, I felt refreshed in both body and mind, as if I could live until eternity and breathe with the universe. My mind was flooded with emotions and thoughts. I thought about my motherland and my nation. Our forefathers had labored and procreated here, turning it into a vast land of charm and beauty. However many difficulties and problems there were confronting us at present, I was sure that they would be overcome one by one. I grew so ecstatic that I forgot my advanced age. This experience will stay forever in my memory.

I had not planned to write anything when I visited Mount Stone Bells. Su Dongpo's famous essay having been handed down from generation to generation, how dare I sell water by the river and show off my petty cleverness before a wise man? Nevertheless, during the visit I was so stirred that I must get it off my chest, hence this little piece. If there was any regret, it was that I did not stay for a night. Otherwise, like Su Dongpo, I would take a small boat in the moonlight to the foot of the sheer precipice, see for myself those huge rocks that "stand terrifyingly like wild beasts or fierce spirits who would soon attack people" and hear with my own ears the sounds that "go on ceaselessly like chiming bells". It was with this regret in mind that I tore myself away from Mount Stone Bells. Murmuring two lines of a poem that had arisen in my mind at some point of time, "Wait until I'm advanced in age, and I will pay the renowned mountain a second pilgrimage", I saw Mount Stone Bells grew smaller and smaller, eventually fading into the dense fog created by the river and the lake.

(At the foot of Nine Fantastic Peaks of Lushan Mountain
August 6th, 1986, upon my 75th birthday)

The Yangtze River Three Gorges

Liu Baiyu

In a letter I wrote, "Today I seemed to be soaring through a magnificent symphony. I have sailed in the ocean, I have flown in the sky, but on the Yangtze - our mother river, I was for the first time captivated by the great force of Nature."

The light was dim when it was broadcast that we had arrived at Fengjie. As the Jiangjin anchored, dawn was breaking. I got up to have a look outside, where the dusky outlines of peaks had just emerged out of the darkness. I went to the lounge after our ship had set sail again. Ahead of us two sheer cliffs flanked the narrow river. We were in the Qutang Gorge. The river bent with the cliffs. There was a golden band of sunlight across the sky in front, yet elsewhere a sea of clouds reigned. The mouth of the Qutang Gorge was the most perilous place of the Three Gorges. Du Fu wrote in his *Song of Kuizhou,* " The City of Baidi guards the Three Gorges from high above, the Gorge of Qutang more unaccessible than the Bailao Pass." And there is an ancient ballad which goes, "If the Yanyu is as large as a horse, it's foolish sailing down the Qutang Gorge; if the Yanyu is as large as a monkey, it's foolish swimming in the Qutang Gorge; if the Yanyu is as large as a turtle, you're never going to return from the Qutang Gorge; if the Yanyu is as large as an elephant, you're never going to sail up the Qutang Gorge." The Yanyu had been a huge pile of black rocks right at the mouth of the Qutang Gorge. Once the roaring waves had surged into the mouth, they went directly for the huge rocks. You can imagine how devastating that was. A boat riding the waves was like an arrow that had been shot, smashing to pieces at the slightest error. By now the huge rocks had been blasted. Nevertheless, in the Qutang Gorge the turbulent current was still rumbling, and numerous whirlpools were formed. Water splashed loudly as our ship braved the whirlpools. At the end of the eight kilometer-long Qutang Gorge, dark clouds were suddenly dispelled, and in their place was an azure sky dotted with several drifting golden clouds. A shaft of sunlight poured onto the cliffs on the left side like a flash of lightening. On the right side, a piece of whitish cloud hovering over the peak started glittering like sequins, but the sunlight had not yet descended. Right then, in the far distance ahead, over range upon range of mountains, a ball of red fog leapt out of the mist. Look, the foggy ball was set off by dark reddish purple mountains, resembling the reflection of the glow of rubies in the deep valley. What a fantastic wonderland! If you happened to notice the river itself, you would find that it, too, was colorful: the two sheer cliffs cast their dark shadows; in between the shadows there was a zigzagging sparkling path, on the surface of which fine ripples shimmered; hills nearby were emerald green. Time clicked by, the red fog ball ahead turned redder and brighter. As our ship gradually approached it, we saw that there was a peak standing gracefully tall and erect in the red fog, and that the latter was formed by thousands of brilliant sunrays. At twenty past eight we were bathed in the brightly golden morning sun.

Looking up, we saw the Wu Mountain. Sunlight flooded in directly from above, while thick fog coiled up from below, creating a spectacular scene. The tall erect mountain that we had seen in the distance stood right at the mouth of the Wu Gorge, upright and charming. I was told that it was the first of the twelve Wu Gorge peaks. It seemed to be greeting visitors from the upper reaches: Behold! Here are the Wu Mountain and the Wu Gorge. The Jiangjin kept close to the foot of the hills as it entered the gorge. Right then the bright sun shone into the glass-paneled hall and onto my face. In the gorge, brilliant sunlight mingled with milky white clouds. The sun dominated one place while clouds prevailed at a stone's throw — how mysterious! The sails of several wooden boats going upstream were transformed by sunlight into white transparent wings. The gorge grew narrower and narrower. Ahead of us two hills stood facing each other, leaving in between an opening no wider than a door. And there was nothing but misty fog beyond the door.

At ten to nine everybody onboard the ship raised their heads. I too went to the deck to observe a slender rock, which resembled a person looking into the river, rising above immeasurably high peaks. That would be the legendary Beauty Peak. Legend has it that a fisherman's boat capsized and he drowned in the river in an unexpected rainstorm. His wife carried their child to the peak top to look for him, day after day, month after month. He never returned. Yet she still stood there waiting for him, morning or night, rain or shine - even until today.

If the Qutang Gorge is comparable to a locked gate, then the Wu Gorge is a winding river gallery. At every turn of the ship as it traveled along the cliffs, a marvelous landscape painting unrolled itself. On both sides were magnificent rolling mountains. The twelve Wu Gorge peaks were all different in shape, earning them high esteem and wonderful names, adding poetic quality to our land. And the poetic quality was never monotonous: now a dark gray rock hung straight down into the river, calling to mind a huge exclamatory mark; now a slope carpeted with green grass, reminding one of a tune expressing exquisite feelings. Even more eye-catching were those piles of weeds that, dyed red by autumn frost, resembled blooming azaleas spread all over the hills. Owing to the sheer cliffs, strong current and whirlpools large or small, the ship labored along like a traveler making his slow way through high mountains and lofty ridges. Yet it happened to provide visitors from afar with plenty of time to admire the natural grandeur on the vast and mighty Yangtze River. Goshawks hovered above gorges and the river surged along hills, the reflection of clouds mixed with that of hills, sunlight mingled with the shimmer of water.

At ten, the river surface widened out. The Jiangjin made steady progress over rapids and through the Wu Gorge. At quarter past ten we arrived at Badong, entering Hubei Province. At half past ten we reached Niukou, where raging tides swayed our ship. Without a breathing spell, the river rushed out of the Wu Gorge into the third gorge - the Xi Ling Gorge.

The Xi Ling Gorge was broader, but the current here carried overwhelming force. Rapids and shoals were everywhere. Sometimes the ship went loose with surging waves like a meteor; sometimes it advanced in a roundabout way avoiding shoals. There are three most notorious shoals: the Xie Shoal, the Blue Shoal and the Kongling Shoal. Upon arriving at the Xie Shoal and seeing the torrents turn into hundreds of thousands of whirlpools, you would feel that the river was spinning around instead of rushing ahead. The Jiangjin started shaking violently. Despite the perilous waters, fascinating legends abound along this section. At eleven fifteen we arrived at Zigui, the original fief of Xiong Yi, the first king of the Chu Kingdom, and the hometown of Qu Yuan. Qu Yuan was later exiled to the Miluo River, where he died. Folklore has it that, on the day of Qu Yuan's death, someone saw him ride gracefully away on a white horse, wearing a high hat and a wide waist belt. Whereas according to another version, after his death a large fish carried him back to Zigui, finally returning him from his place of exile to his hometown. At first all these sounded weird and uncanny, yet they show how much people miss Qu Yuan.

A large pile of ghastly rocks towered terrifyingly across from Zigui. We were not out of the Xie Shoal until after a long stretch of rapids. The Jiangjin exhausted all its strength, quivering and shaking, as it passed the most perilous section. A grotesque peak soared into the sky just as we were out of the rapids, and the river was flowing to its right. To its left there was still another stream, which turned out to be the birthplace of Wang Zhaojun, the Fragrant Stream. In a flash it reminded one of Du Fu's poem, "All hills and valleys lead to Jingmen, where in a village the imperial concubine Ming was born." We had barely had time to look in the direction of the Fragrant Stream when the ship turned around the hills and entered a long and unprecedentedly steep gorge — the Gorge of the Treasure Sword and the Book on the Art of War. It was a narrow alley all the way along. I went out to the bow and looked up. Yellow stones and green rocks rose into the sky. After a while we reached the Blue Shoal, where the river descended abruptly. Waves were rolling, spray flew in all directions. Before you could have a close look, the ship had shot down like an arrow. Huge waves were ploughed open by the bow, then closed up, and then rushed relentlessly on. The foam of breaking waves was drifting and swirling all over the place, as if the river were boiling. A comrade working on the ship pointed to a small town perched on the rocks and told me, "Many of the Yangtze River navigators were born here... Even a wooden boat would hire a navigator from here to sail through the Blue Shoal." As he spoke I was gazing at a wooden boat that was traveling upstream. The Blue Shoal seems to be scary, but man is able to conquer nature as long as he has come into the knowledge of a route through all those torrents.

At noon the Jiangjin was ready to enter the Kongling Shoal. All people familiar with the Yangtze River know the saying, "The Xie Shoal and the Blue Shoal are nothing compared to the Kongling Shoal, which is the real jaws of death." From that, you can gather how dangerous it is. The river surface was crowded with gray rocks. Our ship cast its anchor. It turned out that at that moment a steamer was traveling upriver along the narrow one-boat course, and consequently we had to wait. Yet the waiting was unexpectedly long. Apparently the upriver steamer took the utmost care. As the Jiangjin traveled downstream, we saw a forest of grotesque rocks. It was almost like we were not on the vast Yangtze River, but trudging over a narrow path through an endless jungle.

Autumnal Leaves at Fragrant Mountain

Yang Shuo

The red leaves at Fragrant Mountain has long been said to be the best autumn scenery in Beijing. Of course I was glad to have a chance to see them with my own eyes. The weather was so favorable that it could not have been better on the day I paid my visit: bright and clear, fresh and cool. Moreover, we happened to locate an old guide who lived right at the Foot of West Mountains. In his early years, he was a guide for 40 years. His beard has turned white, but he is still going hale and hearty with a straight back.

First, we invited the old guide to a small country restaurant, where, with a few dishes of game and half a glass of wheat wine, he started talking in an unhurried manner, "The only thing good about Fragrant Mountain is its altitude. Its entrance is as high as the top of Mount Jade Spring. Because of its high altitude, the air is clear and refreshing, and people love coming here. They come for a walk in spring, to relieve the heat in summer, and in autumn -" an impatient fellow traveler interrupted him, "Have the leaves on the mountain turned red?"

The old guide said, "Not quite. Some might have turned red on the southern side of the mountain facing the sun."

Therefore, after drink and food, we asked the old guide to take us uphill along the southern side. What a peaceful place! On both sides of the stone-paved mountain path stand ancient pines and cypresses that block the sunlight. It is said that one would not sweat a bit walking in the shade in dog days.

Hands folded on the stomach, the old guide led the way at a pace neither too slow nor too fast. As usual, he spoke leisurely, "There used to have nothing around here. Just some deserted hills in the back and a laborer hired by a rich man to farm and raise pigs. The pig feed was poured into a broken stone trough. However little feed there was in the trough, the pigs could never eat it all. Finding it a bit odd, the laborer put a few copper coins in, and he got an infinite supply of money. So he knew it was a treasure bowl. When the time came to reckon his pay, the laborer asked for nothing but the stone trough. How much could a broken trough possibly be worth? The rich man was only too glad to oblige. The stone trough was so heavy that the laborer was worn out as he trudged in the mountain. He dug a hole in the ground to bury the trough in, and marked the place with a pine and a cypress lest he should forget its whereabouts. When he brought some help from home, he found an entire mountain covered with countless pines and cypresses." At this point in the story, the old guide sighed with feeling, "This is indeed a live mountain. There is running water in this mountain. Some water flows underground. If there is underground water tree seedlings will grow. No wonder people believe there is a treasure bowl buried underground."

By then the old guide had taken us into a rather secluded courtyard with two springs. Two words-"Twin Limpidity"-were inscribed on a stone wall. After walking around the springs, the old man wondered aloud, "It has been ten years since I last climbed the mountain. How come that stone tablet is gone? I remember it reads 'Dream Expelling Spring'." He went on to tell us a story about a Yuan Dynasty emperor who came sightseeing in the mountain, felt tired and fell into a sleep here. He dreamed about sitting in a boat on churning water. When he woke up, he had people dig right under his feet. Water sprang out, hence the name "Dream Expelling Spring".

The old guide then spoke with a smile, "This is just country hearsay. I simply told you what I have heard. You needn't believe it."

Listening to this white-bearded old man chattering away about some fantastic legends, you will feel that Fragrant Mountain is all the more charmingly mysterious. We wouldn't spoil the fun by denouncing them. However, why was there not a single red leave in sight as we climbed?

The old man said, "Don't worry. You will see everything once you arrive at the pavilion halfway up the mountain."

We arrived at the pavilion and looked out to the east. What a beautiful view! The vast Hebei Plain was in front of us. Deep into the misty trees was our city of Beijing. Another thing marvelous was that Kunming Lake, ordinarily regarded as somewhat impressive, now looked just like a basin of clear water. The Mountain of Longevity and the Fragrant Pavilion of Buddha were just some decorative potted landscape. We all forgot to look at the red leaves. They came into full view right there on the slopes above, half yellow, half red, quite enjoyable. The pity was that the leaves had weathered too much rain to be thoroughly red. If they were red in and out, what a brilliant color it would be in the sun!

Eying the red leaves I asked, "What are these trees? Why don't they look like maple leaves?"

The old guide said, "They are not maple trees in the first place. These are called red trees." He pointed at the trees on the side of the path and added, "Look, just like those over there."

The roadside red trees had not turned red yet, so none of us had paid them any attention. I went over to pick a leaf. It was round, with only a little tint of red coming through the veins.

I couldn't hold back a cry, " Why! It smells good." I put the leaf under my nose to smell. It sent forth a slight herbal fragrance.

A travel companion also cried out after taking a smell, " Why! It does smell good. No wonder it is called Fragrant Mountain here."

The old guide agreed in his unhurried voice, "Indeed it is fragrant. Why haven't I smelled it before in my 40 years of life as a guide?"

My old man, although I am not familiar with your past experience, from your wrinkled face I could infer all sorts of hardship. In the past, with a bitter heart, how could you smell the fragrance of red leaves? Neither do I know clearly about your current life, but at such an advanced age you managed to climb the mountain without panting or getting short of breath. You seemed to climb at an average pace, but we had always lagged behind. An old person with a brisk pace must also feel light-hearted. How possibly could any fragrance from the red leaves escape you?

In the air permeated with the fragrance of red leaves, the old guide led us to visit Jade Tablet, Snowcapped West Mountains on a Sunny Day, the Shao Temple and some other scenic spots of Fragrant Mountain. It was near dusk when we trekked downhill. Looking up we saw a white first quarter moon in the eastern sky. It suddenly occurred to a companion, "Is it the Double Ninth Festival today?" A check of some newspapers we brought along revealed that it was the day after. This autumn outing of ours coincided with the old custom of mountain climbing on the Double Ninth Festival.

It was a trip short of perfection for those who regretted being unable to see dream red leaves. But I had picked a more precious red leaf and kept it in my memory. It was no ordinary red leaf, but a leaf that had been weather-beaten in life. The later the autumn is, the brighter and lovelier it becomes. Needless to say, I was referring to that old guide.

Ascending the Golden Dome of Mount Emei

Xu Chi

Du Fu wrote in a poem that:
"I hope one day to ascend the summit,
and find all the surrounding mountains dwarfed."
Li Bai, too, had a poem to his credit:
"I whisk to the top,
not a single gossamer is in sight as far as the eyes can see."

Both poems stir me on to ascend the summit, especially Li Bai's "I whisk to the top", which he wrote at the age of 58 after scaling the summit of the Wushan Mountain. You can imagine what kind of person he was if he was still "whisking" at 58. It was an almost aesthetic experience whisking across famous mountains. Whisking across mountains, you become not only a companion of the wooded hills, but a part of it, the same as elk and birds. Dancers aspire to fly up to heaven, but unlike the flying Apsaras in the frescoes of the Dunhuang Caves, they are unable to rise with only the help of a ribbon. However, one could whisk to the top of the summit and stand shoulder to shoulder with the sky.

On this occasion we were whisking to the Golden Dome of Mt. Emei, one of the most famous Chinese mountains, a combination of an excellent botanical garden, a first-class museum of plastic arts and architecture, rest homes and summer resorts. As the popular saying goes, "There is no other place under heaven as beautiful as Mt. Emei." It is beautiful because it stands out on the edge of the West Sichuan Plain taller than all other mountains, its altitude being 3,050 meters above sea level. The majestic Golden Dome, summit of Mt. Emei, has a sheer precipice on the east side rising approximately 2,600 meters from the ground. Although the path uphill has been paved, it is quite some climbing for you to cover the 45 kilometers if you brush aside byroad attractions, or the 60 kilometers of winding trail to the Golden Dome.

We drove from Emei County to the Dragon Gate Cave, where we started climbing by taking a shortcut to the Wannian Monastery via the Qingyin Pavilion. At the Qingyin Pavilion, the surrounding green mountains reduced the sky to a slit and the two creeks were crystal clear. The Wannian Monastery was a quiet and secluded place sheltered by mountains on three sides and hidden away deep in firs, pines, cypresses and *nanmu*. Comparatively speaking, there was nothing noteworthy about the scenery below the Qingyin Pavilion, for the scenery above was far superior.

At the Wannian Monastery we were happily surprised at a Song Dynasty-cast copper artifact and a Ming Dynasty beamless brick hall. The former was a statue of the Bodhisattva Puxian on a white elephant: the Bodhisattva sat with his legs crossed on a lotus throne; a red kasaya drapes over his golden body and a red necklace of pearls and jade hung from his neck; the golden crown of wreath was two-tiered with a small Buddha's image set in between. The white elephant stood life-size on a lotus pedestal, wearing a golden belt and golden head ornaments, with three pairs of protruding tusks and a floral rug across its back. All, from Puxian's golden crown down to the four limbs of the elephant and the lotus pedestal, were cast copper. The total height was 6.82 meters and the net weight 62,500 kilograms. I will leave out the accurate proportion with which it was cast. The statue was neat, tidy, and plump, as if breathing. The giant elephant's skin wrinkled slightly, as it were in motion. Complicated patterns were engraved on the golden crown. And on top of this huge artifact there was the arched roof of a beamless brick hall rarely seen in China, complete with 24 brick niches.

Among us there were painters who jotted down sketches and found frequent inspiration on the way, as well as composers who immediately transcribed the sounds of nature into musical notes. Art is wonderful, but the really wonderful artistic creation was here weighing a good 62.5 tons! Just think, classical Chinese paintings on silk produced in the Song Dynasty had turned yellow, and the Ming Dynasty music had disappeared into thin air, while the copper statue and the brick hall still stood lofty here, undamaged and glittering. It was a real bliss to see such a cast copper artifact, and such architecture.

After the Wannian Monastery we went uphill to the Huayan Summit, passing by the Place to Calm the Heart and the First Hall on the way. The Huayan Summit was also known as the Middle Summit as it reigned over surrounding mountains. Here the vermilion buildings of the Jiulao Cave in the distant verdant woods had the air of a fairyland. In other words, beatitude welled up as one looked. The altitude was 1,900 meters. Above us there was the Sky Piercing Slope paved with slippery mossy flagstones. Once up the slope we could have pierced the sky to arrive at the Elephant

Washing Pool, 2,200 meters above sea level. The distance traveled so far was 15 kilometers.

At the Elephant Washing Pool, the sea of clouds became visible. From time to time, a puff of cloud floated past a window in the monastery, or even found its way into your sleeve. It happened to be the 15th day of the lunar month. The Elephant Washing Pool was known for its moonlit nights, yet we were there on a cloudy day. It was chilly, for the temperature was only eight degrees Celsius. And the primeval forest nearby made it even gloomier. In the deep forest a dove tree had burst into white blossoms.

Up from the Elephant Washing Pool was the Continuous Slope, where the climb was so steep that it was nicknamed the King of Hell Slope. It was more precipitous and mossier than the Sky Piercing Slope. Firs dominated the primeval forest here. Vines hung across the lush woods, while green moss carpeted tree trunks, branches and vines. How numerous were the trees and the winding trails there! The sun was blocked entry into the woods and the treks overgrown with moss. Wet clouds flitted in to moisten the green greener.

After the Continuous Slope was the Leidong Level Ground, and after that was the Seven-Li Slope. Of all the slopes, the Seven-Li Slope was the most perilous. But the climb over the slope to the altitude of 2,800 meters offered distinctive joy. The prettiest flowers that had first appeared in clusters on the Continuous Slope were running wild all over the place here, the azaleas.

Here the azalea trees stood as tall as six meters plus. Here the azalea woods spread over slopes upon slopes. Here the azaleas were in full bloom, as if a recent snow that had all been piled on branches were glimmering in the bright sun.

Although we'd like to whisk to the top, here we could not help pausing and taking in the splendid sea of flowers in awe. A glance at the sea of flowers sufficed to dispel road weariness. And right at the moment there were azaleas all the way. Please imagine how we were flying over this colorful sky.

The pale purple flower belonged to the *Meili* Azalea. The bell-shaped white flower with purple specks was called the *Changli* Azalea. The pale rosy *Weili* Azalea hung over rocks. The Wrinkled Leave Azalea was pale pink with a tiny calyx. The blooming *Chengxian* Azalea was bright yellow. The Long Stamen Azalea was white and fragrant, its pedestal a tiny tube out of which dozens of stamens stuck.

Azaleas were a specialty of Mt. Emei. Unlike ordinary azaleas whose color was red, they were a multifarious assortment of purple, yellow, rose and white, as well as red. They were rare ornamental plants enjoying equal renown with the Spring Heralding Flower and the dove tree of Mt. Emei. Back at Chengdu I had met with Prof. Fang Wenpei, a plant taxonomist, who had a profound knowledge of those rare flowers. According to him, these mountain azaleas were valuable because they were able to cure many difficult and complicated cases. But for me they were more valuable in the aesthetic sense.

Azaleas carpeted not only the Seven-Li Slope, but also the newly-paved flagstone path above the Crown Prince Level Ground. Eventually we flew over the azaleas and whisked to the Golden Dome.

The Gold Dome had used to refer to a copper hall on the summit of Mt. Emei. The hall had stood over 8 meters tall and 5 meters deep. Viewed from the distance it had appeared glittering in the sun, hence the name the

Golden Dome. However, the Ming Dynasty Copper Hall had been burned down to just two copper doors, a copper tablet, and a copper tower. There was exquisite relief on both sides of the copper doors. On the two sides of the copper tablet there were the calligraphy of Wang Xizhi's and Chu Suiliang's respectively, depicting and praising the copper hall. The engraving was even finer on the 21-story copper tower. It was safe to conclude from the remaining copper doors, copper tablet and copper tower that the copper hall on the Golden Dome of Mt. Emei represented the highest achievement in metal as far as arts and architecture were concerned.

The eleven of us painters, composers and poets who had ascended the Golden Dome as a group were witnesses to the acme of perfection in ancient arts.

I could not help admiring the ancient bronze craftsmen, the ancient cast-copper artists who had created masterpieces like this with bronze as their medium, their paint brush, their musical instrument and their rhythm. Copper artists today are certain to scale new heights, thanks to the solid foundation laid by their predecessors!

However, my copper fever was soon subdued by the chill on the Golden Dome. It was the end of May, but the temperature on the Golden Dome ran a mere three degrees Celsius. Indeed, as the poem went, when you were on a high mountain, you found "the coldness permeating the marble towers and jade halls located on a high altitude hard to bear." On such an overcast day of occasional pelting rain, we shivered with cold. Even worse, we missed the famous Buddha's Halo of Mt. Emei.

Nevertheless, we saw the view at the summit, which was what actually mattered. The reason why one hopes "one day to ascend the summit" and to "whisk to the top" in earnest is the view on top, where one finds "all the surrounding mountains dwarfed" and "not a single gossamer is in sight as far as the eyes can see." Yet this time, as far as our eyes could see there was coiling mist and a brilliant sea of clouds.

Please take a good look at this sea of clouds. Right now we were at the Golden Dome of Mt. Emei, a mountain that stood out taller than all other mountains, where the view was the best.

Yes, we had taken a panoramic view at the Wannian Monastery and the Huayan Middle Summit, where we had been impressed by the broad vision made possible by elevation. Yet it was not until we had reached the Elephant Washing Pool did we realize that the Huayan Middle Summit was not that high after all. There it resembled a mere bonsai, let alone the Wannian Monastery. On the other hand, viewed from the Golden Dome, neither did the Elephant Washing Pool appear imposing, let alone the Huayan Middle Summit. What met our eyes was a boundless sea of clouds, curling and surging like a real sea. Clouds were changeable, and how nimble they were! Now churning, now flying, now dark, now light, you never knew what would become of them the next minute. Because of them, a peak appeared at one moment and disappeared at another.

The clouds were snowy white. The mountains were dark green. When clouds dispersed, the range upon range of mountains came out to form a perspective drawing. Whether they were visible or not was entirely up to the caprice of clouds. The latter changed as fast as a dancer who whirled around waving her long sleeves. No, even faster, much faster!

Two lines of poem by Chairman Mao were called to mind:

"Mountains brandish silver snakes,

Plains allow wax elephants to gallop."

These two lines get a ready response among readers who have some mountain climbing experience of their own, while others form a mental picture out of them. In the same way I had felt myself able to comprehend the poem. Yet how wrong I had been! It was not until I had ascended the Golden Dome of Mt. Emei that I saw "mountains brandish silver snakes". The mountains were indeed "brandishing" something, but not silver snakes. Instead the snakes were green. Then how about "Plains allow wax elephants to gallop"? As I stood trying to figure it out, a snow-capped mountain suddenly emerged on the horizon to my west.

The gigantic snow-capped mountain unveiled its waistline first, then the peaks, then its entirety. It came galloping like a wax elephant with unrivalled majesty, the shimmering Gongga Mountain of Kangding County that rose 7,600 meters into the sky.

The clouds melted away one after another. On the western horizon stood the giant snow-capped mountain, and on the eastern horizon lay the West Sichuan Plain. The Dadu River, the Qingyi River and the Min River joined hands at Leshan County. As mentioned in "Rivers", Volume 33 of Li Daoyuan's *Commentary on the Waterways,* " To the south of the county there is Mt. Emei and the Meng River, a.k.a. the Dadu River... According to the *Book of Mountains and Seas,* the Meng River originates from south of Hanjia and flows west to join the Min River." Guo Pu wrote in his magnificent poem *Ode to the River,* " Mt. Emei is a landmark north of the river." Previously I had not been able to get at the meaning of these two quotes. However, at the Golden Dome I saw in the sun the Dadu River soar like a golden dragon towards the sea of clouds. "The Meng River originates from south of

Hanjia", while Hanjia referred to Jiading, or the present-day Leshan. "Mt. Emei is a landmark north of the river" because on top of it one can see the Dadu River flowing to its southeast.

Only a summit permits a panoramic view. Look, the imposing giant snow-capped mountain! See, the confluence of three rivers at Leshan! In the same direction you could see Leshan, Wutongqiao and Jianwei in a row. With a pair of high-powered binoculars you could even see Yibin, another confluence point of three rivers, namely the Min River, the Jinsha River and the Yangtze River. Look, over there the Jinsha River flowed from the Daliang Mountain and the Xiaoliang Mountain, while the Yalong River rushed from the giant snow-capped mountain. Beyond the range upon range of snow-capped mountains rolled the Tongtian River. The source of the Yangtze River was right there!

At the Golden Dome of Mt. Emei the entire upper reaches of the Yangtze River are visible. You will never find a better place to have such an extensive view. You may climb up higher mountains, but you may not always locate a superior position that provides you with a broader vision and a fuller picture of "the land so rich in beauty."

Only when one has ascended the summit can one talk about the view there. It is true not only with nature, but also with the mind. If the mind has not reached the summit, it has to linger on winding trails in the woods. Although there may be a view of the distance in the Middle Summit, or a fascinating encounter with azaleas, it fails to take in everything at a glance. Only at the mental summit can we look afar and have a panoramic view that spans 5,000 kilometers and 5,000 years.

Only at the mental summit can we fully understand our times.

Stone Inscriptions at the Taishan Mountain

Wang Zengqi

I first came across the stone inscriptions from Sutra Stone Valley at the home of an old and well-established family in Kunming. A couplet with four characters in each line printed on thick paper and in thick ink, they were rubbed in an early time from dispersed characters inscribed at the valley. It was dark and gloomy inside the century-old house, but the vigorous handwriting left an indelible impression on me.

Sutra Stone Valley is located on a byroad of the Middle Route of the Taishan Mountain. The typography here is quite odd: how come that there is an almost level stone ground covering an area of one mu in the midst of high mountains and lofty ridges? Most of the granite that makes up the Taishan Mountain is green in color, while this level stone ground is ginger yellow. Strangely, there are no similar rocks around. Who discovered this place and came up with the idea of inscribing the entire content of the Vajracchedika Sutra on its surface? Each inscribed character is half a meter tall. Engravings of huge characters are usually seen on vertical cliffs, but engravings on horizontal stony grounds are rare. Besides, the style of handwriting here is seldom found elsewhere.

Opinions are quite divided on the time of the engraving of the Sutra Stone Valley Inscriptions. Yet most people agree that the style of handwriting represents a transition from the official script to the regular script.

Those people who hold the view that the Sutra Stone Valley Inscriptions came into existence at almost the same time as the Yi He Inscriptions show remarkable insight. The Sutra Stone Valley Inscriptions keep quite some characteristics of the official script, but not the initial stroke shaped after the head of a silkworm or the final stroke similar to the tail of a wild goose. The writing brush was applied in a flexible manner while the characters are a little bit on the flat side, which may have carried on the style of the Shi Men Inscriptions in a less liberal manner. But the theory that Wang Xizhi wrote both the Sutra Stone Valley Inscriptions and the Yi He Inscriptions seems unfounded. Wang Xizhi's handwritings usually slant to the side, but the Sutra Stone Valley Inscriptions do not. The more slender Yi He inscriptions, lean but sturdy, impress people with their elegance, and it is quite reasonable to assume that they were written by either Wang Xizhi or Wang Xianzhi (I believe they were written earlier than Wang Xizhi's time). Calligraphy since the Jin and Tang Dynasties has given priority to a lean and sturdy style. A line of poetry by Du Fu, which goes to the effect that "the only divine style of writing is the lean and sturdy style", reflects the trend. Despite their plump and heavy appearance, the Sutra Stone Valley Inscriptions convey a sense of strength and intelligence.

There is not a single stroke missing, and never a trace of stiffness. If there were one word that sums up the Sutra Stone Valley Inscriptions, it would be "steadiness". These characters were written by an unruffled and persevering Buddhist. Could a nonbeliever have possibly copied the Vajracchedika Sutra? No. Buddha is present in every inscribed character of the sutra.

Only characters like that match the Taishan Mountain. If inscribed somewhere else they would not achieve the same effect. Once, ten years ago, I spent a long time at the Sutra Stone Valley and considered the two-day trudge worthwhile after admiring the inscriptions. Sutra Stone Valley is an integral part of the Taishan Mountain. The Taishan Mountain devoid of the Azure Clouds Temple and the South Gate of Heaven would still deserve a visit as long as Sutra Stone Valley is there.

I really hope that someone could make a rubbing copy of the entire text inscribed at Sutra Stone Valley (which may require the piecing together of many sheets of paper), and put it on display in Beijing. It would not be going too far to build a large gallery especially for the purpose.

Traces of Autumn on the Daishan Island

Chen Congzhou

She is an island named Daishan. An illusory girdle separates it from the vast green sea. The sea should be boundless, but looking out on this island, you would find it similar to a lake, only more mysterious. The lake is in the midst of the sea, and beyond it the sea reigns. " The insignificant is present in the significant, and the significant is to be found in the insignificant". I was a bit confused. The elusive grace has long since won her the name Penglai the Buddhist Kingdom.

In the morning the sun emerged above the sea. The jet black mountains, the bright red glow, and the glistening sea interweaved into a solemn picture of sunrise. I leaned on a railing, lost in thoughts of the other world. Only a night's journey from Shanghai, and I seemed to have undergone a religious baptism. I did not dare to say that I had seen through human vanity, but fame and fortune seemed no longer that important. I improvised a poem (to the tune of *Wash Stream Sands*): "Caught in the web of this world and having no desire to disentangle from it, why pretend to be above the common herd. In the face of illusion the unreal comes true. The tired eyes follow the mountains into the sea. The shadow cast by the solitary sail chases the man. Who is to share the sound of waves with me." After the ship had pulled in to shore, we headed directly for the mountain. We walked in a leisurely manner on a winding mountain trail through the pine woods, farther and farther away from the sea. Our bodies moistened. How quiet and comfortable it was to have the urban sound and fury replaced by the clean morning air in the mountain! The Ciyun Temple on the mountain, hidden among thousands of bamboos and pines and overlooking the lake-like sea, is like a mirror that tells virtue from evil in this world and dispels all sorts of wickedness. The choice of location for religious buildings is worth studying. On my previous visit four years before, the local authorities had planned to replace the temple with a hotel. I said that upon completion of the hotel a few guests would rob the majority of tourists of an attraction. What was more, why demolish a temple that was still intact? Without it tourists would not come, and who would like to stay in a hotel standing all alone on the top of the mountain? The practice of building hotels on the former site of temples had been followed for a long time. A good case in point was the many hotels built around the West Lake [in Hangzhou] that had turned into forbidden zones. I suggested closing the hillsides, restoring the temple and relocating the hotel. Now, on my second visit, the local authorities expressed their gratitude, for pines and tea shrubs had grown all over the mountain, while the revenue from tourists and pilgrims to the Ciyun Temple was quite considerable. As to the hotel, the site was quite nice, the buildings in harmony with the temple. A solution that satisfied rival claims had thus earned me an invitation to stay here for a few days.

This time I found the scenes so enchanting that I could not tear myself away from them. The most memorable moment on the Island was when I had a long talk over early morning tea with an old monk on the terrace in front of the Ciyun Temple, where fleeces of cloud flitted under my feet and the soughing of the wind in the pines reached my ears. Birds sang sweetly in the still mountain, reminding me of "waking up to the trill of an oriole" in the drama *The Peony Pavilion*. When does the trill of an oriole arouse us from the dream of life? I felt sad and distracted. The conversation with the old monk started a train of thought in me. At the request of the abbot, dharmacarya Wudao, I wrote "Buddhist Valley, Transcendental Sound" on a perpendicular rock in front of the temple. A fellow visitor, Guyin, praised the inscription as appropriate, for the sounds of sutra chanting, birds, wind, mountain and tides created an ambience that was both religious and natural. Inscriptions are meant to provoke visitors' thoughts. Probably it was "fate" in the Buddhist sense that led me to leave my handwriting here.

Autumn was in the cool night air as pines cast their shadow on the window panes. A Song Dynasty poem wrote, "what causes people sorrow is autumn in the mind of a traveler." Autumn brings forth in people far more complex feelings than spring does, especially in those of us who have passed middle age and gone through a lot of things. Autumn means different things for each of us. I was glad to find the initial encounter with autumn here much more enjoyable than that in the city. In the city you feel the arrival of autumn through a change of people's attire, but here you feel it through the change in nature. A person long used to urban life seems to know creature comforts, but not the appeal of nature. Whoever sits in a café inundated with dazzling multifarious lights will not be able to appreciate the idyllic life. The tranquil sea, dimly-discernible islands and hardly distinguishable seagulls in the remote distance are only to be enjoyed from an island mountain. Autumns on Daishan Island are comparable to pieces of white silk, on which you are free to paint the most charming picture, write the most touching article. She is forever enchanting.

West Lake Vistas

Yu Min

It rained once on my previous visit to Hangzhou. Two lines of poem which went to the effect that, "Complain not of climbing in the rain, for the rain only adds to beauty of mountains", prompted me to climb the Jade Emperor's Hill. Going up the wet steps over slippery moss, I was soon sweaty all over. It takes pain to get at beauty, sure enough! Against the gray misty clouds the bamboos appeared particularly verdant, with innumerable water drops rolling on the tip of their leaves. The hilltop overlooked the vast Qiantang River, which meandered out of the haze over the horizon. Across the river Xiaoshan was only dimly discernible.

The gusts and heavy rains on top of the hill forced me to take shelter in a teahouse. Looking out of the window through swaying bamboos, I was struck by the unexpectedly fine scenery. The West Lake had turned black, as if dyed in thick ink! "Grains of rice dot the dark landscape". I saw it was indeed so! "The dark landscape" is a human invention modeled after nature. There is a style of traditional Chinese landscape painting, named after the originator Mi Fu [1051-1107], that splashes ink dots of various size, density and shades of black to depict the hazy landscape shrouded in a drizzle. I had thought little of this overly freehand technique, but this chance discovery proved me wrong. The lake water was dark black, while the Su Causeway resembled a white girdle, and the six bridges linking the Causeway looked as if carved out of white marble. The peculiar contrast between black and white as a result of natural creation had opened my eyes to a beauty never seen before. The Mi style seemed to be the one and only technique capable of reproducing such scenery on paper.

It happened to rain again upon my arrival by train in Hangzhou this time. "The lake is lovely as wavelets glimmer in sunlight, and when the hills grow misty with rain their pristine loveliness retains." My interest was so aroused that I went boating on the lake. Mine was the only boat on the vast lake. Understandably, there were few people as crazy as I was. Yet despite the drenching I did not regret it a bit. Climbing the hill in the rain on my previous visit had enabled me to enjoy the unusual West Lake vistas, while this time going boating in the rain allowed me to take in the extraordinary mountain scenery. The mountains appeared delightful all because the rain had made them partly hidden and partly visible. One moment they were visible, the next moment they vaporized as the haze rose. One moment they were hidden, the next moment their pale green outlines were unveiled as the mist lifted. You felt the work of magic when they were hidden, and a surge of warm feeling when they became visible. Again the Mi style would be the one and only technique capable of capturing the illusive beauty.

The Qing Dynasty scholar Gu Tinglin advocated "traveling ten thousand miles and reading ten thousand books." It was significant the way he used "ten thousand". Beauty is infinite, so is the universe and life. To form an independent opinion one has to take pains with the "ten thousand". And the courage to explore an objective reality ten thousand times with a view of cognition is beautiful in itself.

The boatwoman was curious about my eccentricity, while I sympathized with her life story. Her name was Liu Aqiao. Having eked out a living by rowing a boat for 22 years since the age of eight, she was a walking history book of the West Lake. Japanese invaders, the Kuomintang, high officials, dignitaries, moneybags, and women of eminence had brought disasters to the boat people and desolation to the West Lake. At dawn Aqiao and her pals would stand waiting nervously at the foot of the high steps leading up to big mansions. Would there be business? Would there be money to buy the day's food?

Yet what was the point in my reminiscence? Liu Aqiao was sitting on the bow, awakened from memories of the past. She relaxed her eyebrows into a smile, as if a breeze had just rippled the lake surface. How could she not smile at her happy life? The famine in recent years had failed to cause her sorrow, alarm or despair. At the moment her family was not quite well off, but there was always food on the table. On the monthly payroll of the West Lake Commune, she was no longer afraid of the off-season, the rainstorms, or any unforeseen events in her life. The baby she had just given birth to was well-fed at the commune nursery. Her elder son was a middle school student in Shanghai, the fact of which gave her unabashed ecstasy. Relieved of family worries, she happily rowed tourists hither and thither. It was in the croaking of her oars that she had bid farewell to humiliation and welcomed happiness, and in the croaking she looked forward to a better tomorrow. She was a happy hostess of the West Lake, and happy hostesses are always hospitable. She pointed out scenic spots to me and gave me explanations with enthusiasm, not leaving out a single detail about the beautiful West Lake she had grown up with.

In the drizzle, the water and the sky had blended into one color. Aqiao took me to the Three Pools Mirroring the Moon, where I got off. It was late spring, when the green leaves were fresh but the red flowers should be fading, yet here around the West Lake, flowers blossomed all year round. I walked over a winding stone bridge, underneath which the water lilies had not stirred from slumber. Azaleas were in full bloom. They scattered in clusters of snowy white or bloody red among green trees and slender bamboos. The wild gingers on the waterside resembled orchids, but less fragile; instead they had grown thick and sturdy. An aroma assailed my nostrils, but its source was hard to tell. In such an environment even the carpet of fine grass and the green mosses smelled pleasantly. The Three Pools were cradled in the center of the West Lake. Clouds had already shrouded the North and South Peaks out of view. The Willows where orioles sang and the Flower Harbor hid behind thick forests, revealing their upturned eaves from time to time. The glazed tiles of Jingci Temple glittered at the foot of the Nanping Hill. And the drizzle caressed all. As its rhythm varied, the scenery underwent a myriad of changes. It's just beyond me to describe such a natural and graceful scene.

On second thoughts, the West Lake is no rival for either the Taihu Lake or the Erhai Lake, neither are the Twin Peaks up to the beauty of the Yandang Mountain or the Huangshan Mountain. Then why has it enjoyed such a high reputation and attracted such a great number of visitors? Is it because the lake and the hills complement one another well? Is it because of their infinite facets around the year, in all weather? It was not until on my visit to Linyin Temple [Temple of Soul's Retreat] that I got an answer. Here the hills stood gracefully erect, trees soared into the skies, creeks gurgled and babbled, exactly the way described by the two lines of poem that "The spring sobs under perilous rocks; the heat of sun abated by the green pines." There were many caves at the hill named Feilai Peak [Peak that Had Flown from Nowhere], the largest of which was called "Longhong". In it many stalactites, shaped like icicles, were hanging from the roof. Lining the walls were Buddha's statues carved out of the rock in the thousands of years gone by, many of which were rare works of art. Deep in the cave there was a natural cleft in the roof through which a slit of the sky was visible, hence the name "A Slit of the Sky". Who wouldn't marvel at such a quiet and secluded place? However, people linger on not only because of the hills, the trees, the springs, the caves, and the stone carvings, but also because of the stately temple here; and more than that, because of a popular figure related to the temple. He is the legendary Divine Monk Ji Gong, a person who denounced bigwigs while helping those in distress and succoring the poor. Natural beauty, artificial beauty, and moral beauty had come together to attain the highest form of beauty.

My theory was further proved later at Yue Fei's Temple [Yue Fei, 1103-1142, patriotic military commander of the Southern Song Dynasty]. There was nothing remarkable about the architecture; neither was Yue Fei's statue a success in the artistic sense. Yet the place is always crowded with visitors. Who wouldn't drop by on their tour of the West Lake? I believe only very few people would skip it. Without such national heroes of extraordinary courage as Yue Fei, Yu Qian, Zhang Cangshui and Qiu Jin, without such renowned poets as Bai Juyi, Su Shi and Lin Bu, without such well-praised figures as the White Snake Lady and Su Xiaoxiao, conceivably people would not be so interested in the landscape of the West Lake. We raise our voice to sing Yue Fei's poem *Manjianghong* as we pay respects at Yue Fei's Temple, recite silently the *Poem on the Eve of My Death* by Zhang Cangshui as we stroll around the Nanpin Hill, recall Su Dongpo's "the Six Bridges lie across the vast lake, only then does the North Peak with the Nanpin Hill connect" as we linger on the Su Causeway, chant in a low voice Lin Hejing's "dappled shadows are cast over clear shallow water, secret fragrance permeates the moonlit dusk" as we ascend the Solitary Hill to reach the Crane Releasing Pavilion. Here, nature and human achievements blend into one. Not only do the hills and the lake complement each other well, but man and nature are in harmony too.

The bond between man and nature is similar to that between man and other men. The longer the coexistence, the firmer the bond becomes. Since I lived close to the Flower Harbor, I would go for a walk there morning and night, and with the days going by I felt increasingly reluctant to leave. A screen of roses served as the gate. The blooming roses gave off a refreshing fragrance. Right beyond the gate gracefully slender bamboos, elegantly erect cedars, and magnolias ready to break into blossom lined both sides of the path. A rockery made of stones from the Taihu Lake lay way ahead; its winding cobble path led up to a spacious pavilion of primitive simplicity. There was a riot of colors all around. I wondered if there was any master painter capable of distinguishing all those shades of green and red. Azaleas had already withered, but Chinese herbaceous peonies were vying with each other for the beauty crown. At the foot of the rockery, along the winding trails, clusters of red, purple, yellow and white flowers were greeting visitors with smiling faces. Holding a flower in your hand, and you would feel it trembling bashfully. The aroma of flowers assailed the nostrils, especially on bright spring days. The sweet fragrance was intoxicating. Down the rockery, across a green carpet of a lawn, beyond the willows, there was a zigzagging stone bridge and a fish pond containing hundreds of thousands of golden carp. At the clap of hands they approached you in schools with gaping mouths. Farther ahead, trailing the winding stone balustrades, around a magnificently painted building, you would find yourself in a secluded courtyard overgrown with bamboos. Beyond the lattice wall lay the Su Causeway shaded by a green canopy of trees. And the bright open space beyond the Su Causeway would be the rippleless West Lake. At the Wave Reflecting Bridge you'd better strain your eyes to look at reflections in the lake. The Mid-Lake Pavilion and the Three Pools Mirroring the Moon came clearly into view. In the far distance across the lake stood the elegant Solitary Hill, the rainbow-shaped Broken Bridge, and the solemn Baochu Pagoda of the Precious Stone Hill.

Other people usually prefer to go sightseeing on sunny days, but I am more interested in unusual beauty at unusual times. One foggy morning I went to the Causeway to find both the hills and the lake submerged in the mist. As far as my eyes could see there was only an opal mass. The croaking of oars came closer, echoing the pleasant chirps of birds. A dot popped out of the white nothingness, and then the outline of a boat gradually came in sight. That would be the first pleasure boat of the morning. On another moonlit night I sat on a bench at the Su Causeway. Dim moonlight cast mysterious shadows on the lake. The latter glittered as if innumerable silvery fish were thrashing about. The quietness emboldened all the fish to sneak just under the water surface and leap out from time to time, as if spying upon the human world. A silvery object shot with a splash over the water, and in the twinkling of an eye it was gone.

Upon arrival I had attributed the thriving greenery to the special favors of nature, but as time went by I realized that it was not exactly so. A tourist would often exclaim, "How spotlessly clean this pebble path is!" Yet he may not be necessarily aware that every morning there are gardeners sweeping off withered branches and dead leaves with long-handled bamboo brooms. "The green lawn feels as soft as a flannelette blanket!" Yet it would never occur to him that there are female workers wearing bamboo hats squatting on the lawn plucking out weeds, even with the scorching sun directly overhead. It is only after days of observation that one finds that the gardeners are always busy spraying pesticide over the greenery with pumps, replacing wilted flowers with blooming ones which they have transported in heavy carts, so that a blaze of colors is always on display, or climbing up high ladders and supporting cedars with bamboo stakes in order that they maintain a gracefully erect posture. With this knowledge in mind, I felt bad every time I saw a flower or a leaf drop to the ground, for each and every of them had resulted from hard labor. However, I would be relieved by the idea that those leaves and flowers had fallen to dirt to form nurturing ground for new beauty. I remembered hearing tinkling sounds at night during my previous visit to Hangzhou. Inquiry revealed that they were produced by dredgers. The crew manning the dredgers was nowhere to be seen, but the clear water was their gift to us. Thanks to the work of millions of people, we are now able to enjoy the beauty of the West Lake!

The beauty of the West Lake is immortal, because labor is immortal and laborers are immortal.

I frequently ran into Liu Aqiao by the lake. Every time she saw me, a sincere and cordial smile would appear on her round suntanned face. She would forget me in the long run, for I was just one of the millions of tourists. But I will never forget Liu Aqiao. I would observe closely whenever I gazed at the boats in the distance. The image of her rowing with graceful ease had been forever captured on my retina. The Liu Aqiao's and gardeners had inspired me and led me one step closer to a truth: the working people are the people who appreciate, cherish and create beauty the best. Only in this sense is the beauty of the West Lake immortal.

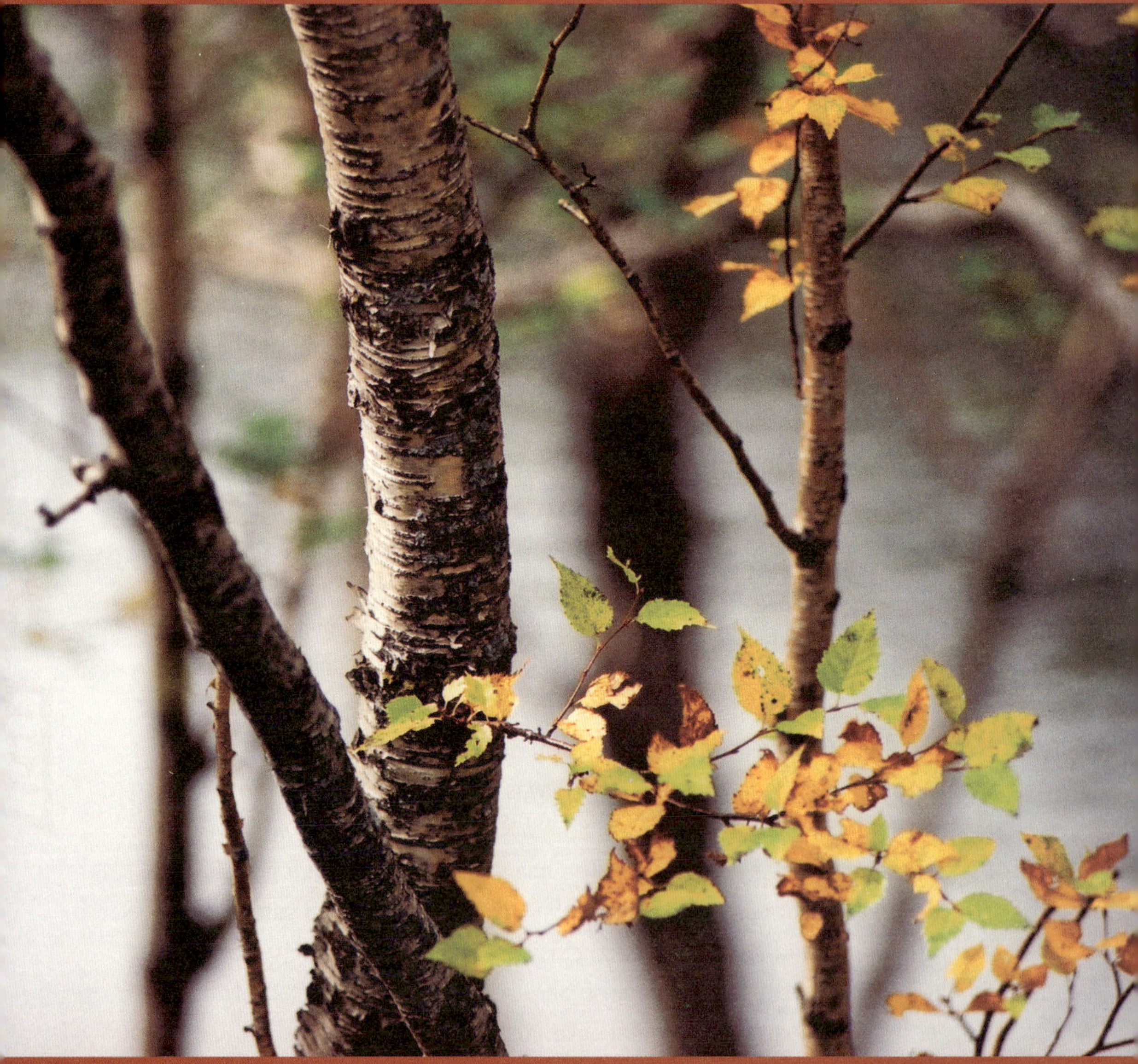

A Butterfly Gathering by the Lancang River

Feng Mu

I was fortunate enough to witness a butterfly assembly in the beautiful Xi Shuang Ban Na.

Many people have heard of the Butterfly Spring and butterfly gatherings at Dali, Yunnan Province, as well as having read about them. From the *Annals of Dali* compiled during the reign of Emperor Wanli of the Ming Dynasty to press coverage of recent years, we have encountered detailed descriptions of this unique phenomenon taking place in the enchanting border area of Yunnan. Records of butterfly gatherings date back to ancient times. To my knowledge, Xu Xiake of late Ming Dynasty was the first person to have left a meticulously accurate account of the wonderful butterfly assemblies. This outstanding traveler living over three hundred years ago, recreated faithfully not only the extraordinary phenomenon of butterfly gatherings, but also the natural setting of the Butterfly Spring. He wrote:

"... At the foot of the hill there is a huge towering tree close to the cliff. Clear spring water oozes out of its roots to flow east. Within a few steps to the east there is another smaller tree, at whose foot lies another spring. The two springs converge at a pool of around eleven square meters, which is exactly the source of the river we have been looking for. Early in April the big tree sheltering the pool bursts into blossoms in the shape of butterflies; moreover hundreds of millions of genuine butterflies hang down hooked in strings from its branches to the spring. There is a profusion of splendid colors."

What a dazzling and fascinating scene! No wonder many visitors to Dali take pains to see this spectacle with their own eyes. The pity is that many fail to catch sight of it. For some law of nature inexplicable to us, every year butterflies assemble for only a short time and at a different time period at that. Traffic problems often make it difficult for those who have the chance to visit Dali to reach the Butterfly Spring on time. Even Xu Xiake himself missed the grand occasion. He was a few days late, and when he arrived the flowers had already withered, so much so that he went away disappointed, a twig from the tree in hand. His description of butterfly assemblies was more than likely a record of what others had told him.

I went to the Butterfly Spring eight or seven years ago. Late as I was, I did not go away disappointed as Xu Xiake had been, because there were still hundreds of butterflies lingering on the site. Over a mirror of a limpid spring stretched the graceful limbs of the giant tree. Multicolored butterflies fluttered lightly over their own reflections in the pool. The sight was indeed unusually beautiful.

Ever since then I have met quite a number of people who have been to the Butterfly Spring, but only few have been in luck. Nevertheless, their accounts were far less spectacular than those in books and folk tales.

In fact, that is not surprising at all. With better roads, more visitors, more wasteland under cultivation, it is only natural for the number of butterflies to dwindle at the Butterfly Spring. What's more, if we get to the bottom of legends about butterfly assemblies, we will find that rare sights like these are nothing more than the outcome of the natural environment. Furthermore, it has been clearly stated in some books that the so-called butterfly assemblies are not unique to the Butterfly Spring at Dali, but that they have occurred somewhere else in Yunnan. For example, Zhang Hong of the Qing Dynasty recorded a gathering of butterflies at the Yuantong Hill in the city of Kunming (the present-day Yuantong Park) in his literary sketches entitled *New Collection of Anecdotes of Southern Yunnan*. He wrote:

"In the first month of summer every year, hundreds of millions of butterflies gather at the hill, inundating all houses, trees, rocks and valleys. Some are as big as wheels, others as small as coins. They flutter gracefully in the wind, displaying a splendid multitude of colors. They will not leave until after three days. No one knows where they come from, or where they leave for. I have personally seen the wonder for two years."

Zhang Hong lived under the reign of Emperor Qianlong. Naturally there was no way for him to explain the peculiar sight he had seen in Kunming in a scientific manner. On the other hand, with the passage of time I am afraid that there would be few current Kunming inhabitants who have heard of such natural wonder taking place right in Kunming. However, Zhang Hong inadvertently proved for us one thing through his vivid description of butterfly assemblies, i.e., butterfly gatherings are not unique to Dali's Butterfly Spring, but a specialty born of Yunnan's particular natural setting, where the climate is mild, plants flourish, and the land is fertile. Therefore I hypothesized that, although the number of butterflies were dwindling at Dali (as it did in Kunming in the past), we would have no trouble finding another place as picturesque as the Butterfly Spring somewhere else in the beautiful border area of Yunnan.

My hypothesis was proven by a chance encounter on my recent trip to Xi Shuang Ban Na.

By luck I stumbled upon a real butterfly assembly that compared well with the one at the Butterfly Spring as described by Xu Xiake.

The weather is like spring all the year round in Xi Shuang Ban Na. There you never see plants withering. Yet spring is still the best season. It was on the eve of the Water Sprinkling Festival of the Dai ethnic group in spring that we went to the Olive Flatland, the so-called "emerald" of Xi Shuang Ban Na.

Others had told me that whoever missed the visit to the Olive Flatland did not see the real Xi Shuang Ban Na. The moment we got off a boat on the Lancang River and set foot on this land of dense foliage I realized that they had not exaggerated a bit. We seemed to have stepped into a huge natural tropical garden with sun-blocking trees and multifarious flowers. It was vibrant with life: birds were chirping endlessly, plants of all sorts crowded the brown fertile soil and competed against each other for headroom. Walking along the paths connecting villages and hamlets was like walking along meticulously maintained boulevards in parks. The scorching sun was able to penetrate the thick leafage occasionally. We went hiking in villages along the Lancang River.

At the end of our hiking route there were two hamlets nestled against the river close to each other, Manting and Manzha. As soon as we set foot on a riverside trail that wound through dense woods, I found every plot of land, part of the trail, and stretch of woods to be so rich in tropical views that each of them was a masterpiece of colorful landscape painting. We passed by quite a number of villages hidden deep in the forest, whose exquisite Dai-style bamboo stilt houses were almost indistinguishable from the copses. Villages here were unusual in that houses were scattered in the immense forest instead of gathering close together. There was a fertile orchid around each bamboo stilt house, and in each courtyard there were tall coconut trees and betel palms, luxuriant mango trees and litchi trees. Here the fences were made of banana trees heavily laden with fruit, and walls were made of fragrant cordate telosma trees. Fruits hung heavily from the shaddock trees that rapped at the eaves of the bamboo stilt houses, jackfruits clustered against each other among branches to give off an intoxicating aroma.

We enjoyed our afternoon at the garden-like Manting and Manzha. At Manzha we visited an excellent nursery, had a lunch of ethnic flavor with commune members according to the Dai way in a neat and pleasant canteen, sharing their mirth over their prosperous life. At Manting we attended a joint meeting of commune leaders on the production of sugar canes and double-harvest rice. Afterwards we set out on the journey back, feeling contented.

We took the same trail on which as we had come, the trail that wound through the thick forest where the air was richly scented by numerous exotic flowers. Along the path, deep in the forest, birds and cicadas joined in a loud but pleasant chorus. Through openings in the foliage we frequently spotted huge stretches of level fields, where early rice and the seedlings of other tropical cash crops swayed in the breeze, basking in the setting sun. On the edges of villages there were gigantic pattra trees and bodhi trees, under whose crowns the golden towers and roofs of Buddhist temples were glittering.

All looked the same as on our incoming trip, yet we felt something different in the environment. Eventually we found it: we had new company - swarms of butterflies. There were multicolored butterflies fluttering in knots over flowers, among leaves and around us. Some hovered in the woods, while others followed us. At first we were not surprised at all, for we all knew how unparalleled the butterflies here were in beauty and number, and we had often run into colorful butterflies that would chase us for miles. We had been accustomed to regarding butterflies as an integral part of the wonderful landscape of Xi Shuang Ban Na.

Nevertheless, as time went by, we were increasingly aware of the extraordinariness of the spectacle. There were more and more butterflies flying over the trail in the same direction as ours. Now high, now low, now right, now left, they fluttered their colorful wings in such a rapid manner among flowers and trees that we were dazed. Sometimes thousands of butterflies blocked our way of advance, forcing us to drive them away with twigs.

After fighting the butterflies for about 2.5 kilometers, something fantastic came into sight as we approached the edge of a lush pattra wood. In the middle of a meadow there was a gigantic bodhi tree whose outreaching branches and thick leafage sheltered the entire meadow like a huge umbrella. On the few square meters of meadow in the center there was some bizarre growth made of hundreds of thousands of beautiful butterflies. They crowded against, clung to and piled on each other, making the parterre-like structure expand continuously both horizontally and vertically. More butterflies were flying towards it in an endless flow. Most of them belonged to the same species, the pale green inside of their wings imitating tender green grasses as they stayed put, with the golden outside with beautiful patterns turning them into little golden flowers when they fluttered their wings. In the thick of them there were an occasional one or two huge ribbon- wearing butterflies with red specks on a black background, as if they had joined for the sake of variety. In the twinkling of an eye we had entered a fairyland. In front of us, around us, in a wonderful natural setting, there were butterflies everywhere, so much so that we could easily reach out to capture some of them. Pollen flew like snow in the sky, joining the wild flowers in the forest and the bodhi trees to emanate a scent so strong that it irritated the nose.

We were dumbfounded at this natural wonder. Standing in the midst of hundreds of thousands of butterflies, we felt like intruders. But the butterflies were not afraid of us at all. As we threw twigs at them they swarmed into the sky fluttering their colorful wings. Yet within a minute they again congregated on the meadow. There was barely any way for us to dampen their enthusiasm for attending the grand occasion.

It was after a long time of appreciating and marveling at the huge assembly of butterflies that we finally tore ourselves away. An idea flashed across my mind: might it be a case of the legendary gathering of butterflies we had heard of in the past? Some of us had often lamented over the dwindling number of butterflies at Dali's Butterfly Spring, yet wasn't it easy to find some other sites for their joyous get-together in the extremely beautiful and abundant land of our border area?

Certainly my thoughts at the time were ludicrously childish. It had never occurred to me to seek a scientific explanation for the peculiar phenomenon I had seen (I leave it to entomologists and botanists); neither had I considered whether butterfly assemblies were good or bad to our land. I should say that I had been overwhelmed by the fairytale scene, and that, excited and joyous, I took great pride in the spectacular scenery offered by our border areas. How abundant, how beautiful and how enchanting the land we are living on, working on and building on!

Sorrow-Free Lake

Huang Shang

Sorrow-Free Lake is located outside the Shuixi Gate, the so-called dock area in the past. Before the railway was open this area had used to be a hub of water transport for the Southern Capital*. Looking down from the Shuixi Gate, you could still see the scene of prosperity in the streets. The streets had been built in the old style, with fresh product stores and grain stores. A walk along them easily reminds one of the streets in Bianliang as described in such traditional novels as *The Seven Swordsmen* and *Five Chivalrous Persons*.

There is another funny association, too. In a traditional opera entitled *The Four Palace Graduates*, I heard Song Shijie sing to his adopted son and daughter after being beaten at the court, "You're not in the Shangcai County of Henan Province, neither are you at the Shuixi Gate of Nanjing." The singing left me feeling dejected. It was in such a downtown area that this small potato who was rejected by the mortal world led a dreary and lonely life. Today I may not have waited until the sun slants to take a look outside the Shuixi Gate, but I can still feel what he felt.

Beyond a near-rotten wooden bridge, turn right at the end of a street (its very name being Sorrow-Free Road), and you will see the walls of a small temple at the far side of a clearing. That would be the Huayan Temple.

Inside the temple there is a brick path lined with willows leading up to Chess Winning Building facing the gate. Legend has it that the First Emperor of the Ming Dynasty once played chess with Xu Da on the spot, and upon losing the game bestowed the building on the latter. The source of the legend is doubtful, but we do know that the building was constructed on the former site of Tulip Hall, named after a line of poem by Shen Quanqi which goes to the effect that "a young married woman of the Lu family is as beautiful as a tulip" written in memory of Lady Sorrow-Free. Zhu Xie located three sources of the allusion to Lady Sorrow-Free in his *In the Name of Textual Research*. The first cites the song in praise of river water by Emperor Wu of the Liang Dynasty that "the river water flows east, and a young lady from Luoyang was named Sorrow-Free" to prove that Lady Sorrow-Free was originally from Luoyang. The second concludes from the annals of musicians in the *History of Tang*, which states that "there is a woman named Sorrow-Free in the Stone City* who is good at singing local ballads," and that she was a Jinling* native. The third refers to the sketches of Hong Rongzai that say she was from the stone city of Jingling instead of Jinling. I am interested in neither of them, for I suspect there might be a lot of ancient women bearing the name Sorrow-Free, just like the way it is with names containing such characters as "Juan" or "Hua" nowadays. But it is indeed a nice name, and Lady Sorrow-Free of the Lu family has been remembered for centuries thanks to the poem by Shen Quanqi. The stone profile of Chen Yuan at Kunming and that of Xue Tao at Chengdu have conditioned me to expect a similar profile of Sorrow-Free here, and there it is. All engraved on stone tablets, they have been blackened by years of stroking and rubbing. All of them seem to be the same type of delicate ancient beauty, dressed like maids of honor. There are also a great number of antithetical couplets, many of them excellent. Probably it is the favorable geographical location where heroes and romances abound that has given writers inspiration.

The most famous couplet was composed by Wang Renqiu. According to Liu Yusheng, the original work had read "Disdain not the woman from the north, for when her boat arrives all girls of the south pale by comparison; Gone is the extravagant life of the Six Dynasties, all has changed except for the blue mountains where peach trees and plum trees blossom year after year." Later at the protest of "all girls of the south" the couplet was revised. That's why in the current couplet at Chess Winning Building, "pale by comparison" has been replaced by "gain by comparison", while "all remains the same including the blue mountains" has substituted "all has changed except for the blue mountains." Naturally such a revision misrepresents the original intention, and the self-contradictory first line causes confusion. There is an epilogue for the couplet which states, "Upon completion of the renovation of the pavilion at Sorrow-Free Lake in the tenth year of Emperor Tongzhi's Reign, Commissioner Gui Xiangting invites me for a visit and a few words of commemoration. According to the annals of musicians, Sorrow-Free was a woman from Hezhong area who married into the Lu Family, a well-established family in the north. People differ in their views as whether she was a prostitute living on a boat in the Stone City or not. Perhaps it is because of her beauty that her name had been circulated through literary works. She should be ranked with Qijiang of the Song family rather than Zhenniang of the Su Family. Therefore I write this postscript to acquaint the busybodies with the fact." The wording is rather sensible, yet the influence of Confucian canon still shows, for he cares too much about social status. In fact Sorrow-Free had much more in common with Zhenniang than with the noblewoman Qijiang.

There is another fine couplet written by Xue Weinong (a.k.a. Xue Shiyu), "The landscape is tender, the weather remains the same, a few people enjoy their boating trip, whereas a pretty young singing girl strokes her string instrument to sing a folk song in the style of the Qi and Liang Dynasties; the game of chess is over, the heroes long gone, some visitors ascend the building to look into the distance, paying homage to the portrait of the deceased court official whose deeds are greater than those of Chang Yuchun and Mu Ying."

This is exactly what I mean by forming an antithesis between heroes and romances. The portrait of Xu Da, the Prince of Zhongshan*, whose deeds, according to the second line of the couplet, were greater than those of Chang Yuchun and Mu Ying, is hung right there on the upper floor. But in my opinion it is most probably a fake. What amuses me more is a portrait downstairs recently painted by Xu Da's offspring. In it Xu Da lies prostrate on the steps. According to the inscriptions on the painting the story goes, "Once (the First Emperor) came to the Xu Residence together with Mr. Xu. Compelled to drink, Mr. Xu committed the crime [the Chinese character for "crime" is a homonym of the Chinese character for "drunken"] of sleeping on the imperial bed in his stupor. When he woke up he was so frightened that he lay prostrate on the steps pleading for mercy. The Emperor looked at him feeling pleased, so he ordered officials to refurbish the residence and erect the Great Achievement Arch in memorial of Mr. Xu's deeds."

It is funny to see the way Mr. Xu lies prostrate in the painting. He is huddled up, his head out of view except for the jewelry on his hat. Although the painting is far from a masterpiece, the real scenario must have looked exactly like that. No wonder the First Emperor was so pleased that he ordered this first-class servant to be rewarded.

I will deal with the matter in more detail later. The day when Renyuan and I went to Sorrow-Free Lake our first stop was Leaf Sweeping Building. Tired from the walk along the city wall until the Shuixi Gate, where we left the city for the lake, we sat by a window of the lakeside teahouse to have a cup of tea. The lake seemed to be cramped with graceful floating lotus leaves. The stone city wall stretched to the west along the lake, which looked vast indeed in the distance. In the lake there were some young girls in small wooden bathtub-shaped boats gathering lotus seeds.

Our teahouse stood alone in the area. Most of its neighboring pavilions had already collapsed. The few that had not were nodding to their fall, their plinths already gone askew.

In the neighborhood there used to be an Honorable Mr. Zeng's Pavilion in memorial of Zeng Guofan. In it there had been a portrait of Mr. Zeng, as well as a couplet whose line "in a small pavilion between the sky and the river sits a man of outstanding personality" was praiseworthy. At present, the Honorable Mr. Zeng's Pavilion is nowhere to be found, nor is his portrait. However, another picture of his is still hung at Chess Winning Building. Wearing a long cloth gown and long-bearded, he is elegant in an other-worldly way. Despite his rebuilding lakeside houses and restoring gaily-painted pleasure boats in the Qinhuai River after recapturing Jinling, Zeng had never been reprimanded as a traitor. Instead he behaved like a pillar of the Confucian orthodoxy, compiling anthologies of classical prose and renovating the Confucian Temple. Besides re-strengthening the rule of the Qing Dynasty, he also revived the "Holy Way" that had been on decline ever since Han Yu. Nowadays he is as much censured as praised. Some scold him severely, while others extol his deeds, and the collection of his letters home has become a recipe book for winning promotion. Nevertheless, there are few traces of him left in Nanjing. His memorial hall has been taken over by the Committee of Mongolian and Tibetan Affairs, its halls having been turned into either offices or dorms. A picture is all that has been left. As we sipped our tea, the waitress brought us some melon seeds. At the opening of the window the wind rose sighing over the lake. In the distance, Cool Mountain had turned red in the sun, the top of which was still green. That must be an ideal place to take a rest.

He Shaoji once wrote a poem in memorial of Sorrow-Free Lake, "The vast lake has gone deserted, although in the past a tour of it was cherished. The landscape will come to a better time, just rest at ease and sorrow free." Poets have always been able to communicate their sentiments. Dilapidated as the buildings are, deserted as the lake is, one can always have a moment of peace sitting here. Ancient young girls favored the name "Sorrow-Free," yet they might have seemed free of care in the eyes of others while they themselves did not feel like pretending to be naïve and charming all the time. This is probably a perpetual tragedy similar to that of "the young married woman in her boudoir" depicted by Wang Changling!

*Translator's note: The Southern Capital, the Stone City, Jinling, and Zhongshan all refer to the present-day Nanjing.

Notes on the Sky Mountains

Bi Ye

Friends, have you ever been to the Sky Mountains? They are the huge mountain ranges in Northwestern China that stretch for thousands of miles between the Junggar Basin and the Tarim Basin, separating the vast Xinjiang into a northern part and a southern part. Viewed from the distance, the towering peaks that are covered by snow all year round glitter like the pearl-adorned hats worn by groups of dancing Uygur girls; the colorful and extending mountains are as charming as peacocks spreading their tails.

Besides being exceptionally beautiful, the Sky Mountains are also infinitely tender. There are lush pastures and exuberant forests. Clad in shadows they are as shy as young girls; lit up by sunlight they are like the ample bosoms of young mothers. People would love them with two intertwining sweet sentiments: one, that of a baby nestling up against its mother's breasts; the other of a man leaning close to his lover.

With your permission, I'd like to take you on a tour of the Sky Mountains.

Snow-capped Peaks, Streams and Creeks, Forests and Woods

In July when it is scorching in Xinjiang's Gobi Desert, it is the ideal time to ride a horse and visit the Sky Mountains. Both Ili in northern Xinjiang and Yanqi in the south are known for fine horses. If you ride a Kazak horse

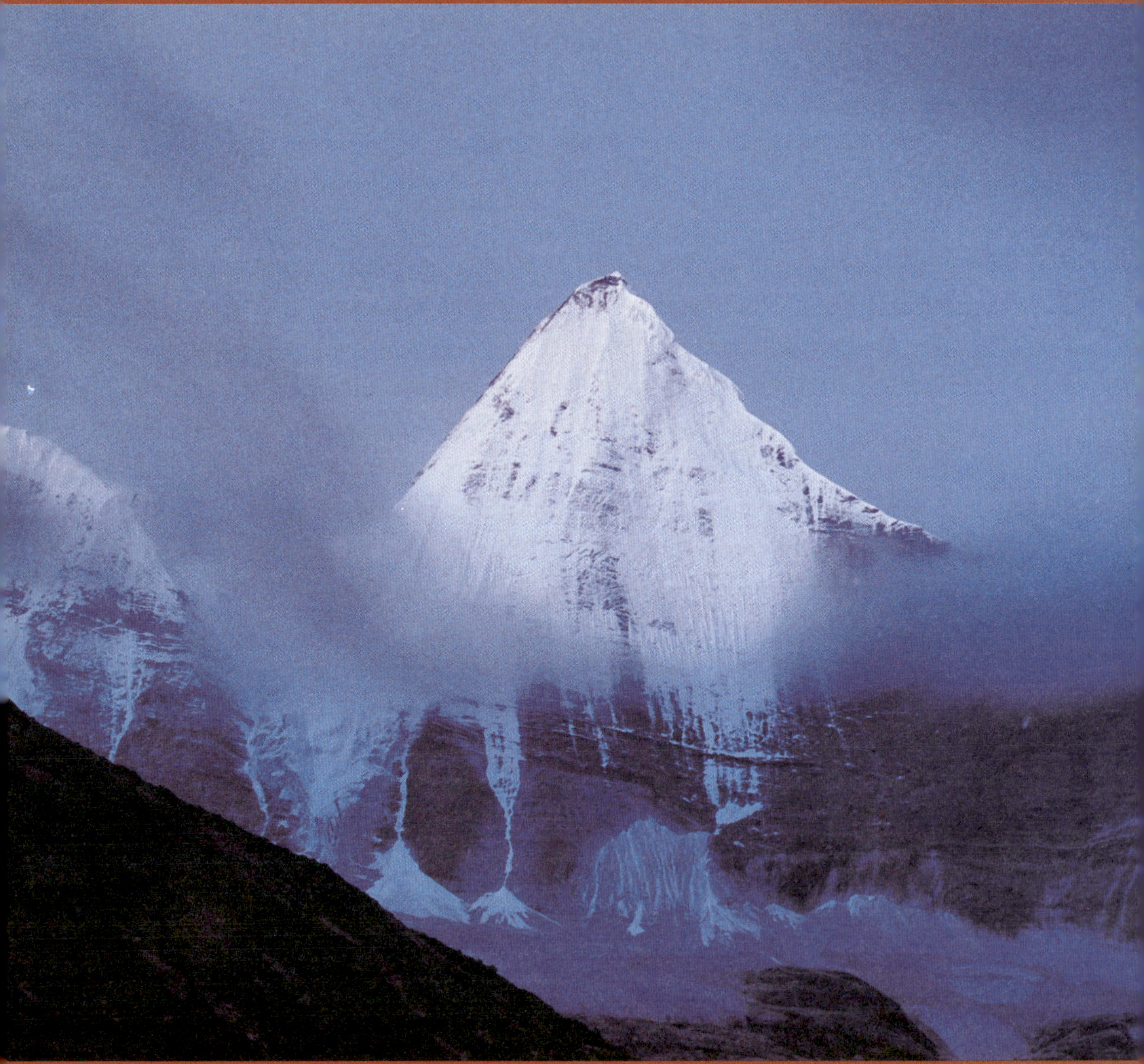

from Ili or a Mongolian horse from Yanqi to climb the mountains, the trip will feel as smooth and fast as one on level ground.

The moment you enter Sky the Mountains, the heat of the Gobi Desert is left behind. The snow-capped mountains greet you with a cold air that instantly makes you feel as pleasantly cool as in autumn. Enormous snow-clad peaks stand out against the blue sky. Clouds in the sun cast their shadows here and there over the snowy peaks, like silver gray flowers embroidered on a length of white satin. Newly-melt snow rushes along mountain streams and down from cliffs like hundreds of glistening silver chains. The snow water clashes against the swift creeks down below, sending sprays upward like thousands of blooming white lilies. Yet as soon as the current slows down, fishes will skip in the backwater. If you water your horse here, you can look down from your saddle into the bottom of the crystal-clear creek and find fishes swimming among multicolored pebbles. Their scales glitter in the limpid snow water, adding life to the silent mountains.

As you go farther into the mountains, the view is even better. Below the snow line there is the endless luxuriant virgin forest, where pine trees stand like giant umbrellas and where the foliage is so thick that sunlight is only able to penetrate through a few places. The sound of a horse splashing about in a creek dotted with rocks only accentuates its tranquility. Few birds venture deep into the forest. Occasionally a bird will chirp in the distance. If you get off the horse to take a smoking break on a rock, your cigarette would flicker in the darkness even if it is sunny and bright outside the forest. Judging by the one or two charred trees, hard-working hunters may have camped here at night and roasted game on the fire. Herds of wild goats, deer, oxen and camels abound in the Sky Mountains.

If so far you feel the weather is autumnal, it is like spring as you travel even farther. The color of the mountains softens, so does their shape, as if you could touch creamy skin. Here streams and creeks flow gently around the foot of every hill, along the banks of which are wild flowers taller than the horse's head. Red, yellow, blue, white and purple, they spread like an endless piece of brocade, as dazzling as rosy clouds on the horizon, as brilliant as rainbows high in the sky. Layer after layer, the wild flowers are meters in height, their blossoms as big as 22-centimeter agate plates, their petals larger than the palm. A horse appears all the more strong and vigorous walking through the sea of flowers, and the man on horseback full of vitality. You needn't bother to dismount, because armfuls of lovely flowers are within easy reach.

Although at present it is not spring in the Sky Mountains, there is no spring garden on earth that rivals the multitude of flowers here.

A Charming Summer Ranch

Among the snowy mountains there is a huge and peculiarly charming ranch. It is doubly laced with dark green virgin forests and bright-colored wild flowers. Lush buttery grass spreads to the horizon with clear streams meandering through it. The grassland is as endless as a calm and tranquil sea. Yurts glisten in the sun like bubbles.

Wherever you gallop on this boundless grassland, you will see hundreds of thousands of sheep, horses and cattle. Thanks to the milky buttery grass, their hair glows as if oil exuded from the tip. In particular, those yellow oxen, spotted cows, white sheep and red goats that stand out against the green pasture are as beautiful as colored patterns embroidered on a piece of green satin.

On occasion, along with the wind comes the jingling sound of Kazak shepherdesses' silver ornaments. It's a touching scene to watch them ride horses against the background of blue sky, snowy mountains and green pasture. They laugh and chase the galloping horses. Once slowed down, they wave their whips gently while singing love songs.

Surrounded by snowy mountains, green woods and full-blown flowers, this huge ranch appears to be low-lying and flat, yet in fact it is two or three thousand meters above sea level. Whenever a puff of dark cloud drifts over the sky, it will shower on the ranch. Herds appear and disappear among the rain clouds to make the latter appear heavier, making it hard to tell one from the other. Once the shower is over, the grassland appears fresher and greener, comparable to a huge sapphire from a distance, and when you look closer, the drops of water on the leaves are like countless diamonds.

Dusk at the ranch is even more enticing. The setting sun turns clouds and the snowy peaks around the ranch to a dazzling crimson, whose reflection in turn brightens up the vast ranch into a magnificent world, bathing yurts, herds and shepherdesses in a rosy glow. As the sun goes down, the crimson tint on mountains gradually fades away, and the whole grassland is enveloped in silvery gray twilight. By then, numerous spots of firelights spring up, and you know that the herdsmen are heating their bronze kettles on their fires and fixing their supper.

You needn't stand on ceremony but just make yourself at home at any yurt. Whichever yurt the firelight guides you to, the hospitable Kazak herdsmen will receive you as warmly as if you were part of the family. If you are thirsty you could first have a bowl of mare's milk, if you are hungry there are roasted lamb chops, yogurt lumps and buttered cakes. You can eat and drink to your heart's desire as the Kazaks do.

When the wild oxen dung is burned to glowing ashes under the family kettle hanging on an A-frame, plucked string instruments will be played and Kazak shepherdesses will sing their sweet and clear songs in the night breeze, as a dozen families gather at a larger yurt to enjoy the final happy moments of the day.

After that the whole place quiets down. Put on a leather coat and walk out of the yurt, you will have a vague view of herds strolling about quietly on the grassland in the moon or under a starry sky. The ranch at night is so tranquil and peaceful that only the flowing water in creeks provokes you into a meditation on nature.

Wild Horses, Mushroom Rings, Marmots and Snow Lotuses

Much must have happened on the pasture under the starry sky or in moonlight, but people are oblivious of it in their sweet slumber. At dawn they will find much larger herds of horses than the night before. Pleasantly surprised, they approach the herds, only to find that the horses would suddenly split into two groups and that one group will gallop away, their satin-like long manes swaying in the pale blue twilight. Then you will realize that those are wild horses that came to mix and play with pasture horses at night. Alert and agile, they wander around following the lead of a few of the sturdiest stallions. Upon meeting the many familiar pasture horses, they would smell each other and touch each other's heads in an intimate manner before grazing and frolicking together. They are ready to leave at dawn the moment herdsmen come out of the yurt. The wild stallions always let the mares and foals leave first. They would stop at a safe distance from people. The beautiful knee-long manes of the wild stallions that stand guard of the herd shine in the rising sun.

As the sun lights up the vast grassland, mushrooms can be spotted the most easily. Mushrooms at the Sky Mountains are tender and juicy, huge and delicious. You just need to look out on the pasture on your horse to detect some especially green circles. These would be mushroom rings. If you ride towards them, you will find, among the lush circles of buttery grass ten to thirteen meters in diameter, mushrooms as countless as stars in a summer night sky. Those snow-white mushrooms hiding in green grass would tempt anyone. If one hand can't pick fast enough, naturally you would put both hands to work. If your pockets are bursting with mushrooms, naturally you would use your hat and even boots as containers. It's the happiest thing for visitors from afar to gather so many fresh mushrooms for the first time. Washed clean in the creek and boiled without any oil or salt, they taste extraordinarily delicious. If you cook them together with a wild goat leg, the dish would both taste good and smell good.

There are lots of rarities at Sky Mountains. Otters are known to live by or in the water, but marmots live in the Sky Mountains. You will see holes here and there at the foot of hills along the edge of the pasture. These are their habitats. Marmots spend half a year hibernating in the holes, from

September or October when heavy snow has sealed the mountain passes until April or May the next year when the thaw is over. It is only until after the Summer Solstice that they grow plump and sturdy by feeding on green buttery grass. By then hunting on a large scale could begin, for their fur has turned into a shiny brown, their bellies touching the ground, and their four legs dragging along laboriously.

The snow lotus is another rarity. If you climb above the snow line of the Sky Mountains, you will see silvery white snow lotus erecting proudly in the cold snow. Accustomed to the extremely cold environment, snow lotuses strike root deep into rock cracks, deriving nourishment from snow water and absorbing snow light. They are gentle and graceful, pure and spotlessly white. These unusual flowers, found in deserted snowy mountain areas several thousand meters above sea level, are said to be rare herbs for gynecological diseases.

Natural Lakes and Fruit Gullies

Huge natural lakes are found among the high peaks of the Sky Mountains, as clear as mirrors used by a beauty to make up in the morning. White clouds and snowy peaks are reflected in the smooth and crystal clear lakes. The lakes, peaks, sky and reflections are integrated into a translucent whole. Swans are the only moving objects in the secluded lakes. The whiteness of the swans adds to the clearness of lake water, and their cries add to the tranquility of the lakes. Mountain scenery is said to be varied, whereas in fact lake scenery is also changeable. If you look down from a high altitude at a lake, you will see an expanse of refreshing water. If you pay closer attention, you will find that the lake surface near you gleams as if thousands of silvery fish were swimming therein, while in the distance the lake surface is as smooth as a mirror without a single fleck or gossamer. The lake grows deeper in color as it expands further, from silvery white to pale blue, dark blue and dark green, with clear demarcations in between. Legend has it that a teardrop shed by an unfortunate ancient Kazak lass turned into one of the lakes, and that the varied colors of water stand for her numerous sorrows.

The offspring of this legendary lass are currently grazing flocks of sheep right beside the very lake. The lake water provides moisture for the green grass on the lakeside. The green grass fattens the sheep. Sheep milk nurtures her offspring. Of course, the same lake that used to stand for Kazak misfortunes is now a symbol of happiness.

Embraced by high mountains and clear lakes, caressed by sunlight and stars, the herdsmen move their yurts and flocks around the lakes. Their flocks keep breeding year after year. They themselves fall in love, have babies, play musical instruments and sing in praise of the happy life.

The newly-melt snow from the high mountains flows into the lakes, and then rushes down through clefts into mountain streams thousands of meters below, forming dangling chains alongside cliffs. Those silvery chains are visible from hilltops dozens of kilometers away. If you walk to the verge of a cliff, a profound shock will be sent from your feet through your whole body. Looking down, you will see water chains splash down onto the rocks in the stream below, forming colorful mists in the sunlight. Right along the swift-flowing stream, scattering in the green valley, there are herdsmen's yurts as well. The yurts are as white as washed jade.

If you follow one of the zigzagging mountain streams, you'll find that water from hundreds of springs joins in to form a creek. More mountain streams and creeks merge into rivers that roll out of the Sky Mountains.

Wild fruit gullies are frequently located near such streams in the untraversed mountainous areas. In spring the gullies are full of blossoming flowers, and in autumn, fruits are aplenty, making them paradises for birds and wild animals. Those wild fruit gullies are rarely discovered by human beings. One such gully stretches for 250 kilometers and is overgrown with wild apple trees. When spring came, there was no one to appreciate the bloom, and neither was there any one to pick the apples upon the arrival of autumn. Old apple trees died as more new trees thrived. Years passed. By now there is a thick layer of meshed wild apples along the 250-kilometer-long gully.

After the discovery of this gully, a pig farm was built to feed herds of Ukrainian white pigs on wild apples. There is also a plan to build a brewery and make wine out of the wild apples, so that those precious gifts from nature could enter the human circulatory system and improve health.

Friends, I've just mentioned a few things at the thousand-mile-long Sky Mountains. High hills or deep valleys, grassland or lakes, forests or streams, there are more quality products and beautiful scenery than I could describe here. If some day you are seized with the desire to go sightseeing at the Sky Mountains, do please remember to inform me. I might act as quite a good guide for you. Or rather, to be your guide is just an excuse for me to revisit the Sky Mountains.

Autumn at the Taihu Lake

Ai Xuan

This morning when I got up, the ground had frosted over. It being around Slight Snow according to the Chinese Lunar Calendar, tangerines at the East Hill must have all been harvested. Or, probably hanging among tangerine trees planted at the northern nooks in the hill, there might still be some clusters of late-maturing "Liao Hong", whose color is changing from green to yellow.

I had not been to the East Hill for a couple of years, but I often thought fondly of the islets, villages, tangerine trees, tea farms, loquat orchards, and red bayberry plantations in the Taihu Lake area.

This time I took some friends from the literary circle there. Some of them, advanced in age and weak in constitution, might find it tough traveling in the hills. Before departure I had asked for information as to whether the island highway winding round the Dongting East Hill was open to traffic, and whether it was possible for the elderly to reach the back hill by car.

The back hill is the cream of the Dongting East Hill, where tangerines, loquats and bayberries are at their flourishing best.

The Dongting East Hill had been an isolated island in the Taihu Lake until about 200 years ago. At present its northern tip is connected with the mainland. A fishback-shaped mountain stretches from north to south across the center of the island, dividing it into an eastern part and a western part.

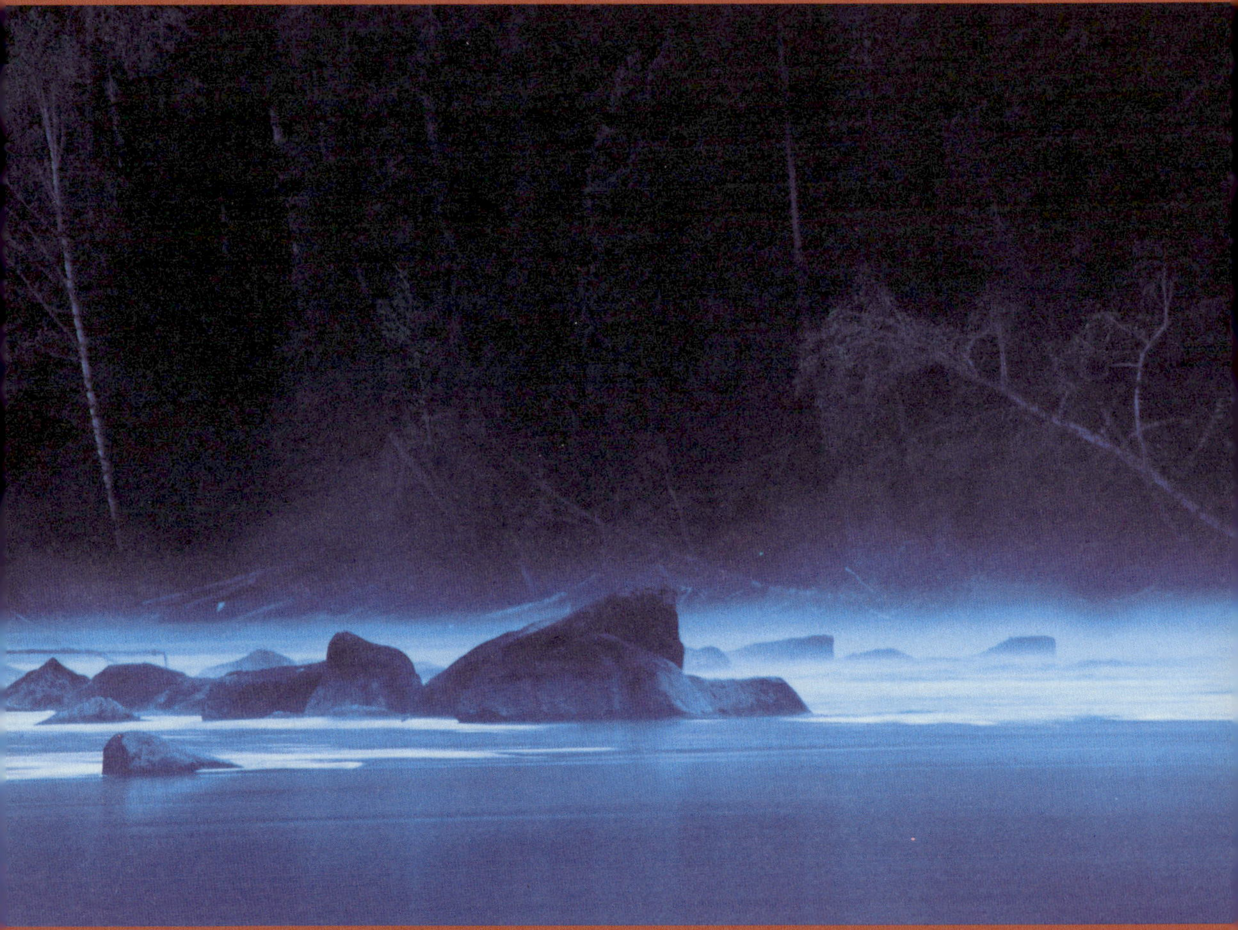

The eastern part, with its gentle slopes, is called the front hill; the western part, where the terrain is very rugged and steep, is called the back hill. In the past, the huge expanse of Eastern Taihu Lake was visible from any minor slope of the front hill. However, owing to excessive land reclamation in recent years, what comes into sight is a lake that has almost been squeezed out by land. It is only from the back hill where one can see the vast misty Taihu Lake and the fishing islands that dot it like green shells.

Tangerine trees have been grown on the back hill for over a thousand years. Nowadays when people recommend Dongting Tangerines from the East Hill, they quote a line of a poem from Bai Juyi which goes to the effect that "frosted new tangerines glitter like gold among thousands of trees", and a story from *Wondrous Tales Old and New* about a trader making a big and unexpected fortune by exporting Dongting Tangerines abroad. Unable to break away from convention, I'd also like to cite Prefect Bai to prove the long history of Dongting Tangerines.

For over a thousand years, tangerines had been transported out of the back hill by either manpower or wooden boats. A mountain range that meanders for miles blocked the way between the front hill and the back hill. To reach the East Hill Town, center of the front hill, from any village in the back hill, one must either follow a dangerous trail over hill and dale, or take a smoother but tortuous and narrow path round the lake. Either of the two land routes was utterly inconvenient for back hill farmers when it came to transporting fruit out and food in, seeking medical care or visiting friends and relatives.

I paid my first visit shortly after liberation [1949], just in time for the harvest of loquats and bayberries, as well as the rainy season in the Taihu

Lake area. Loquats and bayberries rolled all over the ground as a result of wind and rain. They were scattered in the grass, rock cracks, woods and along paths. Boats carrying fruits were stranded by heavy rain, strong wind and high waves. Meanwhile, loquats and bayberries, delicate and perishable, would go moldy and rotten within two days of harvest. At that time, everyone in the Dongting Hill prayed for a highway around the island and a road to Suzhou for long-distance buses. However, if a road, even a single lane, were to be built across the dense orchards of Dongting Hill, fruit trees that had taken scores of years to become productive must be felled, and precious land of which each individual could only claim a meager share must be sacrificed. People were caught in such a dilemma of gains and losses that they had never made up their minds.

It was not until this summer that the round-hill highway, over 20 years since conception, finally came into use.

The East Hill Town looked much different than it had several years before. There were wider streets, more stores, and taller buildings. Only the Engraved Mansion, a palace for some past nouveau riche, remained unchanged. The mansion is known to tourists home and abroad for its many wood carvings, brick engravings and heavy cumbersome structure. History has destined it to be heavy and cumbersome, and for which there will never be any need to change.

The 2.5 km-long flagstone street found its ancient and narrow way across the East Hill Town from the north to the south. Bamboo poles, on which hung washing of all colors, poked from upper-floor windows on both sides of the street. By now the middle section of this long street has been broadened to allow two trucks to move side by side. The other section has kept its historical look from two to three hundred years ago. Those high-walled mansions lining both sides of the street are still what they were during the reign of Emperors Kangxi and Qianlong. Some of those mansions with five, seven or nine residential compounds have been transformed into premises for commune-run small plants. There are tall fire walls around those mansions. Inside there are brick engravings on lintels, zigzag-rule-shaped buildings facing a deep, dark, damp shaft of a courtyard, floors paved with square tiles. Those imposing, gloomy and enclosed old mansions from the time of Emperors Kangxi and Qianlong stand side by side with spacious, bright, and open buildings that have been constructed in recent years.

Once out of the East Hill Town, our bus ran briskly along a crude new road, sometimes over hills and valleys, sometimes along the lake. Scenes outside the window changed rapidly: new terraced fields and stone blocks, pipes carrying water from the lake to the hilltop, villages, tributaries and creeks, farmer's boats, the few "Liao Hong" tangerines remaining on branches, "Bai Sha" loquat trees with swelling buds, white and red plum trees ready to break out into blossom, "Bi Luo Chun" green tea trees with blooming white flowers, beehives in the wood, children cutting grass for their sheep. One felt touched by and drawn to this early winter landscape with an increased heartbeat.

The bus did not travel at top speed. In one and a half hours' time we finished the round-the-island trip and were back at the starting point. When asked about their impression, everyone nodded, "Quite nice. Quite nice." The polite but unenthusiastic response from my guests woke me up to reality: The East Hill should be visited on foot instead of by bus. One could see nothing but the cloud of dust raised by the bus, the vast expanse of lake water, and the thick leafage of orchards by taking a bus around the island.

I had accompanied friends on their visits here quite often in the past. Back then the highway had not been built yet, so we would always enjoy our walk along a little brick-paved mountain path through dense orchards. The path was exquisitely paved, some sections with pebbles or rectangular stone slabs, some others with flat gray bricks forming geometrical patterns. Dust would not rise on sunny days; neither would mud appear on rainy days. If it rained, the rainwater would be drained so quickly that in a few moments one could walk on it wearing a pair of cloth shoes. Quite a few sections wound through thick woods that had never been exposed to sunlight. As a result the roadside bricks and stones were carpeted with moss and lichen.

The mountain path rose and fell with the terrain, now turning into a nook, now going close to the lake. Fruit trees on both sides of the path met overhead to form sun-blocking arches. People walking underneath had to push aside those branches that touched their foreheads. Once in a while they would stop to check the growth of oranges and tangerines. On occasion, they took a rest on a bench in a roadside pavilion and amused themselves by reading lines of doggerel on the plaster wall. When there was a break in the orchard, they would stand by the roadside to look at the pale blue islands in the far distance where the lake met the sky, or look down into the castle-like bamboo fish weirs in a shallow bay. If there happened to be a village on the way, they would chat about the crop with a known villager or an old stranger. Farmers left their doors open all year round. Even if a stranger walked in, they would offer a seat, cigarettes and tea with good grace. None of these scenes full of human interest and local fellowship would be visible to travelers in a vehicle that whizzed by. They would fail to appreciate life on the Dongting Hill, local conditions and customs, as well as friendship among local folks. There would be no detailed discussion about how fruit trees are getting along, no laughter or sigh brought forth by a bumper harvest or a lean year. What is lacking in a round-island bus is interpersonal communication.

Human life is multi-faceted and multi-paced. There is toil and rest, work and leisure. When people of the Dongting Hill work, what they need are ebullient labor songs, roaring pumps, noisy automobile engines. But what outside visitors need are winding mountain paths, roadside pavilions where they can enjoy the scenery while taking a rest, labyrinthine nooks and orchards, dimly discernible hills in the distance, thin clouds, vast expanses of lake water, speeding boats, and arrays of seven-mast trawlers.

In this area where the lake and hills have long been tranquil, conflicts frequently arise between modern science and classical arts, manmade wonder and natural beauty. But harmony does exist in some cases. A high-tension wire spans nine kilometers of lake surface from the Moli Peak on the East Hill Island to the Turtle Hill on the West Hill Island. Scores of hundred-meter-tall iron towers stand tall and upright in the vast lake. The electric cable zooms from tower to tower over the broad and peaceful lake, a perfect integration of utility and aesthetics, grandeur and grace.

The electric cable spanning the lake had become a part of the landscape several years before. This autumn the Taihu Lake again looked different, thanks to the round-island highway that girdles the beautiful Dongting Hill like a satin band.

The Scenery of Guilin

Fang Ji

It was really a treat to come to Guilin and keep company with a scenery that is second to none on earth, observing its myriad facets in the morning mist, evening glow, on cloudy days and clear days, when wind rose and rain fell. I started envying the local Guilin residents. Although I had worked for over six months at the Representative Office of the Eighth Route Army at Guilin during the War of Resistance Against Japanese Aggression 23 years before, I was then a young man in no mood for sightseeing. I had scarcely enjoyed the scenery except for a mental note that the scenery was indeed fantastic and that the Seven Star Cave was good for an air-raid shelter. In the summer of 1959 — exactly 20 years later, Comrade Li Kerang mailed me a painting entitled *The Profile of the Painted Cliff at Guilin* after he had returned to Beijing from a sketching trip to Guilin. I was immediately attracted to the painting, which brought back fond memories of my life at Guilin as well as the scenery there. I grasped what I had failed to grasp previously, and saw what I had failed to see. The scenery of Guilin made a vivid reappearance in front of my eyes. While marveling at the great moving power of art, I composed a mediocre old-style poem and mailed it to him:

"The light-ink strokes are unrivaled in the world,

the ink resembling peeled-off paint and the brush applied like an axe;

The nine peaks of the Painted Cliff rise towering,

the originality derived from a high degree of perfection."

On this second visit to Guilin, the scenery there reminded me of the painting by Kerang. Thus memory helped verify the relationship between the painting and the hills, between art and reality. I came to realize how a painter's creativity could turn natural things into heart-stirring works of art that have a life of their own.

It has long been noticed that the scenery of Guilin is worthy of a painter's brush. The Song Dynasty poet Huang Tingjian wrote, "The Gui Mountain hems in the city like the Yandang Mountain, steep emerald hills pop out of the level ground. With Li Chen and Guo Xi passed away, who could ever paint all the peaks here?" By this he might be lamenting the scarcity of painters who focused on the scenery of Guilin, but he might also be doubting whether Li Chen and Guo Xi could convey its beauty. Most painters of the succeeding Yuan and Ming Dynasties preferred the Huangshan Mountain. Shi Tao of early Qing Dynasty, a native son of Guilin, formed a distinctive style by integrating his childhood impressions into landscape painting. Among modern artists, the master landscape painter Huang Binhong took pride in "having painted all the scenery of Guilin", and Qi Baishi said "what I have in my mind is the finest under heaven, for this old man is used to the hills of Guilin." Undoubtedly the picturesque scenery of Guilin has lent variety to the technique of Chinese landscape painting.

Whereas in literature, the most celebrated description of Guilin's scenery known through the ages would be Han Yu's lines - "The River is a blue ribbon of silk. The hills are hairpins of jade." It is quite creative of him to have personified Guilin's scenery by comparing it to an unadorned but graceful woman. Although women in our times are no longer dressed in that way, people could still grasp the looks and characteristics of Guilin's scenery through an understanding of ancient life. During my sojourn in Guilin this time, I climbed the Folded Brocade Hill and the Bright Moon Hill. Sure enough, seen from the hilltop, the clear blue Li River, which flowed slowly towards the Bright Moon Hill from the northwest, turned east at its foot, passed through the city of Guilin, skirted around the Wave Subduing Hill and the Elephant Trunk Hill, and then headed southeast, looking exactly like a blue ribbon of silk swaying in the wind. While the surrounding hills, alternately basking in the sun and veiled by the mist, appeared in various shades of dark green, bright blue and silver gray, just like the fine and delicate headdress of a beauty.

It is no easy play of words to sum up some local natural scenery and create a clear-cut image. The risk is twofold: either an excess of details or a lack of the concrete. No wonder the works of later poets who visited Guilin, including such celebrities as Huang Tingjian, Fan Chengda and Liu Houcun, failed to come up with a portrait of Guilin as concise and vivid as Han Yu's. Fan Chengda once wrote a book entitled *The Hills and Rivers of Guilin* describing the fantastic scenery of Guilin, but people didn't believe him. So he had to resort to illustrations to convince them. Evidently it takes artistry to present things unusual through language.

Ancient people realized the importance of producing an artistic conception through the depiction of nature, hence the landscape paintings and poetry that express the thoughts and personalities of the artists. After being demoted as a "sinner" to Liuzhou, Liu Zongyuan spent his days "sightseeing in a leisurely manner". Later he turned out essays of fresh artistic ambience and lasting appeal. The dozen or so of essays from *A Pavilion at Guilin's Zijiazhou* to *A Rock Pond to the West of the Mound* are truly unrivaled in their fine description of the scenery around Guilin. Ranging from over a thousand words to less than two hundred, they may be about an outing, a hill or a valley, a pond or a rock, but few ancient landscape essays could match their meticulous observation, deep feelings, accurate depiction and terse language. Despite all those unprecedented artistic moods he had created in the essays, Liu Zongyuan wrote in the end, "I sat by the pond surrounded by bamboos and trees. The place felt desolate and cold. It was too cheerless to linger, so I left after making this note." (*A Rock Pond to the West of the Mound*) The word "cheerless" is quite accurate if his bitter experience as well as the natural features of Guilin at his time is taken into account. However, when it came to summarizing Guilin's hills, he simply wrote, "(they) shoot up steeply in great numbers".

Of all essays, *The Travel Notes of Xu Xiake* by Xu Hongzu (a.k.a. Xu Xiake) offers the most realistic and concrete account of Guilin's scenery. There is little generalization or analogy in his essays, but plenty of accurate details. As you read on you will not only be moved by his desire for sightseeing and be touched by his efforts, but your own wanderlust will also be stirred by his vivid and specific narration. However it is not that easy to form a mental picture of Guilin's scenery after reading his book. He himself once said, "Yet those which I long to see are beyond generalization." His travel notes followed a different style. He recorded natural scenery, roads and their length, the origin and direction of flow of rivers. His travel notes are not only valued as fine literary work, but also treasured for the many scientific data they contain. In a way, Xu Hongzu seems to be the best traveler of all time. He spent all his efforts and money traveling far and wide. Wherever he went, he recorded exactly how things stood, frankly expressed his feelings, and stayed clear of clichés and generalizations, which has henceforth become the most fascinating feature of his essays.

Therefore, from ancient times to the present, people have always added personal elements to the perception of scenery. Nevertheless, all those paintings, poems and essays that succeed in reflecting the true looks of nature on the one hand and creating a lofty artistic mood on the other hand have become part of the intellectual assets of our people. They bestow beautiful images and characters on the splendid land of our great country, stimulating patriotism.

The scenery of Guilin is indeed beautiful. In the morning, as soon as the windows are open, a grayish blue mountain haze will invade the room, leaving a transparent light flickering on walls, the desk and the writing paper on it. It also makes the trees outside the window greener, the flowers on the table redder.

Yes, it is all because of the sun, which at this time is still on the other side of the hills and shrouded in clouds. Thanks to refraction, it paints the mountains near and far, the clouds high and low, in tones light or heavy. At this moment the hills of Guilin are at their multifarious best: the ones close by appear so blue that they are almost transparent; the ones farther away are grayish black; and those even farther away assume a successive look of dark gray, light gray and light green. But there is even more. From time to time a high green hill would suddenly stand out from the range upon range of mountains. Surrounded by all the other beautifully tainted hills, it stands like a rude, naked man in front of you - all because the sunlight has penetrated the clouds to reach it.

Then you will see the Li River start to ripple and glisten in the distance. The sun dyes it into a transparent ribbon of blue silk and girdles it round the hills of Guilin.

Now you may go out. Wherever you go, sometimes as you round a house, a towering peak will come abruptly into view. At other times a graceful hill is visible through the thick foliage as you sit under a tree. Or the moment you lean forward to have a look at what is outside the pavilion in a park, you see a green curtain of a hill hung up on its upturned eaves. If you stand by a lake, the reflection of a hill in the rippling water often starts you on a train of thought.

Hence the scenery of Guilin is always by your side, in your eyes and your heart, in your mind and your feelings.

Yet how does it feel to live in Yangshuo? I have been there only once, and my impression is that it feels like a "fairyland". Compared with Guilin, the hills there are denser, greener, quieter and more secluded. Hill after hill spring up to reach the sky, yet they reach out for each other and set off each other. Their colors vary with changes in sunlight, clouds and mists. Moreover, unlike the rocky Guilin hills, they are overgrown with woods that adorn them like green velvety dresses. The best time to visit is around the Festival of Pure Brightness in spring, when the green velvety dresses are embroidered with blood red azaleas. People will grow passionate in an atmosphere of tranquility.

The best way to go to Yangshuo is to take a wooden boat trip along the Li River. The reflections in the water are worth separate mention. The hills reflected in the river are much clearer than the real hills on the banks; and they seem to come to life with the flowing water. Besides, their postures appear different as the boat sails. The clear water of the Li River is unrivaled, so much so that no matter how deep the water runs, the pebbles on the river bed, the patterns on the pebbles, the glistening of the sand, and traces left by small insects on the sand are always visible. Lush waterweeds grow at the bottom of the river, their long, glitteringly green, cattail-like leaves flowing with the current.

The scenery along the Li River from Guilin to Yangshuo is compared to a natural picture scroll. But the real landscape is much more lively because it takes on different looks at dawn, at noon, and at dusk, especially on rainy spring mornings, when the river is enveloped in the misty rain with hills near and far gone from view. The drizzle falls on the boat's roof, the river surface, and the grass and trees on the bank. The subtle sound adds to the quietness of the Li River. Suddenly at the creak of an oar, a small fishing boat glides from a tributary into the river. In the fine rain, peach blossoms trail along the banks of the tributary into the depths of the valley, where an indistinguishable mass, probably a hill, or some cloud, or the mist, keeps them out of sight.

The moment reminded me of Comrade Kerang's painting *South of the Yangtze River in a Spring Rain with Apricot Blossom...*

By now the "Painted Cliff" has become discernible in the distance. Millions of years of erosion have left layers of imprints on the steep cliff standing erect on the bank, as if numerous hills had been compressed together. In people's imagination, these imprints, with varying degrees of brightness and color, have become nine steeds. Hence the Painted Cliff is also known as the Scroll of Nine Horses at the Painted Cliff. The nine steeds on the cliff, some standing, some lying, some bending their heads, some looking up, some galloping, some drinking from the river, are really vivid. But at the same time Comrade Kerang's painting *The Profile of the Painted Cliff at Guilin* was revived in my mind in an even more vivid manner.

The painting is not very large, and the lines are drawn in the traditional ink and brush style. Towering rocks take up almost the whole tableau, except for a space one-fifth of its length from the bottom, where a man leads an ox towards the viewer on a field ridge in front of a village clothed in green. But the latter is not the focus of the painting, neither is it particularly eye-catching. It is those towering rocks all over the scroll that instantly grabs viewers' attention. They surge like successive waves on a stormy sea, one topping another, until they reach the sky on the top of the painting, where the nine peaks of the Painted Cliff are demarcated. You can almost reach out to touch the precipitous cliff and feel the rough limestone. Consequently, the entire Painted Cliff appears mighty and imposing. At that moment, the Painted Cliff in front of me seemed to have been detached from the surrounding hills and come to life, a life with its own thought and feelings. The hills as a natural wonder and an artistic creation have blended into one.

However, all these happened in a flash. With the Painted Cliff behind us and impressions gone, a majestic ambience and an uplifting inspiration lingered in my memory...

As I sat in the bow lost in thought, it suddenly occurred to me how marvelous is the creation of man's labor and man's spirits. It is like a mythical bridge between man and nature, and a legendary golden key to immortals' cave dwellings. Thanks to the bridge and the gate, people are able to get at the heart of nature.

Geologically speaking, the scenery of Guilin is just a kind of karst topography: the calcium carbonate in limestone form caverns as a result of long-term exposure to water. Guilin and the Stone Forest in Yunnan Province claim the best developed karst topography in the geological sense. Natural phenomena can't be designated as beautiful or ugly. The reason why some scenery is beautiful while another is not, or not beautiful enough, is that man has ever been making observations and comparisons in his existence as a social being. The concepts of beauty and ugliness result from man's exertion of labor and consciousness on nature. Since this kind of exertion has long been acknowledged in history, natural beauty has become an independent objective reality. Moreover, man's concept of natural beauty varies with time and class; hence his understanding of nature grows deeper and richer.

As a form of art, landscape painting has always acted as a means by which man comprehends nature, appreciates natural beauty, and transforms nature "according to the law of beauty". Like all other forms of art, it derives power from an in-depth observation and detailed portraiture of nature. The paintings by Comrade Kerang are a good case in point - not only is there in-depth observation, but also detailed portraiture; hence they appear realistic and powerful. Consequently, without your being aware of it, you are led from a concrete experience of the scenery into a spiritual ethos created by the artist, be it majesty, splendor, or all kinds of love for the landscape of our mother country that well up in your heart. At moments like these, you will feel that your patriotism is concrete, powerful and inspired by personal experiences and feelings. It is at these moments that painters are rewarded for their efforts.

Comrade Kerang has done quite a number of sketches, or what he himself terms as "painting from scenery", in recent years. Certainly he has neither made things up nor copied from nature. There is always a concrete object in a concrete environment. But then he has also been bold in generalization, depicting what lies underneath the object through meticulous representation. That's why these so-called "sketches" are able to convey at once the specific and generalized typical characteristics of our country that all people can see and feel.

It is probably for just this reason that *The Profile of the Painted Cliff at Guilin* has come off. It reveals what lies underneath the scenery of Guilin through a realistic and bold depiction of Guilin's limestone hills, empowering me, a member of the audience, to understand life better on the basis of personal experience.

(Guilin, April 1962)

The Grand Canal

Lei Jia

The Grand Canal is old and young at the same time.

Each of its glitters resembles a footstep of the Chinese nation. For 1,400 years its flow has echoed the mournful songs of human misery, as well as cheers of victory. In it there is leftover top-quality wine from emperors' banquets, but there is more sweat, blood and tears shed by hungry commoners.

The Grand Canal is majestic in appearance. Regarded from an aerial surveying plane it looks like a two-dimensional statue, fresh and pleasing to the eye. It is also an enduring landmark on earth, linking up the North and the South and lasting forever.

In close encounter it turns out to be refreshing and lovely. Like the Yellow River and the Yangtze River, it maintains its youth, with brisk steps and an eternal smile.

Reeds abound in the Grand Canal. They are as old as the human race. Young reeds paint large expanses of water green. Standing on top of the water, they edge the land with green laces. As small turbine boats send waves heaving, they roll along in a natural and rhythmic manner. The Grand Canal has a joyous and leaping heart of a child.

Widened and deepened, by now the Grand Canal has almost turned into a new river. It has been excavated westward to four times its former width. The original river course has been left alone. The old west bank has now become a canal divide. There are quite a number of thatched sheds, brick huts and acacia woods. People have crossed over to plant vegetables and wheat on the abandoned land. The bank being excellent in soil property, numerous brick kilns have been set up to produce building material for the commune, day and night.

The scenery is charming where the old canal meets the new one. Sometimes they are an integral whole, on other occasions they are clearly divided. The old canal is shallow, tranquil, secluded, and undisturbed by boats. It leans close to the Grand Canal and amuses itself by attracting the eyes of tourists, or by having fishing nets spread across its bosom. There is quite some poetic luster here. Upon close observation the two banks of the Great Canal appear different. The west bank, quiet and peaceful, with reeds hiding vast expanses of lake water from view, seems to hail from days long gone by. As to the east bank, there is a straight highway through acacias and villages, on which automobiles come and go ceaselessly, as if racing against boats in the canal. Yes, they are all racing against time. The Four Modernization process has just begun and there is a long way for them to go...

Not long ago a TV series on the Grand Canal was shot, but I wonder if there is any mention of Liubao, where the novel *Stories from Liubao* was located, or Shaobo Town at the rear of Baoying Port, where a seven-day battle was fought during China's War of Liberation in a place named Damiao. It is said that the beginning portion of the movie *Preludes to the Eastward Advance* was filmed right there. All these were meritorious medals won by the Grand Canal during the War of Liberation.

Baoying Port should be described as a crossing point on the Grand Canal. It is only here, of the whole canal, that there is a road to the Baoying Lake. To the south of the Baoying Lake there are the Jieshou Lake, Gaoyou Lake and Shaobo Lake. The White Horse Lake is to its north. And it also directly accesses the largest lake of all, the Hongze Lake. Those lakes are comparable to earth's interconnecting lobes of lungs.

Over a thousand boats moor at or pass through this crossing point on a daily basis, which cries for a much wider river course. The other day when a passenger ship was passing through, a fleet of dredgers happened to be on their way out of the port. In reaction to the unexpected encounter, the captain of the passenger ship reversed his steering wheel to the full before leaning forward to monitor the situation outside. He shouted orders to the dangerously close approaching ship, "Seize-the rudder!" "Lift - the rudder!" He almost fell as he again reversed his steering wheel to the full and kicked away his wooden chair. What a close shave! There are signals directing traffic at ship locks, but there is not a single water police box here at such an accident-prone vital communication line.

All sorts of fleets gather here. What did Emperor Sui Yang's fleet back then look like? Fleets today are indeed of great variety. There are fleets from Anhui Province, Hubei Province, Hunan Province, Jiangxi Province, as well as from the local Jiangsu Province and Shandong Province. Local fleets differ from those of other provinces. Among the latter there are differences too. I am not talking about the difference between a square-bowed boat and a pointed-bow boat, but the difference among boats of similar hulls. Currently barges are the most practical. A dozen or so barges towed along by a main ship may appear identical, but not so in the eyes of an expert. They look like rectangular containers with upturned bows and sterns. The helmsman's post is usually at the stern. In one fleet there might be a dominant number of women minding the helm while sewing cotton-padded clothes. On another fleet the majority are young or middle-aged male laborers, with someone playing the violin at the bow. Undoubtedly they belong to two different work units and two systems. For example, fleets belonging to staple food suppliers are assigned a fixed amount of work every year, therefore they would appear relaxed and at ease while completing tasks. Trudging along are some other fleets with fewer and smaller barges laden with goods, as if they could never get a break throughout the year. Most likely they belong to provincial or city transportation authorities. Boats traveling southward carry coal and sand, or dried sweet potatoes bound for breweries in Changzhou. But the majority of them carry cotton and grain. The most eye-catching boats traveling up north carry chinaware and earthenware made at Yixing. There are also boats carrying human excrement or small boats loaded with sand. Mostly made of cement, they are flat, low, shallow, laden, deep of draught, with sides almost level with the water surface. When such fleets meet with provincial or city fleets, one could easily tell which are state-owned and which are collective-owned. Waves produced by turbines on big ships threaten flat-bottomed cement boats. People are often seen standing on small boats waving a mop or both arms to ask for slow passage for fear of accidents. Therefore, horsepower limits must be put on steamboats traveling in the Grand Canal. Apart from state-owned and collective-owned boats, there are even smaller boats, or privately owned boats, most of which carry sand and dare even fuller loads. The more they carry the more profitable they are, but they also incur greater risks. It is an encouraging sign to see the number of privately owned boats on the rise. Individuals pay 4,000 yuan for a scrap public ship, another 1,000 yuan or so for a small motor, and there is no longer any need for sails or sculls.

How could one deny that the boats are of great variety? Here are all types of ships transporting goods between the North and the South, with distinct ownerships but cooperating consistently. Big fleets or small fleets, public-owned boats or private boats, they all follow protocols when they meet, blowing whistles before passing each other. All fleets appear poised and graceful in their efforts to show off.

Among them there are also fleets from state-owned land reclamation enterprises. Because their farms produce a large amount of grain and cotton, there are a lot of freight transport and many ships, as if the Grand Canal had been excavated especially for them. State farms are in possession of large stretches of seaside saline-alkali land, while the existing salt works and beaches for making sea salt that are expanding annually will become saline-alkali land in the future and will in turn be reclaimed by state farms. There is no limit on state farms' land and future, since land is pressing forward steadily and conquering its way to the boundless sea. This is not just fantasy, but fantasy turned into reality. On this fan-shaped piece of land, probably a result of spurts from the ancient Yellow River, the alluvium has never stopped advancing to the east. Its foremost tips are carpeted with earth salt thanks to the backward flowing sea, hence the rapid alternation between beaches for making sea salt and saline-alkali land. Whereas aren't those lakes linked together from the north to the south also what remains of the withdrawing sea? Maybe this myth is valid. Then was it true that Emperor Sui Yang had the canal excavated to take advantage of those lakes?

The last ship lock between Guazhou and Huaiyin is located at Huai'an. What a spectacular scene that is! Ships that have sailed into the lock find themselves in a deep valley while the signal tower rises into the sky. With the lock down, some staff member comes along with a fishing rod to fish up tickets from each ship via a small clip attached to the rod. Shortly after that, water from the upstream floods in. When ships sail again, the signal tower is level with the hull. There is a full drop of five to six meters between the upstream and the downstream.

Guazhou is to its south, while the Canal flows north out of the lock. Observed from onboard a boat, the bearing is as accurate as a compass. There is no road or river as straight as the Canal. And in a straight line the Grand Canal goes up north to meet the Lanzhou-Lianyungang Railway at Pi County. The Lanzhou-Lianyungang Railway is a straight line stretching from the west to the east. It is at the intersection of these two straight lines that you come to sense the grand image of the biggest crossroad on the Chinese territory. The image is even grander in the context of the universe. The balanced and symmetrical intersection of these two incredible projects is like a huge golden cross medal decorating the bosom of our motherland.

The Yellow River and the Yangtze River are dignified, while the Grand Canal is romantic, its eternal waves an inexhaustible source of romance...

Sketches of the Coconut Country

Xu Kailei

It had been raining for days on end, and the azure sky did not unveil itself until, after a day and a night's sailing on the South China Sea, we had landed at Hainan Island in the cradle of the blue sea.

One could not help bracing up at the sudden sight of the azure sky. What were particularly striking were those coconut trees lining the roads in the sunshine. Their thick trunks reached to the clouds, and their sword-shaped palms spread drooping canopies. Scores of light yellow coconuts as large as balloons popped out from under the palms. The blue sky, green trees and yellow coconuts stretched as far as the eye could see, forming a magnificent landscape. I had considered the city of Haikou as the pearl on the crown of the Hainan Island, yet the scenery was of extraordinary beauty at the Jianhua mountainous area of the Qinglan Port.

Wherever our car went, dense coconut woods surrounded us. Each palm stood 15 to 20 meters tall and was topped with an umbrella-shaped crown. The sun shone through to form shadows of all kinds on the ground. Even more fascinating were those coconut cutters who leapt among trees like monkeys. Agilely they climbed from the ground to the treetop, wrapped their legs around the trunk, and started cutting dexterously. Having done with one palm, they leapt a good two to three meters to another tree, and resumed working as if nothing had happened. We were indeed dumbfounded.

People here had forged an indissoluble bond with coconut trees since 2,000 years ago. Starting from childhood they perfected their tree climbing and leaping skills as a way to earn a livelihood. However, the road to fortune was no wider than those trails in the forest. The coconut country inhabitants had been living a hard life. Long before I had been told that even at the moment there were people whose staple food was still sweet potatoes.

We left the Qinglan Port and traveled west to the eastern outskirts of Wenchang County, the renowned coconut country. As the saying goes, "half of the Hainan coconuts are from Wenchang." Half of the Hainan coconut trees are to be found in Wenchang County, while almost all the land in the eastern outskirts of Wenchang County is planted with coconut trees, which not only reign outside, but also inside houses. I walked into a farmer's house and found all furniture — cabinets, beds, chairs, stools and tables alike — was made from coconut trees. On tables there were more items made from coconut trees: cups, bowls, chopsticks, plates and boxes, even vases. Closer observation revealed that the entire house, whether beams and pillars or doors and window frames, was made from coconut trees.

As I marveled at the ingenuity of the coconut country people in drawing on local resources, our host served us guests from afar with some refreshments, which, unexpectedly, were also made from coconuts - coconut milk, coconut candy, coconut mash and copra. Upon inquiry I learned that they were all new products from the collective processing plant. I was told that, since the central government made the decision to speed up development in Hainan a few years before, Hainan had stuck to a development route focusing on tropical crops. The former state monopoly for purchase and marketing was replaced by a diversified economy, providing scope for coconut country farmers to display their abilities. As a result many collective processing plants sprung up. In one single year's time, people were much better off. Even those fishmongers who had never stepped inside the village came here peddling at dusk on a daily basis.

The coconut tree is comparable to the legendary money tree that sheds coins when shaken. Its pulp can be made into coconut mash, coconut jam, coconut candy and coconut oil, and the shell can be carved into handicraft or used as active carbon. Distillate coconut oil is a highly valuable industrial chemical. Coconut fiber is used in many ways, too. Apart from being made into ropes, brushes and brooms, it is also raw material for carpets, mattresses and sofa cushions. In the past people knew it as the money tree, but there was no desire to "shake" it. All they did was cut the coconuts and complete the tasks assigned by the government. At the moment coconut planters are shaking every money tree in the green coconut woods by running factories and businesses. The money that has been "shaken" down find its way to the hands of coconut planters as well as the state treasury. Consequently there is even more diversified production, and life becomes more enjoyable.

Our host seemed to be under 50. All his life he had been in contact with coconuts. He started leaping among coconut trees and cutting coconuts as a 14-year-old, and was able to climb from the ground to the treetop in two to three minutes. His family had lived in coconut woods for generations. As a child he heard the legend from his grandmother that coconut trees had used to be shorter, leafless and fruitless. Later a chief of the Li ethnic group was killed in an enemy sneak attack and his head was hung on a coconut tree. Miraculously the tree grew taller, so much so that the arrows shot by the enemy failed to reach the head. Instead they were imbedded in the tree and became palms, while the chief's head turned into round coconuts. Another legend goes that there were fairies in the coconut woods who would frequently change into all sorts of beautiful animals and play in the woods. Once a young hunter lost his way as he chased a spotted deer. The latter stopped near a creek and turned around to become a beautiful fairy. Eventually the hunter laid down his bow and arrows, took her home and got married.

Our host had indeed wondered about legends like those. As he stood listening to partridges singing in the coconut wood, he could not help searching for beautiful deer with his eyes, or footsteps of fairies with his ears. However, one day the landlord followed his grandfather and him into the wood. At the shout of the landlord his grandfather, who was unable to repay his debts, fell from the tree. No one was sure whether he was surprised into a fall or committed suicide in a moment of despair. Anyway his grandfather was dead and gone forever from coconut woods. Since then our host deleted the story about a hunter marrying a fairy in a coconut wood from memory, and bore in mind only the legend about the murdered Li chief: coconut palms being enemy arrows, coconuts being the head of the victim.

People living in coconut woods have grown used to the gloomy atmosphere inside, and many fascinating fairy tales and legends reflect their desperation over reality. Unfortunately even after liberation [1949], when people owned their own coconut woods and life had been improved somewhat, transient smiles were unable to offset long-standing poverty. Although landlords, along with their scolding and whipping, were long gone, they found themselves in utter destitution after a whole year's hard labor. It was in distress that the father of our host bid his dying farewell to coconut woods. Stagnant water hardly ripples, and similarly there was little excitement for decades. During the 1958 Great Leap Forward Movement, there was quite some uproar. Yet when all was over they realized that the "blueprint" others portrayed for them was as illusionary as flowers in a mirror or the moon in the water. The "poor transition" during the ten-year long Cultural Revolution [1966-1976] put them in such a dire situation that kids in coconut woods went about without pants on. Then what about the current opening up? Today, various processing plants have indeed enriched coconut planters. There are bank deposits for each household, Spring Festival couplets celebrating a bumper harvest on every front door, and plans for the next year in the mind of every one. Our host, being leader of the production team, the plantation and the plant at the same time, was busy day and night. Yet as he woke up deep in the night, he would stare at the ceiling and worry about how long the current way of life could last. Will it be drowned in some sound and fury that was still fresh in the memory, or some disgusting voices? ...

As he treated us to their specially made coconut delicacies and shared with us their current wealth, our host questioned me with melancholy eyes as to whether there would be any change in the future. What could I answer? Should I tell him that the leading comrades of the central authorities have promised a consistent policy and even more opening up, or that as we are in the midst of a second revolution, we need a revolutionary will to face the new time? As a man of few words, I didn't feel myself able to convince, in several simple sentences, this old farmer who had lived in coconut woods for decades and who had suffered much. Reality is extremely cruel. People draw lessons from reality, and form perception out of the lessons learned. Perception thus formed is deep-rooted and resistant to change except when confronted with indisputable reality. The daughter of our host stood by her father, observing us with bright and unabashed eyes. Almost 20 and a recent high school graduate, she was at the moment attending a training program on etiquette in preparation of becoming an attendant at a hotel to be built. We congratulated warmly to this daughter of the coconut farmer on her finding a new job. She laughed, " I'm not sure yet if I'm up to the job."

"Your reply, your modesty and easy manner are sufficient to prove what a capable person you will be when receiving overseas guests," said one of us.

And she laughed again, a bit shyly, but her eyes revealed her full confidence in the future. Expressions like that are hard to find on the faces of her father's generation.

Sketches of the Huangshan Mountain

Han Zi

The Huangshan Mountain appears as tranquil as fairyland in films and landscape paintings, distant and in mid-air. However, if present on the scene, you will see that it is in fact a place of vim and vigor where all things grow and develop, and where the most realistic and lively fairy tales are created.

Follow any trail and you will see tiny flowers and plants crowding its borders, despite the sparse bits of sunlight that manage to penetrate the leafage. All buds and seedlings are growing and crying for attention: Life! Life! Life! I believe many people have observed the sprouts of Chinese torreya right on these trails. Green and fan-shaped, they feel "alive" upon touching. Bamboo shoots are the most vigorous among the young growth. Stand awhile and watch one poke its head out of the shell, bluish and shrouded by white down, to become a part of the world. How refreshing! The exotic flowers here all bloom on tall trees, such as Spring Heralding Flower and Manglietia fordiana, whose beauty rivals that of the rare magnolia but whose blossoms are much more enduring. Or take the light yellow "Orchid Fragrance Lanterns" - we coined the name. We first saw its pupil-like flower from a lower altitude, and when we climbed up it had bloomed into strings of lanterns that glittered in the mist and filled the valley with wisps of orchid fragrance, as if celebrating some joyous event. Azaleas and mountain roses are shorter but hard to ignore for their multifarious colors and peculiar fragrance. Purplish-blue Youth Flowers and dark red Lantern Flowers also manage to grow thickly over mountains and ridges, cheering hikers on enthusiastically. Among all plants, I find leaves the most intriguing and lively. They differ in shape and size, some exquisite, some majestic, some indistinguishable from flowers. The foliage assumes a variety of colors such as red, yellow, violet and green. Even among what are generally referred to as green leaves there are different shades. Layer by layer, the greenery either deepens in color or pales away. Lush dark green leaves alternate with pale green ones that are almost transparent as glass, conjuring up a wonderland in the forest. The grasses here are also distinctive, such as the long beards (Chinese alpine rush) hanging over cliffs, the tender grass that can survive three scalds of boiling water (Grave Returning Grass), and the grass from 50 kilograms of which 1.5 kilograms of copper can be extracted. The rare and elegantly poised glossy ganoderma has a place here, too. I wonder if it would condescend to a lower position among others. Tall, graceful, splendid and odd-shaped, pine trees must be the most distinctive trees on the Huangshan Mountain. The sea of pinewood bathed in the setting sun presents an extraordinarily fetching silhouette. Most pines grow out of crevices. They can gain a foothold as long as there is a thin layer of earth, and often tower above sheer crags, which leaves an impression of being firm and unyielding. The Guest Welcoming Pine, the Exotic Vine Pine, the Chinese Unicorn Pine, the Phoenix Pine, and the Black Tiger Pine are among the most outstanding. Seven people could gather in a circle and have a drink on top of the Rush Cushion Pine in front of the Lotus Peak. How interesting!

Birds reign over these wooded hills. Whatever altitude I reach (it is estimated that there are around 20,000 stone steps), I hear them singing in the woods above, and without being aware of it, I have come to regard them as my guides. On this mountain trail that extends for 15 to 20 kilometers, I often wonder who planted the first trees among these fantastic peaks and high mountains. And on one occasion I was given an explanation. It was the ancestors of those birds that had carried seeds in their bills and with the help of wind forested the hills. There is something in this legend, isn't there? Receptionists at the Jade Screen Mansion and the Cloud Dispelling House are tipped by "Divine Crows" to start preparing tea for guests. Although guests are a good 5 kilometers away, those clever crows deliver the message within an hour and then fly somewhere else. On summer dawns I found a kind of bird that is good at both singing and dancing. Now high, now low, now right, now left, it flies as freely as a silver swallow, its dance nimble and elusive. Its notes, rich and clear, mild and melodious, compose the heartiest morning song. From travel logs kept by ancient people I gather it must be a Musical Bird or a Mountain Songbird. Monkeys are the cleverest among the local fauna, and they are close observers of human life. It is said that the New Fourth Army guerillas once frequenting the area saw them carrying stretchers and some monkeys acting as "doctors". If a monkey falls ill, a monkey doctor will be sent to find some medicinal herbs for it to take. Tigers, boas, wild oxen and antelopes have been seen among deep valleys and green woods. Someone who once saw beautiful flocks of deer could still describe how alert their eyes were. On our way back from the Seeing Is Believing Peak to the Hot Spring area, we caught thirteen giant salamanders from the creek. They appeared as if dressed in ancient costumes, with a bump in the shape of a chignon on both sides of the head, like the page boy in the drama Liang Shanbo and Zhu Yingtai (a Chinese version of *Romeo and Juliet*). There must be some other animals unknown to me, for indeed there are many inaccessible places in the Huangshan Mountain, which has been said to stretch for 250 kilometers since time immemorial. It would be ideal to organize a Huangshan Mountain expedition team and explore the kingdom of monkeys, the native place of deer, and dens of various other animals.

Waterfalls and murmuring springs produce the highest sound of the Huangshan Mountain. The renowned waterfalls such as the one in the shape of the Chinese character standing for "human", the Nine Dragon Waterfall, and the Hundred Zhang (roughly 330 meters) Waterfall are not usual sights. However, after some pelting rain, water emerges from places atop and cascades down thunderously like white dragons. The line of poem which goes to the effect that "(the water) rushes into the Zhejiang River with soughing wind" portrays its bold and uninhibited spirits just right. On ordinary days spring water winds like ribbons through deep forests, usually keeping company with flitting smoke and clouds. Brooks babble along the path. Poetry escapes someone's lips, "Man strides over a spring, water flows at the feet." You can imagine how carefree and contented he feels. Yet it never remains still. Now a spurt of pearly spray, now a billowing length of white satin, it is charming both in sound and in appearance, and glad to sing in antiphonal style with passers-by. Hot springs gurgle out of cinnabar. Sometimes if you scoop up a handful it is crystal clear, but when there is a pool, especially in a swimming pool, it resembles a piece of green jade, blue and shiny like the clear sky.

Twice I watched the sun rise from the east at the Refreshing Platform of the Lion Forest. The first time I was a little bit late and could only cheer with burning passion for the majestic beauty. On the second occasion I was able to worship its birth in silent awe. First came its slow-moving, cloud-lined train, and then suddenly half of the sun leapt out. I had no idea how large it was, but in an instant it was shedding its rays in all directions. As it rose it changed colors in the twinkling of an eye: vermilion, orange, light purple... It was so brilliant and transparent that, as it added luster to all things on earth and awakened the world, its own utterly bright self gradually faded out to become one with the universe. Even if I had never seen it before I would have praised it as "the sun". Clouds are a natural part of the mountain scenery. When we stayed on top of the mountain, white clouds dropped by frequently in early mornings. Hovering outside windows, they were within easy reach. When we went for a walk we would be walking over clouds. Sometimes there were so many of them that the whole mountain area was turned into a vast sea, where only the highest peaks were visible, like islands dotting the sea. That would be the famous sea of clouds of the Huangshan Mountain. Multihued wandering clouds at dusk were my favorites. They appeared in the shape of practiced swordsmen or maids in an imperial palace, riding dragons or phoenixes, followed by richly decorated carriages and accompanied by bands. Observed from hills away, the slow-moving procession seemed to be cruising in the sea.

Many beautiful fairy tales came to mind as I watched them. It is said that there are 72 peaks in the Huangshan Mountain, such as the Lotus Peak, the Seeing Is Believing Peak, the Celestial Capital Peak, and the Bamboo Shoot Peak, whose names either match the shape or carry some metaphorical significance. On the peaks there are scenes formed by spectacular rocks and odd-shaped trees, like the Lotus Picking Row Boat, Five Girls Shepherding the Flock, Peach Watching Monkey, Magpie Perching on A Plum Tree, and the Blooming Writing Brush in the Dream, which are far superior to ingenious arrangements by skilled craftsmen. As to those continuous peaks, I preferred to stand at a distant low place and appreciate the way they, together with the pine trees, stand out against the sky. They were indeed as beautiful as brocade.

Resting places are all over the Huangshan Mountain. Even when it is scorching summer outside, one still feels as though it is spring here.

I am no match for the numerous poets and painters who have portrayed the fantastic peaks and wonderful scenery of the Huangshan Mountain. The renowned traveler Xu Xiake once remarked, "Returning from the Five Sacred Mountains, it's not necessary to see any other mountains. Returning from the Huangshan Mountain, it's not necessary to see the Five Sacred Mountains." Lacking experience as I do, I am unable to grasp the whole of his valiant appraisal. As for the photos published here, I can prove they are real but words fail me in describing the poetic beauty. It seems that these sketches of mine serve the sole purpose of supplementing the photos with some other things I saw and heard on the trip.

(a filler for the *Anhui Pictorial*, December, 1957)

The Mountain Hermitage in Sha Tian

Yu Gwuangk-zhong

The study opens onto the balcony, and the balcony has a view of the sea and mountains. The sea is an azure curve, the mountains a lush green chain. There are mountains beyond mountains. The remotest ones loom faintly on the horizon. They would be hailing from the Mainland. There is all the time and space in the world. No matter how the wind blows, how eagles hover, how the eyes strain, the green hills and blue waters stretch like long horizontal scrolls of painting by Ma Yuan and Xia Gui. I have lived in their midst greeting the dawn and dusk for eighteen months. Eighteen months. That is to say, the chrysanthemums adored by Tao Yuanming have bloomed through two Double Ninth Festivals, and the moon lamented by Su Dongpo has become full twice on Mid-Autumn Festival nights.

Mountains come in between the sea and the sky. Even on sunny autumnal days there is a gauze of dimly discernible ocean air in the crystal clear blue light, like a mysterious mirror held by God rather than man. The sea and the mountains are so mingled together that it is hard to tell whether the sea penetrates the mountains or the mountains captivate the sea. The sea besieges the mountains to turn them into peninsulas, while the mountains break the sea into bays. Yet the loop of mountains fail to contain the vast South China sea, for there is a gap on the northeast where masts drift out and sails float in. On the sunniest afternoons, a white ferryboat travels west from the foot of Pat Sin Leng (the Hill of Eight Immortals) in a leisurely manner in an intoxicating sunset toward Tai Po. The vast blue expanse of Tai Long Wan seems to exist for the sole purpose of setting off that dazzling touch of white. On windy days the sea is transformed into endlessly rolling blue land on which countless lilies bloom and wither. Deep at night, all mountains sink into a dark slumber, and all lights scattering near and far go out. The only sound that remains comes from the ocean tides, an everlasting snoring that stirs my thought. Occasionally a dozen or so fishing lights leap out on the dark sea in the formation of an arc. Gathering closer and closer together, they form the brilliant cluster of a golden lotus.

The sea surrounds the mountains, and the mountains surround me. I live through days and nights, sunrises and sunsets, full moons and new moons on this mountain of circuitous paths. I have become a hermit. Pressed for a reason for taking up residence in the mountains, I offer a smile, for the mountains have answered for me. No, not the mountains, but the birds have, or the insects, or the soughing of pines. The mountains are like eminent and learned monks who refrain from speech. I lean on the upper floor balustrade. The surrounding mountains array themselves like 18 seated arhats to keep me company. Neither of us is ever tired of the other. In the morning I climb to the crown of Buddha to watch the sunrise. At dusk I walk all the way back from the Humanities Department of the United World

College to my house half way up the mountain, a location lower than Buddha' shoulders but higher than His stomach. By then the mountain does not utter a word, yet the chirping birds give his delight away. With the birds well perched and mountains grown hazy, the sounds of nature grow subdued and intermittent. Scarcely have birds stopped singing among the trees when insects start chanting in the grass. As to the tiny secluded valley down at the col, it is comparable to Buddha's navel, exerting an extraordinary charm of its own where the ground caves in. The valley is a music loving country girl who enjoys imitation yet lacks both confidence and technique. When there was a bird chirping, a dog barking, or a train whistling by the valley, she would echo one half-beat later.

Viewed from the upper floor of my house, Mo On Shan rises steeply to the east, delaying the arrival of early morning sun. The imposing but closer Deer Hill blocks out half of the western sky, forcing the dusk to fall half an hour early. In a flash the setting sun has been gathered into the "sleeve" of the Hill. The sunset clouds burn from bronze to golden, to purplish gray, and finally to a wisp of green. The legendary sunset, the funeral of the sun. I sit on the balcony watching the dusk changing into evening. The process seems slow, but then it is rapid too. The rosy glow has barely faded from your cheeks and the trees when the covetous evening shadows reach your elbows from behind. It is too superb a trick of camouflage to be detected by the human eye. After the night has closed in and the darkness settled, the surrounding mountains grow heavy and gloomy, sending fear down one's spine. Especially the Deer Hill to the west, which has transformed from an amiable Buddha or monk into a giant hairy monster lurking in the shadows. Uneasiness oozes up.

Who would dare to stand up to the imposing mountains? Yet when clouds arise, their dignified bearing is changed. When mists fall they become islands dotting the white sea. Pat Sin Leng (the Hill of Eight Immortals) is indeed transformed into the eight sea-crossing immortals, whose silhouettes are revealed sometimes riding the waves, sometimes enveloped by clouds. One morning I looked up to find Pat Sin Leng, Mo On Shan and other hills gone from view. Occasionally I got a glimpse of the closest of them, the Deer Hill, from an opening in the thick clouds. Vehicles to Tai Po seemed to be traveling in mid air. My balcony was detached from all and commanding all, coming and going freely on the heaving white tides. Down in the valley where mortals live, cocks crowed and dogs barked. I walked even higher to teach at the United World College. White clouds coiled up from the ground, while the clothes worn by both faculty and students fluttered like those of the immortals. Smoke and clouds flitted through the windows to attend my lecture.

On windy days all the enshrouding mists are wiped out to reveal the entire landscape down to the smallest detail. It turns out that there are many villages, stores and households by the water across the bay at the foot of Pat Sin Leng. The weather at the peninsula changes a few times in a single day. Gusts of sea wind drive straight in through the mountain gap, immediately turning the valley underfoot into a roaring bellows. Ravaging the podocarpuses and reeds, stirring up the sea and sending out foams, they are a pack of invisible beasts trampling and howling all the way through.

However earthshaking the sea tides and winds are, they just add a flavor of wilderness to the boundless silence. It is manmade noises that are the most fascinating. From early morning till midnight, day in and day out, over 40 trains, be they carrying passengers, freight or hogs, clanked and whistled on the Kowloon-Canton Railway that lies between the sea and the mountains. With their billows of smoke and slender bodies made up of 13 carriages, these oldest means of transportation of the Industrial Age still retain the charm of the old world that is unrivaled by Concorde, the supersonic jet. The railway track extends to the north, so do my heartstrings. Thousands of iron wheels of the over forty trains pound my central nervous system everyday on their way down south or up north, reminding me with their heroic clangs and sparks that what lies down in the valley is not the Shangri-La, neither am I who live up on the mountain an immortal not belonging to this world. I will have to go down.

The green hills close in from three directions on the balustrade,

The dark green hems form a melancholy loop.

Layers upon layers of mountains fade into the distance.

Beyond the Xiang [Hunan] clouds is the Chu [Hubei] smoke, the land stretching far and wide,

Where five thousand years of history and eight hundred million people reside...

The Lake and the Reflection of the Tower

Zong Pu

Those who once stayed at Swallow Garden [the Beijing University faculty dormitory] cannot help but get addicted to beautiful scenery. Used to reading in the bamboo groves at dawn and walking along willow-lined banks at dusk, they have come to regard the scenery as an integral part of their days at Swallow Garden. Among the various scenes, the lake and the reflection of the tower in it probably linger the longest in the mind. However, it is beyond me to recreate the exact picture on paper.

In my childhood I walked a lot around the lake. The lake water seemed so green to me that it blended with the overgrowth of grasses on the bank. Besides, the lake appeared to be much bigger than the lotus pond at Tsinghua University. Otherwise, one wouldn't be called a pond while the other, a lake. The bank across the lake seemed to be close by, but it took some time to reach, unlike the lotus pond which you could circle in no time. There was a green islet in the midst of the lake, with lush trees and layer upon layer of rocky hills. A white stone boat moored forever to the east of the islet. Close as it was, I had never set foot on the islet. All I did was to watch schools of fish swimming towards it, leaving neat ripples behind them. "They are queuing up!" I said to myself. I dreamed of joining the fish in an exploration of the islet.

Decades have passed in a flash. The garden has experienced countless hazards. Whereas I, having drunk many a bitter cup of life, have been to every corner of Swallow Garden, enjoying peaceful and delightful moments all year round. The Weiming Lake remains unchanged. The tower should be named Weiming as well, yet nobody has ever called it that. It stands tall and upright by the lake, overlooking its own majestic reflection. By nature a water tower, it was modeled after the 13-story Tongzhou Pagoda to add luster to the scenery. There are many beautiful legends about the Tongzhou Pagoda, but the Weiming Tower impresses people merely by its reflection in the lake. On sunny days the tower rises into the sky as its reflection delves deep into the lake. In the dark green water every small beast-shaped adornment on the tip of the tower's eaves is distinct down to the last detail. In wet weather, dark clouds press down on the tower, and its reflection seems weighed down, too. At the fall of raindrops vapor rises over the lake surface. The reflection of the tower stirs, disperses, and then stands still again, causing confusion in the mind of onlookers. On foggy days both the lake and the tower are enveloped in layers of gauze. When snow falls all is covered with an uncut white flannelette blanket.

The lake on moonlit nights has a distinctive charm. On its west bank there is a dune with a bell tower on top. By the dune there are trees, lawns and a trail. Moonlight seems somewhat cramped here. However, if you follow the trail round the dune, you will come upon a clear open space all lit up by the moon. The lake appears wider, its ripples spreading the moonlight to unknown places. Soon the lights among the trees on the north bank draw the contours of the lake, and reveal its gracious beauty to the full. Along the bank long willow branches sway in the moon over the lake. Under the shimmering water surface stands the erect reflection, and under the silvery sky there is the imposing tower. The lush green islet in the midst of the lake seems real and elusive at the same time. The moonlight shed on the ground differs from that on the lake surface. The latter glitters and leaps like light plucks of the strings in a piece of music. The former is as hazy and graceful as uneven strokes in a wash painting.

Follow the trail to the east and turn right at the small stone bridge, and you will find a pond connected to the Weiming Lake. It is not very large, but the slopes on three sides make it appear deep. There is an overgrowth of trees on the slopes, thick grasses and rocks along the pond. Streaks of moonlight shine through the dense leafage onto the secluded pond, only to be met with a cold shimmer. Add a white crane that flashes across the water to the scene, and you have a perfect illustration of the lines that "a crane skims over a cold pond, the cool moon chills the poet's soul".

If the cool moon were all-knowing, it would recount all tragedies that have taken place here since the day the garden was built. Neither the crane nor the poet's soul was able to escape from the clutches of feudalism. It goes without saying that the garden was constructed on heaps of bleached bones, by fleecing the people. Originally named the Shuchun Garden, it was built during the reign of Emperor Qianlong by He Shen, the then First

Class Duke and court official who wielded influence with the emperor by helping him with confidential military and political affairs. "Beautiful gardens are built to the west of the imperial capital". At that time quite a few high officials owned garden properties in the neighborhood. Gardens like Jingchun, Langrun and Minghe, located to the north of but later merged into Swallow Garden, used to be in private hands. Weixiu and Chengze Gardens are still intact. There used to be a Shao Garden in the southwest of Swallow Garden in early 1950s, where I had been but had no idea whether it preserved the original look or not. Later the dilapidated buildings in it were torn down. After the 1952 national readjustment of university departments, Beijing University was relocated to Swallow Garden. Shortly afterwards a university hospital was built on the former site of the Shao Garden, where for years tens of thousands of Beijing University faculty and students have received medical care. In the north of the Shao Garden there used to be some paddy fields, probably intended to give the garden some idyllic feel. At present dorms for overseas students are under construction. How great all these are!

Nevertheless, do bear in mind that at the end of feudalism we again suffered in the semi-colonial society. Turn north at the secluded pond and you will find yourself at the Lakeside Study deep inside a bamboo grove. That was the nervous center of the former Peking University. Here the deposition by the moon would be redundant, for there are many people alive with firsthand experiences. Peking University moved here from inside Beijing in 1926, and in the same year there were Peking University students killed during their demonstration against traitorous acts of the Northern Warlords. In the 1930s many young people left the lake and the tower's reflection in it for Yan'an, imbued with revolutionary ideals. In the garden there is no trace of the turmoil, worries, sufferings and joy of the 1940s, but there is evidence of the great feats of the Chinese people in the same period. The exquisite carvings removed from the ruins of the Old Summer Palace, such as the ornamental column erected inside the west gate, and the kylin in front of the administrative building, are perpetual reminders of the fire ignited by aggressors. After all, our mother country has left behind the days of poverty and ignorance and is heading for prosperity. All these are hard won. Having undergone all kinds of sad plight, the lake and the tower's reflection in it should be ready to bear witness to a prosperous and strong country.

I went for another walk at dawn. Perhaps it was too early in the day for the lake area to stir, except for the cicadas that had already started singing. As I walked in a leisurely manner between the dune and the lake, it suddenly occurred to me that I was not alone, because the tomb of Mr. Edgar Snow on the dune was keeping me company. The tomb had become an attraction of the Weiming Lake area. The inscription on the tombstone read, "An American Friend of the Chinese People". It was built on the former site of the Floral Goddess' Temple. The lakeside red brick gate facing the tomb must have belonged to the old temple. I trusted the Chinese floral goddess to take good care of our friend. And the word "friend" denoted the profound sentiments between people around the world and us.

I stood under the red gate to gaze at the islet in the midst of the lake. The white stone boat was stationary as before, and the trees kept their luxuriance. But for the past few years a hemispheroid of wire meshes had been pointing through the dark green towards the sky. That was a radio telescope used to receive radio signals from other celestial bodies. Some friends regarded it as an eyesore, but I looked upon it as a symbol of human intelligence placed side by side with the lake and the reflection of the tower. A childhood dream was called to my mind. The telescope had disclosed all the secrets of the islet that I had wanted to explore, to the whole universe.

As I was meditating, the clouds behind the Weiming Tower turned rosy. Usually by this time more people would have come to the lake, jogging, reading, and enlivening the entire lake. But today there were only two seven or eight year-olds beside me. I had no idea when they had come to sit on a rock by the lake engrossed in the fish in the lake. The summer vacation had begun, which explained why they could afford to linger by the water early in the morning.

"Look! Fish! The fish are queuing up!" They cried out happily while pointing at the neat ripples that were spreading towards the islet.

"Are you thinking about going on an exploration on the back of the fish?" I could not help smiling.

"How did you know?" They winkled at me, but soon they were again absorbed by the big fish. Not only did I know this, but I also saw that the island was nothing to them, for they should be dreaming of exploring the universe.

I walked away so as not to disturb them and strolled up to the main library. It did live up to the style of Beijing University. The green-glazed tiles on the roof of this four-story building were glittering in the morning sun. The two lawns on both sides of the main entrance spread out like two shallow pools of clear water. Down the steps of the protruding porch two long lines of cannas were blooming. Beyond the Indian shots there were hibiscus trees laden with lilac and white flowers. A horizontal board elegantly inscribed with the characters "Beijing University Library" hung above the entrance. It boasted a collection of 3,200,000 volumes and its 2,000 or so seats were always occupied. An ordinary morning sees many people waiting outside the entrance. Sometimes those young people would come up with something original by leaving their bulging schoolbags in the queue in their place. Although the school bags cannot swim like the fish, they guide people through the quest for knowledge. Quite a number of young people had already gone to different parts of our country to apply what they had learned to practice. More young people would arrive here to aborb knowledge.

Although right now I am not standing by the Weiming Lake, I have pictured in my mind's eye a painting of it. However presented, the lake and the reflection of the tower are always beautiful. But do remember to paint a bulging worn canvas schoolbag on top of a lakeside rock, and underneath the bag, a colorful map of our great country.

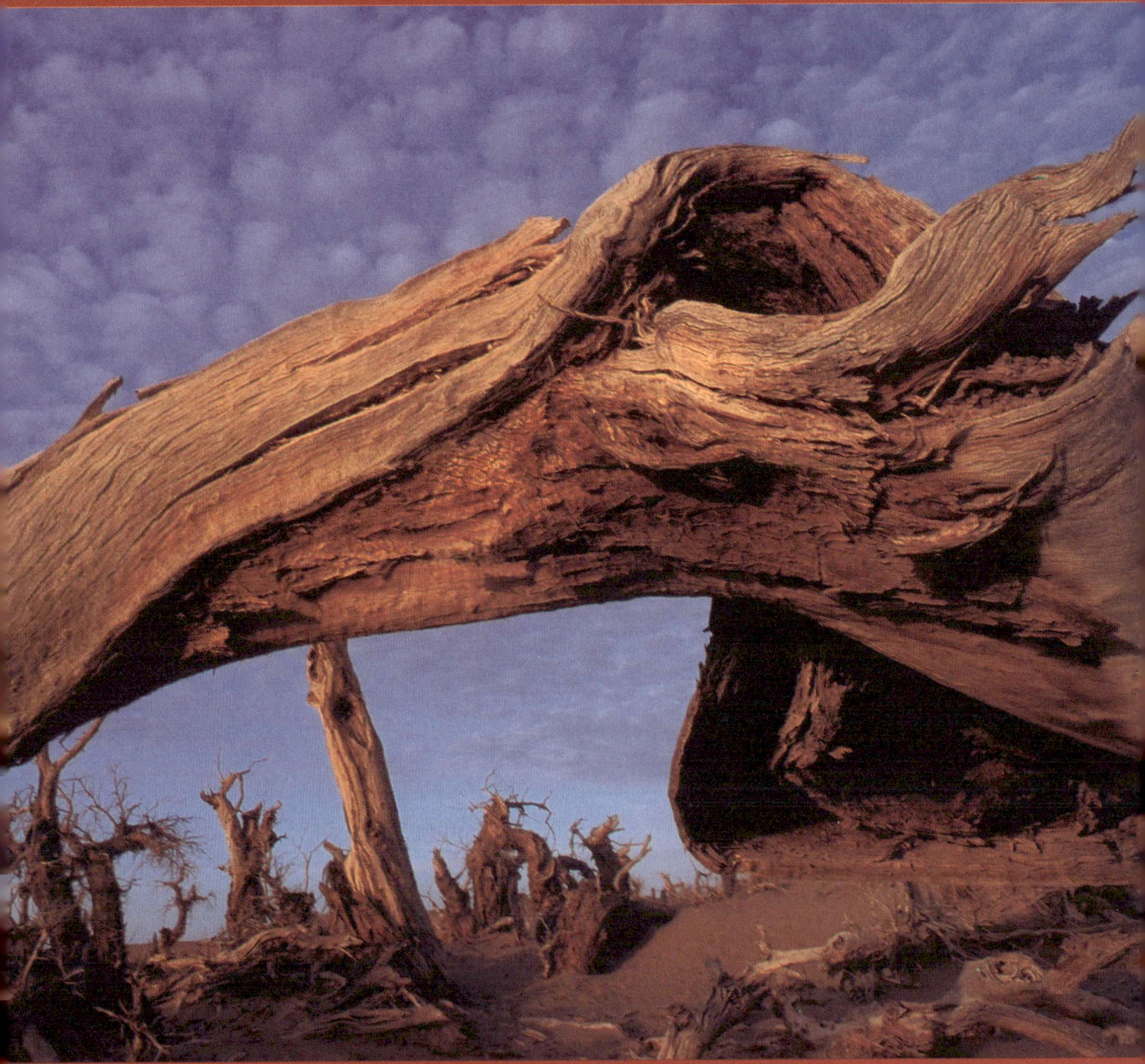

I Visited Three Passes

Lin Fei

Innocent children are inclined to fantasize. In my childhood as I recited Wang Wei's poem "Please drink up one more glass of wine, for there is no old friend west of the Yang Pass", I would draw on my limited understanding of life and imagine how, at the ancient pass, a westbound traveler mounted a horse and waved goodbye to his friends who had enlisted in the army to guard the desert fortress. As dust arose under the gate tower, musicians plucked their *pipa* stringed instruments and played flutes, while singing girls sang melodious songs.

In my childhood I longed often for the ancient fortress. How broad-minded one must be watching smoke from kitchen chimneys go straight up in the desert at dawn, or the round sinking sun at dusk! I found the small town at the lower reaches of the Yangtze River where I was living in overcrowded conditions and found the foul, moldy air stifling.

The Yang Pass had left such a favorable impression on my mind that I had always yearned for a stroll there. I had never tried to locate it on a map. I just had a vague idea that it was far away and hard to reach. Who would have expected that, 40 years later, with graying temples, I would set foot on this long-cherished place?

I climbed up a golden sand dune in the desert southwest of Dunhuang, only to look down on what looked like a dilapidated adobe house, with only four thick clay walls left, standing alone under the blue sky. Repeated desert storms had reduced it to a haggard being no taller than an average person and full of bumps and hollows. There was nothing dignified about it. Is it the Yang Pass, my long-time obsession? Was it narrow and low-lying in its prime? Or have the cruel hands of Father Time wiped off its dignity? Or have poetic works blown it up into a mirage?

The dark red setting sun drew golden contours of the vast desert down the dune. It was bright around the undulating dunes, but darker in the low-lying parts of the desert. The rising damp mist was dyed purplish red by the afterglow. The small lake a short distance away in the south looked like a mirror dropped from heaven, sparkling and crystal-clear as it reflected the sunlight. The place was known for heavenly steeds in ancient times. Many of the gallant horses here became part of the tribute paid to the Emperor Wu of the Han Dynasty.

All my fellow travelers went down to the antique marsh in the hope of finding a rusty crossbow or a coin with its edge rotten away as a souvenir in this wetland overgrown with reeds. According to our driver, great happiness will descend upon those who discover something that has been buried in the sands for over 1,000 years. I guess that has been the way for people to comfort themselves in their long and hard days.

I paced up and down the desert around the dune while keeping an eye on the extending footprints of my friends. It might have rained not long ago, for the sands felt wet and there was no cloud of dust as one walked. A burly man and his huge camel trudged slowly from the distance. The bunches of saplings tied fast to the camel's back shook to and fro as it walked. The bell hung from its neck also shook vigorously, producing short but melodious rings.

The man had big eyes and bushy brows. He looked strong and powerful as he trudged, whip in hand. As he passed me the dark face wrapped under a white towel broadened into a shy grin, as if extending greetings to a visitor from afar. Long gone were the battles, the gong of the night watchman on chilly nights, and the exploits of driving straight into the ancient kingdom of Loulan. This descendant of soldiers of the Han or Tang Dynasty would attain his own achievement by contributing to the conquest of the desert. It is not inferior to the feats of ancient great soldiers to bring to the desert saplings that will grow into towering trees to block sandstorms, and to develop oases and fertile farmland.

On our way back from the Yang Pass we saw people planting trees. They were going to build a green Great Wall. I was suddenly seized by the poetic beauty of this place. How possibly can one not get excited over foreseeing a touch of green over this vast and ancient land?

The Yumen Pass was deeply imprinted on my childhood memory because of Wang Zhihuan's poem that, "What's the point of the Qiang flute's grievance against willows? The spring breeze never crosses the Yumen Pass." Only the disappearance of beauty will result in a perpetual melancholy. Revived memory beckoned me to go on a bumpy trip across the Gobi desert northwest of Dunhuang with some friends. Since there was neither a single man-made road across the desert nor any helpful road sign, the discreet old driver lost his way and brought us to the edge of a marsh. There was a steep square mound, as if piled by human hands on purpose. The climb was hard, but it might have been a beacon tower in the past. We stood in silence looking afar in the gathering dusk, searching for the Yumen Pass we had yearned for over the years. After a while the driver shook his head and told us we had got it wrong.

At a stone's throw in the southwest a mud wall wound its way for scores of meters. On the crude grayish brown wall layers of rotten branches and grasses were dimly discernible. In the evening glow they conveyed an extraordinary sense of desolation. Speculating that this might be the ruins of the Great Wall built in the Han Dynasty, I pictured myself fighting side by side with Wei Qing and Huo Qubing on the solemn but heroic ancient battlefield. The wind rustling in the weeds in the marsh at the foot of the wall brought me back to reality. Later a comrade at the Dunhuang County Museum confirmed that it had indeed been the ruins of the Han Great Wall.

Knowing the trouble we had taken for the visit, our warm-hearted driver took us on a serious search for the Yumen Pass. Finally we saw an ancient mud castle by the Sule River in the north. Its walls went up approximately seven meters, and through the archway we saw an open space large enough for a hundred people to drill and rest. The whole structure resembled a huge barrel discarded on the Gobi desert. Viewed from the dilapidated top of the fortress wall, the surrounding Gobi desert seemed boundless. The omnipresent grayish black gravel made it impossible for grass and trees to grow in multitudes. The few dark-green splendid achnatherum appeared dusty and far from luxuriant to travelers. There was no trace of a green spring east of the Yumen Pass, let alone the area to its west. It turned out that Wang Zhihuan wrote his poem in Liangzhou, a place with plenty of water and lush pasture a thousand miles from Dunhuang, where he could afford to imagine a Yumen Pass shaded by trees.

Over a thousand years have passed, but the poet's image of a green Gobi desert stays in the hearts of many people. How do we explain the amazing charm of this poem? The answer may lie in people's love for life. As long as there are a large number of green trees, people will come and settle in beautiful houses, spreading their laughter far and wide.

Once on my recent sightseeing trip to the U.S. west, I had gone with my friends to visit and meditate over the past at a Spanish church built over two hundred years ago. However, the past I entered today was far remoter. In the space seemingly distant from this world, I found an infinite beauty. It was this beauty that had driven people to look forward to an entirely different life today.

Yes, the vast desolate Gobi desert provided much food for thought, the thought about the onerous tasks lying ahead, about the preciousness of the life we had won, and about the nobleness of our mission. Maybe this was the reason why people had always taken pains to go on a pilgrimage here.

After a tour of the desert around Dunhuang and the Gobi Desert, the Jiayu Pass at Jiuquan , cramped by villages and towns, seemed in want of an imposing background wherein the sky and the land merged into one, although its three adjacent gate towers dwarfed both the Yang Pass and the Yumen Pass in grandeur.

Completed in the early Ming Dynasty [1368-1644], the Jiayu Pass has a far shorter history than the Yang Pass and the Yumen Pass. Owing to sandstorm erosion, the city walls and embrasured watchtowers showed signs of wear, and looking up at the Jiayu Pass from a small Gobi desert outside the city it was quite impressive. There were upturned eaves on each floor of the three-story watchtowers, as if they had lined up to greet trekkers in the distance.

I rounded the fortress wall to the back, where I went up the stone steps to its top. The walls on both sides of the three adjacent embrasured watchtowers marked out two clearly visible vacant lots, probably intended for training troops. Yet at present they were spacious and quiet, devoid of any warlike atmosphere.

Why was it that the towering Jiayu Pass impressed me less profoundly than the mud walls of the Yang Pass and the Yumen Pass? Was it because of the soul-stirring effect of those poems on the Yang Pass and the Yumen Pass? Was it because of the ancient history and age-old legends that gave free rein to imagination? Or was it because of the vast sky and endless land that created an immensely solemn atmosphere? It was hard for me to come up with an answer, for sometimes a person would develop inexplicable impressions. Nevertheless, this impression had been deeply embedded in my memory, broadening my mind and allowing me to see in the coiling yellow sand dust rains, fresh green pastures, and a new leaf turned for the boundless Gobi desert...

Moonlight at the Gaolan Mountain

Yu Qiuyu

It was pitch black in this unfamiliar place. When I first arrived, I had mistaken a light on the top of the mountain for a star. High up there unaccompanied, it was like a solitary beacon in a raging sea. Surprised as I felt, I was too tired by the journey to give it another thought or glance. The moment I touched the pillow, I fell asleep.

It was not until the next morning as I pushed open the window that I was struck by the immensity of the sky-blocking mountain. A pavilion was faintly discernible on the top, from where the light must have come. Yet at night it still felt like a star. Confusion grew as I kept gazing. A few days' bafflement later, I was determined to climb up one night to investigate. So I waited for the moon.

The moon came out. That night it painted everything a half-transparent silver. A knock on the mountain houses, saplings and the earth would definitely produce a loud and clear sound. On this huge mountain there were no angular rocks, swaying lush grasses, or mountain creeks. In a word, it was vast and open, with nothing to hide. A unanimous color of dark silver, the color of tinfoil paper. That was all. Walking on a mountain trail

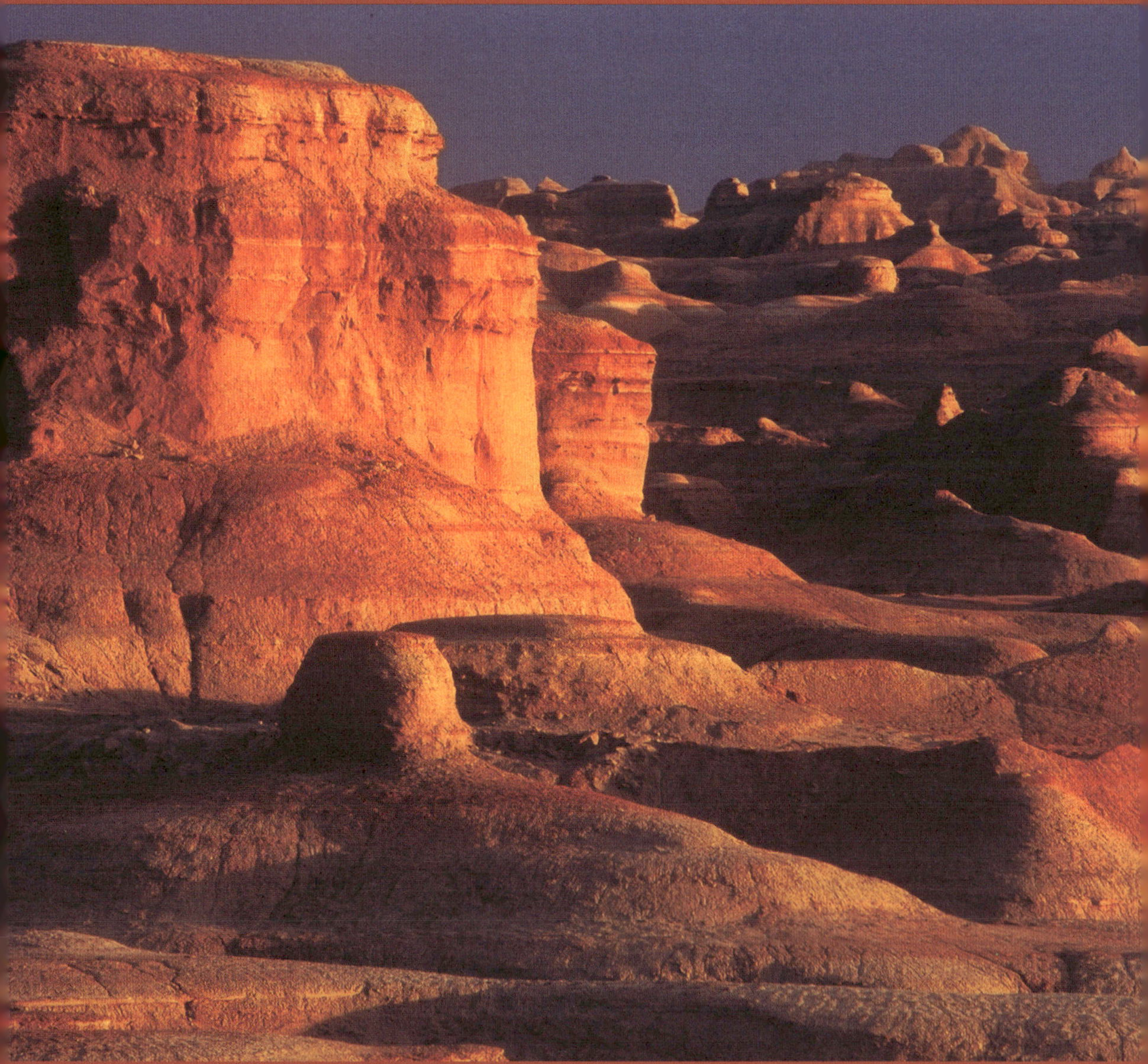

like this, I felt the indescribable freedom of an immortal. I walked on with unseeing eyes, and would keep treading on air as long as the road stretched. Quick but light on foot, I was not going to crush the tranquility.

I must have climbed high. The wind blew harder, and the chill crept under my skin. I huddled up shivering. The moon above seemed smaller than it was below. My bewilderment soon gave way to resignation: the feet are no rival for the moon. The longer they walk, the smaller it grows, never the opposite.

The mind was easily aroused; peace was gone as soon as it started thinking. From the infinite space my train of thought pulled into infinite time. I could not but bow to conventionality by recalling an entanglement of historic events related to the mountain. Huo Qubing seemed to have fought a hard battle here. I remember that *The History of Han* mentioned this mountain in its account of the general and used a single adjective - "fierce" - to stir readers' imagination as to the cruelty of that battle. The mountain had had a hard lot by finding itself in such a strategic location where fighting and killing were inevitable. Mountains can hardly withstand wars, because round after round of deforestation and burning will leave them barren. Creeks dried up, and in their place there were thick bloodstains. Rocks were flung away, and in return there were broken arrows and halberds. What was the use of them? Alarmed and frightened, the mountain swallowed its grief and hurried to bury them under layer upon layer of yellow dirt. If only they could all rot away in there and let the cool breeze and chilly moon reign outside! But no, its naked ridge was doomed to endure recurring wars. It closed its eyes and went silent forever. Like an old man who had had a tough time, it grew numb.

Gentle people like Zhang Qian and Xuanzhang should have visited here more often. But I gathered that they had never gone up the mountain. The road was rough, the landscape was dull, and they had to save strength for the long journey ahead. They would look up a few times and round the foot of the mountain. If Xuanzhang were really accompanied by his legendary disciples, he would have the Monkey King somersault the way up, but not the lazy Pig or the luggage-carrying former sea monster.

Lin Zexu [1785-1850, official who banned the opium trade in Guangdong] may have climbed up. Having more time at hand but few projects to pursue, he might have taken the trip to vent the sulks. There he would look to the southeast, think of his hometown and the bygone days at Humen where he had burned opium. Zuo Zongtang might have also climbed up. As a commander of troops, he had formed the habit of studying the terrain from a hilltop wherever he went. All his life the man had been engaged in some shady affairs, but what he had done here was aboveboard. He would often stand on the hilltop looking out to the northwest, and had his soldiers fetch maps of the border area. When he had a light heart he even ordered soldiers to plant willows to keep out the savage alien wind.

If there had been a road like the one at present, they would have paid more visits, the one keeping watch over the southeast and the other guarding the northwest. But the foundation of the road had been laid a mere 40 years ago during still another war. It was built in a hurry by soldiers and conscripted laborers. During the process, countless skeletons from dynasties back had been uncovered, dazzlingly white in the moonlight. A few skulls grinned hideously. They belonged to ancient colleagues of the road workers. The latter cursed the bad luck, and on second thoughts their hearts sank.

I dare not go on thinking. It gave me the creeps dwelling on these in a desolate mountain at night. So I quickened my pace hoping to reach the end of the mountain trail sooner. Unlike my predecessors who carried military supplies as they traveled, I could well afford light and loud steps. Had it ever occurred to an ancient road worker what part the road was to play tonight as he looked up at the moon, wiping off his sweat?

I pitter-pattered my way to the top of the mountain. The pavilion was built from gray bricks on the site of a former beacon tower. To my surprise, there were quite a number of people but little noise. Apparently amazed at the altitude, they stood and smiled complacently, as they searched for their respective homes among the myriad twinkling lights down the mountain. A wife reproached her husband in a whisper, "I can't find it. Why on earth did you turn off the light?" The husband laughed, "So what? Will our home vanish into thin air?" I smiled to myself. Maybe we had really reached the end of the long mountain trail.

Since my home was not here, I did not have the mood to keep looking. As for the lights, they were not that impressive. Wandering soul as I was, I had turned a blind eye to the splendid view from the top of the lights below at several foreign cities on the Silk Route. Similarly, tonight I had to leave the crowd and seek privacy on the other side of the pavilion. No one else was here. In the moonlight, mountains rolled out to meet the illusive horizon. As I looked out into the distance, I actually caught myself looking up into the sky. These mountains had been standing still side by side for millions of years, yet they were comparable to surging waves. A single wave dwarfed me into immediate insignificance. There came an indescribable sound. Loud and serene, it seemed to ring through the skies and inundate the human ears, the body and the mind. Ancient philosophers had mentioned the rare ringing sound. Might it be the voice of history?

I remembered hearing the sound as I rustled through thread-bound historical records. They had been kept on pieces of paper whose color was identical to that of the mountains here, which must have been a deliberate choice, so that the human eyes that were used to the color of loess would be able to listen to the historical records attentively and find interpretations in the mountains. If so, then I had finally found my home.

Sages said that orchids had abounded here and that the place had got the name for being the native place of orchids [The character "lan" in "Gaolan" means orchid in Chinese-translator]. This is more or less credible, for ancient people were too unsophisticated to pretend. Orchids are still thriving in my hometown, in whose valleys even the waterfalls are perfumed. Who would expect to run into the hometown of my hometown here? But where were the orchids? It was quite humiliating for such a vast mountain to fail to live up to its reputation. But on second thought, I believed it was still fine. Weren't there the silently rolling waves, wasn't there the rare ringing sound? As one is swept off another will arrive in its place. Or will there be another? Probably. Allow me to think longer and listen more.

People on the other side of the pavilion had all left. The lights down the mountain had gone out one after another. With all else gone I stood motionless like a weathered stone pillar.

I'd rather be weathered and go without any caressing moisture than encircled ring upon ring in the human world. I'd like to face the desolate mountains naked, extorting from them the agonized soul and traumatic experience of an ancient race. I believed that Lin Zexu and Zou Zongtang had comprehended the meaning of war from similar extortions. Tonight I would keep listening.

The moon frowned slightly, hid behind a cloud, and then floated west. In her endless journey she had grown clear and uninhibited. Now she bade me to return, with a cool silent breeze. Yes. Neither Zhang Qian nor Xuanzhang had lingered here. Instead they welcomed the breeze and looked ahead, their wearied feet leaving behind a path for the still land to breathe through.

Time to go. Only by walking will there be substantial sounds in the valley, like the jingling of camel bells in the Han and Tang Dynasties.

So I walked.

Pit-a-pat, ding-dong...

— The Gaolan Mountain, outside the city of Lanzhou.

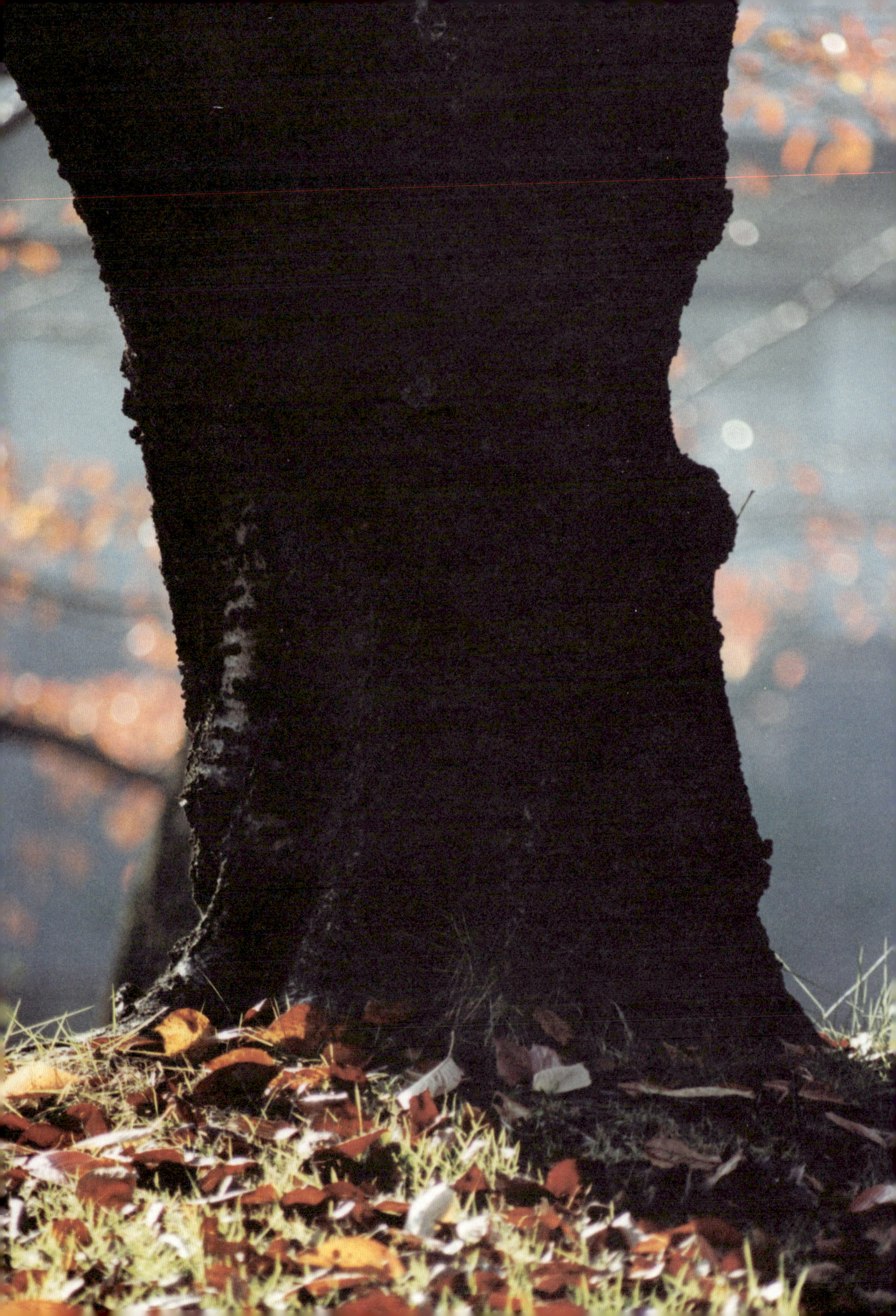

Looking for "Large Red Robes"

Zhao Lihong

"Where are the 'Large Red Robes'?"

"Follow the trail and always turn right when you get to a fork."

"Is it far from here?"

"You may call it far, or you may not. If you are in earnest, there is no need worrying about whether you can find it or not."

After getting down from the back side of the Tianyou Peak we stopped at a junction to ask the way from an old man, who was tilling a tiny lot on the hill. He answered in a few words, pointed to the distance with his hand once, and went back to his work without paying us any further attention.

Nothing met our eyes in the distance but an overgrowth of weed trees and weeds that rustled restlessly in the wind, interlocking crags and rolling ridges. Everything that came into view loomed faintly behind a fine gauze of mist coiling up from cols... Where are the "Large Red Robes"?

The "Large Red Robes" are two world-renowned tea trees at the Wuyi Mountain. It is said that they have been praised as "the kings of tea trees" since the Qing Dynasty. The few jin of tea leaves picked from them and then processed were offered exclusively as a tribute to the imperial court for the royal family and nobles to enjoy. It is a must for visitors to the Wuyi Mountain to have a look at these two tea trees. For one thing, they have an odd name; for another, they are rare.

It was hard trekking. A narrow footpath wound its way through weeds and a shambles of rocks. Vines, thorns and wild roses tripped us from time to time, leaving strips of bloodstains on our arms and ankles. Sometimes the rugged path was so overgrown with weeds and bushes that we could only probe with our feet, fearing some sudden trap or multi-colored poisonous snake...

There was no trap or snake, but the trekking turned out to be even harder.

A terrifying cliff stood on silent guard like a monster and blocked our way. We seemed to be at a dead end! It was not until we had reached the foot of the cliff that we found a path. There was a narrow chink in the cliff, as if someone had cleaved it with a huge axe. In between the cliff the blue sky overhead looked like a blue creek. A bright open space appeared at the end of the gorge. Brooks flowing out of the gorge also revealed their lively side. The babbling was even transformed into ringing laughter. A few steps further and we saw three young girls who were chatting and laughing while washing clothes along a crystal clear brook. Their multi-colored washing floated on the limpid spring water... Why were there three happy young girls in such a deserted mountainous area? Looking around, we saw some greenish gray roofs showing through the tree shade ahead — who would have thought that there were inhabitants here!

The girls were not the least surprised at seeing us, while we, burning with curiosity, could not refrain from asking, "What do you do in the hills?" The girls blushed, glanced at each other, lowered their heads, and started tittering. The oldest of the three looked up and answered us, "We live on the mountain and live off the mountain. We grow tea trees."

Grow tea trees! Where are they?

The girl laughed again at our amazement. " There. Look up. We grow tea trees on the hills."

Up there all was veiled in clouds.

"Where are the 'Large Red Robes'?" we asked in unison.

"Farther ahead. 'Large Red Robes' are deep in the hills." The oldest girl answered.

Deep in the hills. A vague concept indeed. So I asked again, "Is it far from here?"

"You may call it far, or you may not. It takes some patience to find 'Large Red Robes'." The young girl smiled as she replied. Her remarks were amazingly similar to those of the old man at the foot of the Tianyou Peak.

We resumed our journey and always turned right when we came to a fork. There was no room for doubt as far as the old man's directions were concerned. The hills seemed to be stretching endlessly, and the footpath was forever zigzagging...

The path became narrower and narrower. Finally it came to an end in front of a pond overgrown with reeds. We shouted aloud, but there was not even an echo. Lazy breezes swayed the reeds in the pond to and fro, producing rustles that sounded almost like jeers in our ears.

There was no choice but retrace our steps. Carefully we parted those view-blocking weeds in an effort to search for our own footprints, and step by step we withdrew. It seemed that we were not meant to meet "Large Red Robes" today...

There was a fork. Which way to go? We hesitated. Inadvertently we found a wooden sign in the midst of some weeds. There was a line of sprawling handwriting on it, which read, "Go ahead and you'll see 'Large Red Robes'." Underneath there was a black arrow, pointing to the path on the left. Things were beginning to turn for the better. "Large Red Robes" were beckoning us!

"Large Red Robes!" My friends cried excitedly. Inscribed on a roadside stone tablet were exactly these three characters. But there was nothing eye-catching around here. A rock pedestal protruded from the precipice, and from the rock pedestal sprung up two ordinary-looking tea trees: dark gray trunks, numerous crooked side branches, oval leaves so deep in color that they were almost dark green. Were these two plain tea trees really the renowned "kings of tea trees"? After so many twists and turns, we were definitely disappointed.

On a slope not far away there was a large crude wooden house, with a wooden sign that read "Tea" hanging outside. A thin old man stood at the door smiling at us. Suddenly I felt thirsty. When we walked over to the entrance of the teahouse, the old man was waiting inside with several large bowls of tea, "Have some tea and enjoy the delicate mountain flavor." He greeted us with smiles, his attitude earnest and cordial. The yellowish green tea was not that clear, yet it gave off a peculiar fragrance...

I took a sip. It tasted slightly bitter, but there was also an extraordinarily rich aroma. As it went down the fragrance lingered in my mouth, and I felt refreshed. Indeed it was quality tea! We sat near the entrance of the wooden building, unbuttoned our sweaty clothes, looked back at the path along which we had come and which was now enveloped in the mist, sipping tea from the bowl. Gradually, our fatigue melted away. The rich mellow fragrance seeped into the heart, immersing us in refined tranquility, body and mind. Was it not for the fragrance that we had come such a long way? "Large Red Robes" are valued for their inner quality rather than appearance. It is because of their distinctive fragrance that people yearn for them and hold them in high esteem. Right at the moment, as the object of our pursuit, condensed into bowls of fragrant tea, wordlessly comforted our wearied bodies and minds, we tasted the true joy of a pursuer.

Seeing us taking modest sips from the bowl, the old man chuckled, " Drink your fill. There is plenty of tea!" As he poured more tea for us out of a porcelain teapot, he spoke in an unhurried manner, "There is always tea to drink if mountain springs do not run dry and tea trees do not die."

"Why does the tea taste so good?" I asked.

"Thanks to the beautiful mountain, thanks to the spring water that oozes out of rock cracks, and thanks to the care of people." The old man's reply was simple and clear.

"Why were they named 'Large Red Robes'?" I asked a second question.

"The new buds they put forth are red. With all those tender red leaves in early spring, they really look like large red robes." His reply was again simple and clear.

"It's no easy job attending trees like those, is it?"

Instead of a ready reply, the old man simply laughed, rubbing his rough sturdy hands vigorously. After a while he spoke, "We live in the hills all year round, so we're used to it. It's nothing. It always takes time to grow tea trees. 'Large Red Robes' are not that bad. Have you heard of 'Mid-air Spirits'?" He pointed to the peaks barely discernible in the clouds far away. "They grow on top of the highest peaks. Tea farmers have to climb up ivy-like along narrow crevices, as if they were ascending to the heaven!" With that he took a mattock from a corner of the room and walked out. After a few steps he turned around, " Take your time."

Somehow we all blushed. The tea went on inebriating us with its exquisite fragrance. Two lines of poetry by Fan Zhongyan came up in my mind:

"Better to have a sip at immortals' hill,
Cool and fresh, ride the wind I will..."

Autumn at Jiu Zhai Gou

Chen Cun

It was October. After the Dadu River, the road by the Min River was nothing. Of course there were some inevitable "exchanges of chariots" (a term in Chinese chess), wherein vehicles lined up in a single file to brush past the traffic in the other direction, putting on the brakes frequently. On one side stood the mountain, and on the other side rushed the river. The river was so torrential that it was highly likely for passengers to be killed in an overturned vehicle. Sometimes it was even impossible to recover the bodies. Another "exchange of chariots" was the last straw for the photographers in our bus, who got off as trucks plodded by one after another. We did not stir. Our minds had turned numb after seeing all those vehicles that drove with half of the wheels hanging in the air.

What annoyed us were the sandstorms. Wenchuan, Maowen, or Songpan, all were in a mess because of them. I looked out of the window at the barren mountain, mother of sandstorms and the jumbled rocks on the flood land, utterly disheartened. Trees and grass had been wiped out long ago. Those jumbled rocks that were still dangling over steep cliffs would eventually drop down onto the road, or into the river, or probably on somebody. Each and every sand layer cast menacing eyes.

I still vaguely remembered that the Red Army had been here. In 1936, they marched along the Min River while taking advantage of the favorable

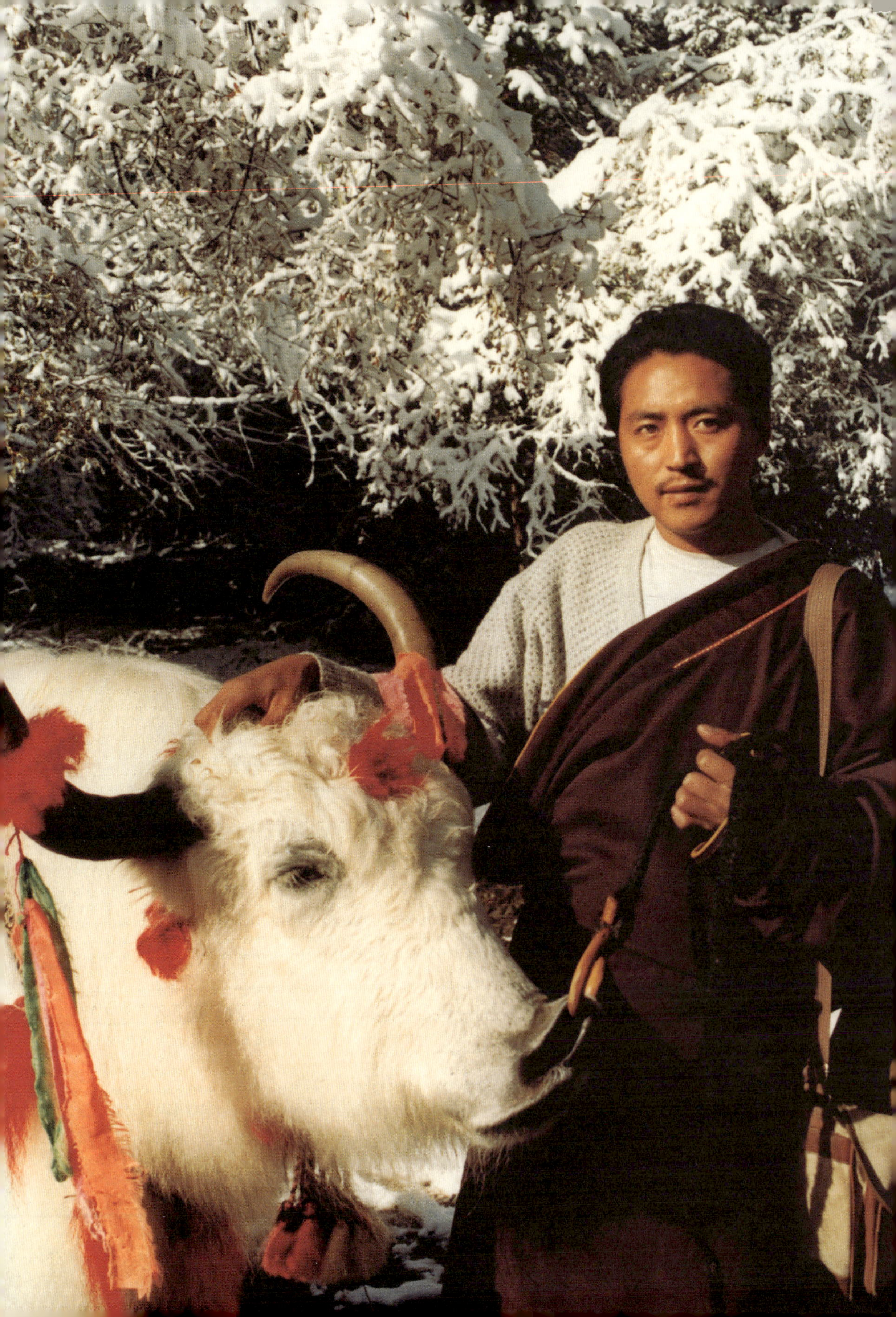

terrain to keep a close watch over Hu Zongnan's army stationed at Songpan, so that the CPC Central Committee could hold its meeting over the road ahead in peace, in Maogong and Maorgai. More than 40 years had passed. The scenery had changed. Many ups and downs of life had taken place. The only things that remained were legends.

The road extended infinitely. We had planned to spend the night at Maowen, but a landslide forced us to stay at Songpan. On the way we took in the cable bridges, the black Black River and the grayish white Min River, as well as the huge gourd-shaped lake of the Taiping Commune, which had been formed after a 1933 earthquake. Songpan, 2,800 meters above sea level, had a frost-free period of 21 days. As we drove out of Songpan, the Min River was no longer in sight. We were on a descent in the midst of an increasingly open country. There were horses and yaks. A clear shallow stream breezed by on its way to becoming a giant river. Occasionally Tibetan natives showed up in twos and threes, looking at our convoy without batting an eyelid. The photographers were again excited. During the break at Wenchuan they had got excited once. Scores of zoom cameras (from Mamiya to Seagull-DF, loaded with Kodak negatives and reversal films) pointed at a young girl in white from the Qiang ethnic group and the "shooting" started. Shutters clicked in rapid succession. This was a well-meaning "execution squad". The girl bowed her head with a coy smile, murmuring "What a slaughter!" In a moment she had slipped the bamboo basket on her back and dodged. Earrings made from key chains dangled from her ears.

The snow-capped mountains in the distance were refreshing, and the buckwheat nearby had turned dark red.

Jiu Zhai Gou was located 40 kilometers south of Nanping, its elevation ranging from 2,000 to 3,000 meters. Yangtong at its entrance was not that impressive, just an overgrowth of trees and weeds along with two houses. All looked dusky despite the scorching highland sun. The sketch map showed a Y-shaped outline, with the Visitor's Center right at the intersection. The names on paper were strange to the eye: the Shuzheng Lakes Gully, the Rize Gully, and the Zechawa Gully. What did they stand for?

"What do they stand for?" I asked.

No one spoke Tibetan. What a pity!

There was a makeshift road built by forest authorities. Late last year the project was abruptly discontinued in response to the appeal of some wise man. All that remained were the road, the houses, and tree stumps.

We missed the Guest Greeting Pine in our rapture over the strings of lakes. They lay lazily in the sun, emanating a heartbreaking green. The mind begged for adjustment, for how could water assume such a color? The reeds in the Reeds Lake had yellowed, and the maples on autumnal mountains had turned red, forming a pleasant contrast with the blue or green mountains and lakes. Nature is always a genius with colors.

The Shuzheng Waterfall flashed by, but its roar lingered longer in the ear. The 140-meter wide Nuorilang Waterfall left an enduring impression on the retina. The three of us unpacked, grabbed a bite, and set out to look for signs of the late autumn.

We found the Nuorilang Waterfall, by the ears at first, then the skin, then the eyes. The moisture in the air felt pleasant. The waterfall cascaded down the cliff in confident composure into the expectant pool at its foot. The sun turned it into a tender dreamy blue.

We stood facing the waterfall, watching it, listening to it, and inhaling it. A giant fir rose proudly into the sky nearby. It was as majestic as the Nuorilang.

Evening found us again by the side of the fir, flashlights in hand. There were just the three of us under a starless sky. I had seen brilliantly shining stars at the Dawei forest zone more than 3,000 meters above sea level. There stars hang overhead as big as saucers. One felt chilly after gazing at them for some time. But now they were out of sight. It was either cloudless or starless in the mountainous regions.

We sat quietly in front of the Nuorilang Waterfall, listening. Was it snoring? No, it never slept. The air still felt moist. The flashlight drew an arc over the seemingly still cascade. The light went out, and the waterfall sank into pitch darkness. It seemed ages before its dim white contours broke out. It was dim but not gloomy.

A pretty young Tibetan woman in a neat ethnic gown answered the door. There was no bed in the room, just a wide stretch of propped-up planks. There were coir mattresses, cotton wadding and sheets on the planks. With ten men sharing it, each could claim a mere half-meter in width. Our heads were close to one another. Our roommates had come from Chengdu to paint gouache paintings at their own expense. Despite parched lips they had not yet considered returning home. Such a "bed" was a novelty to me, while it reminded Mr. Xue of his days in the army.

Over a month in Sichuan had taught me that running water guaranteed sound sleep.

It was impossible to watch sunrise deep in the mountains, much less on rainy days. I had some steamed buns and pickled vegetables packed in preparation for a day's hiking in the Zechawa Gully. I'd like to picnic by the Long Lake. The round trip was 36 kilometers.

The bus was only able to take us half the way, for the road farther along had rotted away. We left the road, pushed aside the weeds with a stick, climbed over fallen logs, and approached the Colorful Lake.

It was a cloudy day. The water was thicker but in no way greasy. The logs ten meters under the water surface were clearly visible. The Colorful Lake lay low and deep, reflecting the mountains nearby. Patches of red and yellow danced over the green surface. The water at Jiu Zhai Gou was colorful indeed. And the transition between colors was seamless. The colors drifted, mixed and blended. I saw the true meaning of "colorful".

There was a small cute raft. Mr. Xue jumped on board. I followed after receiving a hexagonal floral cap from a Uygur man. At the first pole the raft went slyly down. Xue shouted, "Jump off! Jump off!" Soon the two of us were in the icy water, and after a few strokes we climbed out dripping water. The hat was gone.

It was Mr. Cao's turn to show off. A strong 38-year old, he dove twice into the treacherously deep lake to retrieve the cap. On the bank, our sweaters and woolen pants were still dripping water. I felt funny while getting used to the cold shivers. Xue's face looked as if painted. Legend had it that the Colorful Lake, meant for fairies to bathe in, punished the impudent by freezing them. The trip to the Long Lake, which was tens of kilometers in depth, had to be cancelled. The steamed buns went to waste, but drugs for curing colds were in urgent need. In two hours we were back at the guesthouse, where I quickly peeled off the clothes and went huddling in bed. Mr. Xue sent me a can of steaming hot water to ward off the cold.

But I had to go out, for I could not see the beautiful scenery of Jiu Zhai Gou inside the house. In the afternoon we got a ride to the Rize Gully, which was known for its terraced lakes.

We did not take the bus the day before leaving Jiu Zhai Gou. Instead we went slowly up the slopes with a supply of food, cameras and walking sticks purchased at Mt. Emei.

The raft on Mirror Lake felt solid. We took pictures against the background of red leaves and green water. There was a wooden mill in the lake. Its tiles were also made of wood. A giant wheel beneath the house was visible from the floating bridge. It was driven by water drawn over a wooden trough. I climbed up the single-log staircase to push open the heavy black door. Inside there hung a pair of millstones. The lower one was turning, and grains were falling meekly into the aperture. A dark-skinned old Tibetan man sat on the floor, warming his bony hands over a fire of highland barley stalks.

"How do you do!' I bowed slightly.

He nodded. I raised my voice to ask him questions. He got them, but offered few words in reply. He was able to speak Sichuan dialect, but not very fluently. The millstones went on grinding.

We passed by the waterfall and lingered for a while at the Pearl's Shoal. Water overflowed the gentle slopes there, on which grew shrubs that were steeped in water all year round. I walked barefoot for a while. The cold current was in such a rush that it was hard to stay put. What a pity is was that the sun did not come out. Otherwise the water would have glittered like pearls. I could imagine how beautiful the scene would be.

All was quiet. There was no other visitor, nor any floating dust. On the bank of the Peacock River we tried our hand at rafting, which we had learned at the Dadu River. The three of us pushed an almost rotten log on the high bank into the water, expecting the current to carry it downstream. The log floated away with ease. One more log. To our disappointment it was stranded among jumbled rocks close to the bank.

The Five Flower Lake was beautiful, but the small lake lower than it in altitude was even more beautiful. The logs under the water surface had burst into ferocious-looking buds, reminding people of the monster at Lock Ness. The water was so clear that it seemed as transparent as a mass of green air enveloped in multicolored mist. It resembled paintings by Renoir and Lin Fengmian, but in a way far superior to any school, any master. I sat by the water for a long time. Meanwhile Xue and Cao hurried in and out of the water to take a picture of themselves swimming.

We walked beyond the small bridge to the west of the Five Flower Lake. The lake assumed a myriad of blue and green, so tender that it soothed the mind. A cigarette butt was accidentally dropped into the lake. I hastened to scoop it up and bury it among weeds. Multicolored yaks lay quietly in the distance. I went up to offer my greetings in a low voice. There was no obvious hostility, yet they were on alert. Beyond the yaks there was a deserted wooden house, tilted. In front of the house there were high wooded shelves for drying grasses.

The ground floor was always dirty and accommodated domestic animals. A single-log staircase led up to the second floor, where there were dilapidated doors and windows, as well as scattered hay and a dismembered wooden plough. People had used to live here. The third floor, which had been reserved for worshipping gods, was vacant except for some plastic bags discarded by picnickers. Dusk was gathering. We wandered between the lake and the crumbling house, keeping company with yaks. Cao kept eating sour-tasting wild berries. The Five Flower Lake appeared even greener. There was no noise from human beings, just the splashing sound produced by waterfalls on their descent.

Time to go. I walked back to the Mirror Lake, got on the raft, and rowed to the center of the lake despite the extortions of the other two. Let me float. The trees were with me, so were the mountains, the unknown birds. I was by no means solitary. The water flowed slowly and sedately. It would flow past the row of trees in the north...

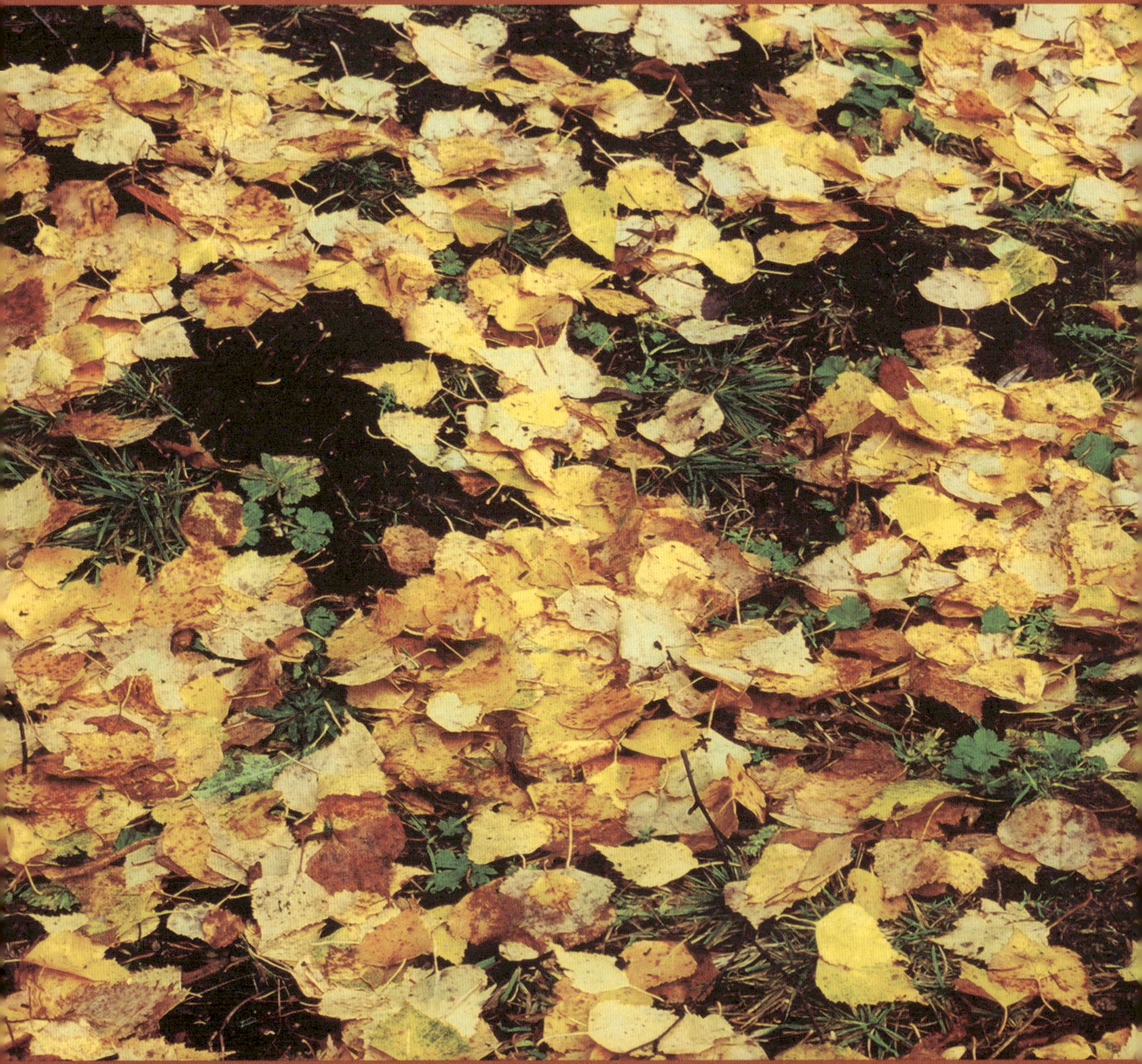

The Jiu Yi Mountain

Xiao Fuxing

Far from the hubbub of city life at the Jiu Yi Mountain, both the body and the mind felt cleansed. It was hard to believe that such a clean and refreshing landscape still existed in a world that was increasingly polluted and noisy.

Man used to wear leaves and animal skins to avoid embarrassing exposure. Later we built metropolises to distance ourselves from nature. The more bustling our life is, the harder it is for us to cover up our shameful behavior, for all our progress has been made at the expense of nature. Meanwhile, nature has remained unruffled. With clean and refreshing landscapes in outlying areas, which form a sharp contrast with human behavior, it has made us all the more embarrassed.

The Jiu Yi Mountain is exactly such a landscape cared for by nature.

In my opinion, the picturesque scenery of the Jiu Yi Mountain is so rare not only because Mao Zedong once wrote the well-known lines "White clouds flit around the Jiu Yi Mountain, princes and princesses ride the wind to descend on green hills" in its praise, or because it boasts such a long history that it was mentioned as early as in the Historical Records, "Emperor Shun died in a place with verdant Chinese parasol trees during a hunting trip to the south, and was buried at the Jiu Yi Mountain south of the Yangtze River", but because it has kept clean and refreshing all through the 5,000 years, unpolluted, unspoiled, and undisturbed. This gives it an advantage over other famous mountains and great rivers. The more well-known a mountain or a river is, the more visitors it has to receive at the cost of its own serenity and natural beauty.

Located 30 kilometers south of the Ningyuan County of Hunan Province in a remote area difficult of access, the Jiu Yi Mountain is less encroached upon by human beings and thus little polluted. Crowds would turn a scenic spot into a bustling market, ruining the sense of cleanliness and freshness. When I visited the Jiu Yi Mountain in May, the eyefuls of refreshing green immediately calmed me down, and a profound admiration for the world welled up. After seeing the city trees that remained dusty all year round, comparable to faces that were always dirty despite the application of various creams and cleansing foams, how could one possibly not cherish the virgin vegetation at the Jiu Yi Mountain? From the Hill of Five Courtiers (a.k.a. the Hill of Sleeping Beauty) seen in the distance outside the mountain range, to the Ehuang Peak and Nuying Peak right before my eyes, to the Shunyuan Peak under my feet, green met my eyes. The Sleeping Beauty swayed its long green hair as if in a graceful dance; Ehuang and Nuying swirled their green skirts pure as dewdrops at dawn. If these hills were green in a tender, delicate and juicy way, then the green of the Shunyuan Peak was deep, majestic and as eternal as chastity and vows, although nowadays chastity is flouted and vows far less popular than lies or sweet words.

Around the Nine Doubtful Mountain, the Shunyuan Peak was worthy of the highest commendation and its green was the most unusual. Somehow it reminded me of the near-superstitious practice of Feng Shui (geomancy), and the mysterious origin of life. Otherwise how would you explain its extraordinary green that made it stand out from all nine peaks? Cai Yong exclaimed after ascending its top 1,800 years ago, "I climb this towering hill to get closer to heaven."

The Shun's Temple at the foot of the Shunyuan Peak dated back to the third year of Emperor Qiande's reign in the Song Dynasty. The pity was that it had been destroyed by war, leaving behind a stone tablet inscribed with "The Mausoleum of Emperor Shun, Originally from the Youyu Family", a hollowed ancient tree, and an elegiac address by He Shaoji of the Qing Dynasty inscribed in regular script on a stone tablet that some countrywomen had later used as a washboard. A new Shun's Temple was under construction. The tender green chicken feet-shaped leaves of recently planted maples rustled in the wind.

Legend had it that Emperor Shun [a legendary sage monarch in ancient China] had died here and had been buried here. Local people reportedly took pride in the fact that, while there were controversies over the burial places of Yellow Emperor [a legendary ruler and ancestor of the Chinese nation] and Emperor Yao [a legendary monarch and model for all rulers in ancient China], it had been unanimously agreed that Emperor Shun had passed away here. It had always baffled me as to why Emperor Shun had spent his last days here. According to legend, he had arrived in a raft up the Xiao River to teach local peasants how to grow tea, to set up a school at the Rosy Cloud Rock by the Shunyuan Peak, and finally to be poisoned to death in his efforts to rid people of an evil serpent. He had died a heroic and worthy death, but why here at the foot of the Shunyuan Peak? This had become an enigma of all time. Legend also had it that Ehuang and Nuying, the two imperial concubines who had traveled from afar after Emperor Shun, had found neither the mausoleum nor his body. To them each and every of the nine identical peaks looked like the Emperor's burial place (hence the name the Nine Confusing Peaks Mountain and Li Bai once wrote that "The nine confusing peaks stretch long and unbroken in their similarity".) Worn out by the long walk and with bamboos mottled by their tears, they finally came to the Shunyuan Peak and decided that was it. In a moment they were transformed into two peaks, i.e., the Ehuang Peak and Nuying Peak facing the Shunyuan Peak. Thus the Jiu Yi Mountain became a symbol of justice and love, two values long cherished by the people.

The beautiful legends about why Emperor Shun had come and died at the Jiu Yi Mountain are part of ancient history. History is both beautiful and ugly. There is no telling whether it is true or false, good or bad. The years that have gone by are comparable to a river far too wide for people to cross to the other side. But anyway, historical legends reflect something people aspire to but can never attain in reality.

Climbing the Shunyuan Peak started a few hundred meters south of Shun's Temple. Although it was the highest peak in the mountain range, the Shunyuan Peak was not very high. A mere 1,000 stone steps covering more than 600 meters led to its top. However, the view from there was not to be belittled. Had it drawn miraculous power from Emperor Shun or was it by nature? It rose steeply and its trail, short as it sounded, was very difficult to climb. The ancient firs that had sprung up from rock cracks were unique to the Jiu Yi Mountain in that their leaves had seven needles instead of the usual five common to their brethren in the pine family. The subtropical secondary primeval forests were luxuriantly green, while flowers and berries could be found everywhere. As we made slow progress up the hill, wild strawberries and wild loquats begged attention like hospitable kids. According to local residents, in autumn there would be a feast of wild chestnuts, tangerines, pears, club-shaped fruit and so on. Especially worth mentioning was a kind of homely nut by the vulgar name of "Gou Ba", or Testicle of the Dog, which was able to preserve its taste and juice until the following spring. Entirely different from fruits sold in stores, these wild fruits were only available in the mountain areas. In a similar way, the green here differed from the polluted green in the city, the plants here differed from the neatly pruned plants in the city, and the creeks and springs here differed from fountains in the city...

At the top of the Shunyuan Peak, I didn't have the sentiment of "hoping one day to ascend the summit, and finding all the surrounding mountains dwarfed." However, there was a panoramic view of the Rosy Cloud Rock to the west, the Ehuang and Nuying Peaks to the north, and the Forked Rock to the south. There were 500 hectares of secluded slender and graceful bamboos at the Forked Rock, where the mottled bamboos were looking up at me with "tearful eyes".

Local residents considered it a pity that I had not arrived a month earlier, when the Jiu Yi had been at its best with red and white azaleas over hill and dale. Legend had it that there had been only red azaleas before Shun's death, but that at his fall all red azaleas turned white as if in mourning. Ever since then, both red and white azaleas have been found over the Jiu Yi Mountain in April.

During the time of my visit, azaleas had faded, but tung trees were in full blossom, scattering petals all over the ground. The white tung blossoms were like snow flakes fluttering over the shady trails of the Jiu Yi Mountain.

I congratulated myself on my not-too-late arrival.

(Upon returning from the Jiu Yi Mountain, June 1994)